Embracing
the Spirit Within

Inspirational Stories and Reflections

by
E. V. ELDER

Photographer: William Gibb
Cover Design: Laurie Sobierajski

Published by:

FriesenPress

Suite 300 – 852 Fort Street
Victoria, BC, Canada V8W 1H8

www.friesenpress.com

Distributed to the trade by The Ingram Book Company

This book is dedicated, with gratitude and respect,
to the giants of faith on whose shoulders I stand:
my maternal grandmother Rosina Kraft-Gerein
my mother Magdalena Frances Gerein-Elder
my father Louis Frank Elder.
They will never read this book,
but they are the inspiration behind its pages.

Table of Contents

Acknowledgements

There are no words to express my gratitude to my family, members of my Koinonia community, and my friends, Canadian and Brazilian, who have graced my life and inspired the writing of this book. Through your example of faith and unqualified trust in God, you have stretched my soul to look beyond the immediate and the tangible. You helped me discover God in both the ordinary and the astonishing events of life.

I would like to single out several people who assisted in the completion of this work:

- My sister Jean Elder and my closest friend Karen Schneider for their outstanding editing contributions. You kept the vision of this book alive and helped bring it to fruition. Your commitment and support live on in these pages.

- My friend Beverly Brazier for faithfully proofreading every page. Your patience has been a blessing.

- My brother-in-law William Gibb for sharing his photography skills in the cover photo and Laurie Sobierajski for her creative cover design.

- Literary consultant Patricia Anderson for her faith in my work and her editorial assistance.

- My Brazilian friends whose faith amidst countless setbacks and challenges continues to inspire me.

- My sister Donna Gibb and niece Jeanine Gordon for their wholehearted support throughout the writing process and their invaluable input into Chapter 15.

- My many friends whose interest and enthusiastic vigil have spurred me on during this long gestational process.

- My former students who taught me to stand in wonder and awe before the miracles taking place around us every day.

- My fellow retreatants whose insightful sharing has helped me deepen my faith and whose support for this work is appreciated beyond words.

- Jerome Stueart and the Whitehorse faith writing group for their encouragement and honesty in critiquing a few small parts of my work.

- My readers. While we may not have met in person, I feel we share a mutual interest in spirituality and its impact on our lives. None of us walks alone. We walk the pilgrimage of life together. May you continue to awaken to your own inner beauty, your spiritual essence.

Introduction: Our Spiritual Quest

The inner experience of truth has the power to set us free, for it reveals not only the falseness that is within us but the beauty and goodness that are deeper still… In repenting we turn around, not to become someone other than ourselves, but to become truly ourselves.

—J. P. Newell

In recent years many people have asked me to help them explore their spirituality. While they come from a variety of religious backgrounds, they have one thing in common: they are filled with a deep desire to get in touch with the life of the Spirit within them. They are already on the road to discovering their own souls. Now their search is leading them to a more profound understanding of who they are and who they are called to be. They long to live in harmony with themselves (body, mind, and spirit), with others, and with God (whoever or whatever they conceive God to be). As they continue their search for meaning and purpose in their lives, the unrelenting desire to know their ultimate and eternal destiny deepens and expands. This longing and searching is an intrinsic part of spirituality.

For well over five years, a group of women and men gathered in my home on the first Saturday of every month. We spent time in retreat because we believed that we are on a continuous journey toward sacredness and depth. It was our way of nourishing our spirits. My responsibility was to prepare a prayer celebration that reflected a specific theme and to share my personal thoughts and insights. In preparation for each retreat, I spent many hours reading and praying. This helped me "grow" my own soul. I was also enriched by the observations that retreatants shared. I believe that we were renewed and strengthened each time we came together.

I am profoundly thankful for my own life's journey that prepared me and led me to this work. It has been a blessing and a vocation. As far back as I can remember, God has been the More in my life, inspiring and challenging me to venture into uncharted territory and to discover the divine Mystery in all things.

I grew up in a small rural community in the middle of the vast Canadian prairies. My family, like most families in the area, had a strong adherence to the Roman Catholic faith. I cannot remember a time when we did not celebrate Sunday as a special day of the Lord. We prayed together as a family and faithfully observed religious devotions and practices. It was in this setting that I became aware of the importance of God in my life. I feel indebted to my parents and my siblings who led me to an appreciation of God and taught me the fundamental role spirituality plays in human life.

After teaching in various schools throughout Saskatchewan for ten years, I volunteered for missionary service in Brazil where I worked in five fishing villages along the Atlantic Coast for five years. There my experience of life grew incrementally as I lived and worked among the poor and destitute. I trained local catechists, organized mothers' clubs, founded cooperatives, and facilitated street prayer groups and Bible study groups; I also celebrated and practiced a variety of corporal and spiritual works of mercy. I believe with all my heart that this experience in Brazil was *the* education of my life. The poor became my sisters and brothers and taught me to look at life in a new way. Their positive attitude and their profound faith helped me see what really matters, what is essential. While they lived in abject poverty, they never lost faith in the God of life. Rather, they gave thanks for the blessings of each day. It was in their midst that I learned that in everyone's life there are innumerable "dyings" followed by unfailing risings again.

Throughout my adult life I spent many days and weeks in retreat. The retreat I cherish the most is a thirty-day silent retreat I made in 1971 at the Jesuit Retreat Centre in Guelph, Ontario. The expectation was that we would spend a minimum of five hours in silent prayer every day. Following each hour of prayer, we were to discern where the Spirit led us and to make note of anything that appeared to enrich our spirituality. These grace-filled days opened the eyes of my soul to the workings of the Spirit within me.

The retreat took place during the month of May—a beautiful, enchanting time to walk amid the blossoming apple trees on site. I spent a lot of time observing one deformed apple tree. Its branches went out in all directions, but every one of them was richly laden with blossoms. While it was handicapped, in a way, it radiated its own kind of beauty. Nature reflects the seemingly contradictory elements in human life.

Life has taught me that most people are in search of personal spirituality and express a great desire to grow in loving relationships. I am convinced that spirituality is God's special gift to every human person. Most often it is an invisible and intangible gift. Therefore, it is difficult to define or describe, much less elucidate. I nonetheless feel called to share my understanding and insight in the hope that the sacred stories told in this book will somehow enrich the spirituality of my readers.

Despite the mixed bag of "the good, the bad, and the ugly" that life holds out to us, people want to believe in goodness over selfishness, love over hatred, and hope over fear. They long to discover what is most profound and meaningful within. Especially in our modern Western world, there is a growing interest in spirituality. People from all walks of life, different age groups, varying social classes, and distinct religious affiliations are expressing a desire to discover their spiritual roots.

Spirituality is a gift that God freely gives to every person regardless of creed, colour, sex, or religious affiliation. While some people search through Eastern spirituality, others seek clarity in the spirituality of the West. Some tap into Native American spirituality; others seek understanding in New Age philosophies. In our day, many turn to nature and the secrets it holds for those who take time to look and listen with the heart. No matter where people look or how they seek to know themselves, spirituality is part of their nature as human beings. It leads us deep within all that has life to the very heart of God.

All great religions are essentially good and wholesome and try to lead their followers to live upright and virtuous lives. The value of any authentic religion is found in its tradition (oral and written) and its unique way of praying and celebrating life's important moments. Because I believe that all religions strive to embrace the eternal mystery we know as God, I have a heartfelt respect for them. Since I am most familiar with the Catholic tradition, however, I naturally tend to cite examples from my Christian roots.

I spent most of my adult life working with children and youth as a teacher and school principal. In a safe school environment, children feel comfortable and learn the wonderful art of trust. This gives them the confidence to voice their opinions and observations and to share their values and ideals. Much of my experience has been in Catholic schools where there are many opportunities for prayer and celebration. It was in this setting that I noted adolescents' natural inclination for spirituality.

Children have an innate sense of the sacred. They are easily moved to awe and wonder at the sight of a beautiful sunrise, the metamorphosis of the caterpillar growing into the butterfly, the marvels of heredity, and the kindness of others. Faith in God comes as naturally as breathing. They easily perceive the presence of the sacred and understand that something greater than self exists and holds the universe in place. This moves them to gratitude for the goodness of life. They instinctively ask God for protection for themselves and those they love.

I learned early on in my career that, like the rest of us, children and youth seek to discover who they are. Like us, they are on a pilgrimage, a precious and indispensable journey of discovery and revelation. They want to know what makes them unique and different. Sometimes they do this privately in prayer and reflections; sometimes they look to others to lead them. While their search for meaning and purpose has many twists and turns, it ultimately leads to God. I am never really surprised when I witness their unrestrained exploration of the spirit world. They have both the capacity and the desire to grasp eternal truths and to discover the impact these have in their personal lives.

As an educator, I have a great appreciation for storytelling. I use every opportunity in the classroom to reinforce a point by telling or reading a story. People of all ages love stories. We easily relate to the characters in a story and intuitively love some, while we have serious doubts about others. Good stories move us to a sense of wonder. They offer valuable lessons about life and give us heroes and role models to admire and imitate. Stories are easy to remember and draw us into the imaginative world of discovery and adventure.

We all need stories. Listening to stories is a way of tapping into our roots, filling us with a sense of gratitude for who we are. Telling stories helps focus our memory and define our spirituality—our values, goals, hopes, and aspirations. Remembering fosters a deeper awareness of who we are and where we come from. It facilitates an appreciation for the changes and transformations that have led us to where we are today.

The stories I relate in these pages are largely from my own experience of life. Because they are personal, they help me remember people who have crossed my path and touched my life in a meaningful way.

They bring to mind countless moments of grace and remind me that life is good. I have carefully chosen each story because it illustrates a particular point. In order to protect the privacy of former students, members of my family, and my friends, I have changed the names of both people and places.

Writing this book has helped me find my own inner truth, the truth that God dwells within me. I know God as one who loves unconditionally, showers me with untold blessings, summons me to conversion, and walks with me along my journey back into the eternal. I know that I have merely discovered a tiny portion of the immensity that is God. I see the Author of life, who created us in the divine image and likeness, as one who has both masculine and feminine qualities. All are equally fascinating and revealing. I know God as a higher Power, an incessant Force that pushes me into the inner world of faith. But, most of all, I know God as my best friend.

This book is not a quick read. Arising out of years of prayer and reflection, it describes my limited experience of the divine—the people, places, and events that have given me a glimpse into the magnitude of God. It is a humble attempt to stimulate the imagination of the reader to focus on his or her personal pilgrimage back to God. May the stories, poems, and anecdotes inspire you to walk deeper into the mystery of your own life and discover where God is leading you. May you learn to see the divine in both the ordinary and the surprising events of your own life. Spirituality springs from awareness.

Part 1

Spirituality: Claiming Our Soul

Your blond head bobbed up and down,
Barely visible
amid the stalks of golden grain.

On a mission,
You were determined to reach the horizon—
where earth meets heaven.
You would find God there.

The storms came out of nowhere.
The wind tugged at your feet,
strange voices beckoned you,
this way, then that.

The horizon continued to recede,
Your end goal eluded you
and you wondered:
"Will I ever feel whole?
Rooted in my soul?"

A Voice within
Would not be silenced,
"Be still and know that I am God."
Your burning desire for something More
fanned into a dynamic flame.

Light pierced
through your doubts.
Then
you finally knew
that God is not out there,
but in the depths of your soul—
loving you still.

Bathed in Light
you discovered
your own inner beauty.

—Edite

Chapter 1: Spirituality through the Ages

There is an undefined restlessness in every human heart. People of all times and all ages have felt it. It has everything to do with our incessant search for something More. From conception to the grave, we experience an enduring invitation to embrace life and all that it holds out to us. At some point in time, we become aware of an innate and insatiable need to know the mysterious Power at work in the world and in our own soul. Awareness leads us to an unrelenting hunger and thirst for God. This yearning, this passion, is our spirituality. The divine presence affects the way we approach life and the way we relate to God and others. Our search for God, often indeterminate and vague, leads us to discover our identity and realize our destiny.

Spirituality, the age-old quest for sacredness and meaning, is a universal gift. Sometimes we feel it as a deep sense of peace and tranquility; other times it is an overwhelming sense of longing. Always, it leaves us with a profound insight into the mystery of life. There are *aha* moments in everyone's life. We do nothing to make them happen. It is all God's doing.

The Creator, eternally present to us, longs to create and strengthen an invisible bond between us. In our practical, matter-of-fact approach to life, we often turn away from that reality. Young children, who walk in and out of mystery with relative ease, have an inherent sense of the divine in all things human. They have no need to define, dissect, and analyze everything. They simply stand in awe and wonder. Their uncomplicated approach to life's gifts leads to absolute delight in creation and its wondrous revelations.

Working with children has been an undeserved blessing in my life. Somehow, they are able to take me back to my own childhood and its innocent bliss. They make me more attentive to my own secret wish to become the good and beautiful person I am destined to be. I was nineteen the first time I volunteered to teach summer catechism classes in rural Saskatchewan. I was assigned twenty-five spirited six- and seven-year-olds.

> The sun is beating down mercilessly. Not a cloud in sight. Not a single tree to provide shade. The old church is stifling, to say the least. The children have a hard time working amid kneelers and pews. Energy and enthusiasm gradually turn into restless fidgeting. I feel the perspiration coursing down my body like a mountain stream. It's time to take a break. The boys stand around and watch the girls organize a game of Farmer in the Dell. Listless and bored, they eventually decide to join the girls.
>
> Everyone appears to be enjoying the game. But where is Carmel? I look around and see her sitting by herself in the sandbox. She's only five. "Perhaps too shy to fit in with the others," I tell myself. I walk over to check things out. As I approach, I hear a tiny melodic voice: "God loves me. God loves me. This I know." Awesome. I stand in silence for a few moments before I edge closer. Carmel has a fairly large Coffee Crisp bar in her hand. She eats slowly, relishing every morsel. The chocolate is melting quickly. As it flows down and mingles with the sand between her fingers, she takes several long, drawn out licks. Absolute joy spreads across her beautiful chocolate-covered face. The refrain, "God loves me," announces the source of her joy and delight. I am, indeed, standing on holy ground.

Whether or not we realize it, we all have spirituality. Like it or not, we are all "wired for God." We can ignore this reality, but we can never completely escape it. Life's pilgrimage ultimately leads us to a higher Power at work in the world. Beauty and goodness awaken us to the divine. Our own innate desires for love, peace, and harmony continually draw us to goodness and love. The Spirit of God leads us deeper and deeper into our true self. There we learn to ask the right questions and to live with those that have no answers. Spirituality is the restlessness, the disquietude, the angst that calls the human spirit beyond itself and leads it to discover its deeper reality, its true identity in God.

Created in God's image and likeness, we are blessed beyond our wildest dreams. At conception, God gave form and substance to our bodies. "For it was you who formed my inward parts; you knit me together in my mother's womb."[1] But God went way beyond shaping our bodies. Breathing life into us, God planted the seed of divinity in our souls. As long as we have breath, we are on a never-ending search for the divine. This journey, this sacred pilgrimage, is our spirituality.

Our bodies are much more than the "earth clay" from which they were formed. They are the temples of the Spirit, the home of the soul. God entrusts them to be the guardians of our souls. A part of God dwells in the core of our being. When we enter deeply into our own soul, we discover the power of love. Love alone is capable of making us whole. We yearn for God, long for God, and search for God our whole life long. And, just as surely, God yearns and longs and searches for us. Spirituality is as much about God's need for us as it is about our need for God. For God, the question is not *whether* we will respond to divine love, but *when*.

There is no limit to what God will do to lead us to the fullness of life. God placed an unrelenting passion within us. This is our spirituality and it is pure gift—unsolicited and undeserved. God blesses us with a zeal for life, a creative energy that inevitably leads us back into the heart of God. Our awareness of God expands and grows until we find God in all things, the seen and the unseen, the predictable and the accidental, the familiar and the mysterious. It calls us to weave the strands of our life together and bring body, mind, and spirit into harmony.

Spirituality spans time and space. People of long ago and far away were in search of a higher Power just as we are. They experienced the same desires, longings, and yearnings that we do. The great mysteries of God and of life touched them deeply. Because these mysteries were the focus of their thoughts and reflections, they inspired them and moved them to embrace the universe. Rooted in the heart and soul of every person, spirituality is the way all people make sense of life—the way they grow and become who they are destined to be.

The Creator blessed ancient people with a certain awareness of something More. Their journey to discover goodness and truth, meaning and purpose, led them through the path of nature. Moved by the great sense of harmony they discovered in the natural world, they felt an instinctive connection with mother earth and all created things. They were deeply affected by the great qualities they found in nature: order, harmony, balance, and unity. Naturally, they tried to emulate nature and, in so doing, they learned to live in peace with themselves, with others, and with the earth.

It was only a matter of time before our ancestors looked for ways to pass on their knowledge, insights, wisdom, and discernment. They wanted their children and grandchildren to walk boldly into the heart of the earth, to know the wondrous gift of creation, to delight in all God's creatures, and to live in harmony with each other. Over time, they developed the great myths that described and personalized the things they found in nature. They discovered a pervading power and subtle presence that they came to know as gods and goddesses. Addressing them by name, they called on these great spirits of nature in times of transition and transformation.

The art and stories of prehistoric people reflect an enchantment with the spirit world. While scholars expected prehistoric art to advance in slow stages from primitive "scratchings" to lively natural drawings, they found instead subtle shadings of light and dark, the ingenious use of perspective, and flowing elegant lines that speak of peace and serenity. Soft curves and images suggest an affinity with the kind and gentle world of the spirits. The simplicity of line and form expresses an intuitive sense of well-being. Highly stylized images reveal a prevailing awareness of the cosmos and its impact on people's daily lives. They portray an inner sense of moral goodness and unity.

Many engravings appear in the mouths of caves and rock shelters. Animal depictions abound. Vivid frescoes in the earliest caves represent magical rites intended to ensure success in hunting. Others allude to fertility and fecundity. Still others depict movement and dance, especially of women and children. Many illustrations portray men, women, and children interacting with the spirits. We assume that these had some spiritual significance. In the deeper recesses of caves, the decorations illustrate ceremonial gatherings. An ancient Ice Age Indian artefact represents the figure of a medicine man. The artist carefully chipped away between the shoulders so that the head could "seat." The figure seems absorbed in the contemplation of thought itself, "akin to the universe looking back on itself."[2]

Spirituality is definitely not a new phenomenon. It has served to guide and inspire people over the entire period of human history. The great formal religions of the world are a mere 5,000 years old. Obviously, spirituality is much more fundamental to the human spirit than any religion. Yet it gave birth not only to one religion, but also to scores of different religions. There has to be a reason for that.

Ancient people responded to an intuitive desire to share their insights, dreams, and aspirations with each other. They discovered a variety of things about life and the world of the Spirit. Over time, these became the tenants of the community's faith. All religions speak of community. We are born connected—created for relationship, for communion. Presence leads to relationship.

As human history began to unfold, pagan cults assumed more and more prominence in the daily lives of people. Primitive ceremonies proclaimed the importance of being in tune with the spirit world. They celebrated a respectful appreciation of the spiritual force within all created things. Because people relied on the natural world to provide them with food, water, and shelter, they developed a genuine love for nature. They stood in awe of the powerful god of the mountain, the mighty goddess of the sea, the moving god of the wind, the refreshing goddess of rain, the prevailing god of the sun, and the gentle goddess of love. Their respectful relationship with the natural world taught then to walk gently into the realm of the spirits.

Over the centuries, people developed their own rituals: prayer, song, dance, ceremonies, and stories to celebrate life. They appeased the gods and goddesses by offering sacrifices and prayers in their honour. They implored them to protect and favour their families and villages. Pragmatic and earthy observances served to safeguard beliefs and values.

True religion begins with a sincere quest for meaning and purpose, a search for the inner value of life itself. It encompasses the rituals and customs that support spirituality. It provides a safe environment where we discern who God is and what God asks of us. Leading us beyond the here and now, religion gives us the bigger picture. As we awaken to the impulses of God deep within us, religion provides the supportive faith community that helps us "grow our soul" and celebrate the milestones along our spiritual journey.[3]

From the beginning of time, people observed the cyclical pattern of nature. The cycles of the seasons, the daily movement of the sun, the rising and waning of the moon, and the dying of the seed in order to produce new life were a reflection of all created things. Naturally, prayers were chanted at dawn and sundown, in the midst of work and recreation, and at key moments of life—birth, maturity, illness, and death.

Little wonder that the circle remains as a powerful symbol in most religions. It brings us out of the earth at birth, continues its pattern of growth and maturity, takes us to our eventual decline, and leads us home in death. We see it as a vibrant representation of life itself. A spiritual icon, the circle depicts our connection with the transcendent and gives us a feeling of eternal unity. As we learn to understand the earth and life itself, we come to see a creative hand at work in all things. This insight gives us a sense of God.

The entire movement of life leads us back to the Creator, the one who formed us in our mother's womb. Celtic people described it in terms of a sacred circle. They passed on this insight to generations yet to come. In the sacred circle, we strive to come home to ourselves and find rest in our own soul. There, we discover an inner harmony and profound unity with all created things and gradually come to see ourselves as part of a larger world.

From its inception, Christianity looked upon the circle as a revered symbol. The communion of saints defines a powerful connection, a dynamic affiliation between the faithful on earth and all the holy people who have gone before us. All are part of the circle. Because we are all one, we often experience a poignant awareness of a relative or close friend years after that person has passed on to eternity. In the sacred circle, we become one with the saints in heaven and we turn to them for inspiration in time of need. Prayer creates prevailing bonds.

The circle, so beautifully reflected in nature, became a symbol of inner peace and contentment through the ages. It gave people a sense that all was right with the world, that everything was unfolding according to divine plan. The circle was, and still is, about connections and interdependence, essential unity and harmony. It reflects an invisible, but real and prevailing link between people. It describes our understanding of community.

Throughout history, people used stories to pass on their beliefs and values. Native Americans use sacred stories to describe the creation of the world and everything in it. Their respect for nature flows from these stories. Their clans are named after the animals they most admire. Even today, they gather with their kinfolk to share their ancient stories with their children and grandchildren. These stories help youth get to know their ancestors and understand their personal role within the tribe and in the larger world. In present-day Yukon, we celebrate an annual storytelling festival that features ancient stories of circumpolar peoples.

Stories refresh our memories and fill us with admiration for the great women and men who are part of our heritage. In my family, as in many others, there is a growing desire to know our family history and to preserve the stories of our ancestors. My brother Jerry spent many years researching and preparing both our paternal and maternal family trees. Thanks to his extensive work, future generations will know the ancestors who forged the way of life we now enjoy. My mother carefully recorded my maternal grandmother's stories. Later, she committed her own memoirs to writing. As a result, the riches of our family history, rituals, beliefs, and traditions are readily available to our growing extended family.

Family stories are important in everyone's life. This is especially true in our era. Many people are transient, moving from one side of the country to the other or clear across the globe. Though we may live miles apart, we seek a common understanding of the extended family and its history. Because stories bring into focus our memories of grace and blessing, of change and transformation, they lead us to gratitude. They help us understand the way spirituality evolves in our own lives and in the lives of others.

Family reunions, abounding in symbols, carry their secret codes. They become religious events because they help us remember and celebrate who we are as a family. Storytelling, the act of remembering, and the sharing of our heritage lead the young to discover their inherent roots. In that sense, the family reunion is a sacred event. When we gather as a family, we make toasts, tell stories, share bread, and roast favourite foods over the campfire. As we play, relax, and pray together, our family connections solidify.

In our Elder family, we gather at campgrounds. Simply being in the natural world is refreshing for people of all ages. The setting speaks of God, relationships, and connections. Everyone enjoys being close to mother nature—drinking in her beauty and the restful atmosphere she provides. Because creation speaks of the grandeur of God, it serves as a natural cathedral. It reminds us to "keep holy the Sabbath day." At our family reunions, Sunday morning's sacred ritual sets the tone for the day. The proclamation of Scripture stimulates inner reflection and leads to the sharing of personal stories. The remembrance of faith and doubt, of grace and failure, serves as an invitation to prayers of blessing and intercession. Over the years, a simple family observance has become a cherished tradition. Grown-up nieces and nephews instinctively ask: "When are we going to have Elder church?"

Spirituality in our day is alive and active in people of all ages. Because it touches all aspects of life, it is recognized as an essential element in the maintenance of a healthy lifestyle. In our day, scientists and health care professionals speak of the mind-body-spirit connection. They no longer assume that they can treat illness simply by treating the body. Research demonstrates the key role that spirituality and positive thinking play in restoring the body to health. All forms of healing involve the unseen energies of feelings, memories, attitudes, and beliefs. Therefore, the key to good health must focus on equilibrium and balance.

Despite an apparent decline in religious affiliation across North America today, spirituality remains an integral part of people's lives. While many "religious" people no longer find inspiration and comfort in their churches, they continue to believe in God. This is especially true of our youth. Even as they distance themselves from our churches, they continue to seek some greater Power, an inner value that serves as an anchor for their lives. What they have lost is a sense of confidence in the organizational church and in its structures, not in God.

Our search for the higher purpose for which we were created is never-ending. It is ingrained in us from conception and follows us to the grave. As natural as breathing, spirituality is an essential part of being human. It never fades away. In a society that puts little store in spirituality or religion, we still experience a deep desire to nourish our spirits, to give fuller life to our souls. We need to make sense of life in an ever-changing world. Spirituality empowers us to put things into perspective and to journey with clarity of purpose. Amid mounting greed and selfishness on the part of some, amid wars and conflicts of every kind, we long to be in touch with the God of peace, justice, harmony, and unity.

Like people of all times and places, we continue to experience a prevailing and inexplicable connectedness. We are filled with the desire to treasure life and to live it to the full. Following the path of our ancestors, we believe in the universal values of honesty, integrity, fairness, and respect for self, others, and mother earth. We feel a deep relationship with the mysterious force that lies beyond us and yet has the power to move us intimately and personally. This is the gift of spirituality.

> Observe the light of the divine presence that pervades all existence. Observe the harmony of the heavenly realm, how it pervades every aspect of life, the spiritual and the material, which are before your eyes of flesh and your eyes of the spirit. Contemplate the wonders of creation, the divine dimension of their being, not as a dim configuration that is presented to you from the distance but as the reality in which you live. Know yourself, and your world; know the meditations of your heart, and of every thinker; find the source of your own life, and of the life beyond you, around you, the glorious splendour of the life in which you have your being.[4]

Chapter 2: Spirituality: A Gratuitous Gift

One day, following a night in prayer, Jesus envisioned others assuming his earthly ministry. It was time to initiate his disciples into their sacred calling. So Jesus called the seventy-two together and presented them with their first mission. Although they were well aware of his most important values, he gave them a few pertinent instructions. They were to take nothing for the journey: no food, no sack, and no money in their belts. Going out two-by-two to neighbouring towns and villages to proclaim the Good News, they were to live simply—accepting the hospitality extended to them, celebrating peace, and curing the sick. Above all, they were to assure people that the Kingdom of God is within them.[5]

The fundamental message is abundantly clear: the Kingdom of God is not a place, but a state of mind. It is not some ethereal setting far away in heaven. It is in the heart and soul of every person. Spirituality speaks of a sacred presence, a holy state, a divine quality, in every person. The Kingdom of God is within. If you want to discover God, to be in touch with the divine, the place to look is within your own soul, in the core of your being. If you cannot find God within, you will never discover God anywhere else.

Spirituality, our lifelong search for God, is a gratuitous gift. It is our inheritance as human beings. We neither earn it nor deserve it. It is freely given out of love. The gift of God's loving presence is there for us to accept and embrace. God literally adores us, is passionately in love with us. And God puts no limits on love. There are absolutely no strings attached. God simply calls us to a deep and enduring relationship. To be alive is to be in relationship with God.

What makes us holy, what makes us whole, is our spirituality. It is the soul power that guides and directs us. It is the inspiration that lights our way through the many paths that lie open to us. Born in grace, we receive a tremendous capacity for goodness and beauty from the beginning. Grace has the power to bring us to fulfillment, to meaning, to insight. The human search for God necessarily leads us to examine our inner selves, to know our potential. The great question "why" surfaces in early childhood and remains with us throughout life. The simple *whys* of our younger days turn into the probing *whys* of our youth.

Spirituality empowers us to live with the questions, letting them simmer, giving the seed time to germinate and take root. It compels us to face our own queries: "Who am I? Why am I here? Who is God? What kind of person am I ordained to become? What kind of person do I want to become?" Powerful questions. Life-altering questions. They explain our burning desire to complete the work God destined us to do.

Spirituality leads us back to our roots, to the womb of all life—to the heart of the earth where we were conceived. We have a sacred bond with our mother, the earth. She nourishes and sustains us. She is our sacred trust, our holy gift. When we contemplate her beauty, we are moved to a sense of gratitude for all that life holds out to us. By nature, we all have the capacity to search for goodness and beauty, compassion and kindness, hope and love. Our spirituality opens us to the side of life that is ultimately important but remains invisible to the eye.

July 1986. The Elder family is camped at Willow Lake. Hot, muggy days are followed by refreshing, cool nights. A huge campfire attracts the young and the not so young as a light attracts moths. Night sets in and dark shadows lurk beyond the fire's glow. Everyone has a story to tell or a song to sing.

Personal stories weave a long yarn of Elder lore. Most of the gossip has a holy ring somewhere in the background. Young children sit wide-eyed and receptive.

The little ones are too tired to protest when moms announce bedtime. A myriad of stars dots the night sky. The quarter moon barely lights the pathways. Flashlights in hand, we guide the children to the outhouses. Crickets. Grasshoppers. Damp grass. Overgrown rose bushes grace each side of the dilapidated toilets. Still, a disgusting, fetid odour penetrates the night air. Adults call out to dawdling children, "hurry up." Tugging at his pants, four-year-old Chris is the last to emerge. "Sniffs good here," he announces as he skips back along the path.

Spirituality is an incessant desire, an indestructible longing to be connected to someone. The relationship we so desperately seek is with God. But who is God for us personally? In the beginning, we take our image of God from others: our family, our faith community, the great prophets of old, and the heroes of our time. Later, we begin to give shape and form to our own God. The circumstances of life immerse us in the power and transcendence, the humility and meekness of God. While we never fully grasp the fullness of God, our search grows and expands until we are overtaken by Love.

Where do we find God? Wherever the sun shines and the rain falls, wherever the birds sing and the flowers bloom, wherever the trees produce fruit and the seeds germinate and grow, wherever there is breath of life, there is God. The light and love of God shine through all people: the famous and the unknown, the wise and the simple, the aged and the very young, the saint and the sinner. God is present everywhere: in sacred shrines and on battlefields, in magnificent palaces and in lowly huts, in buildings of power and in refugee camps, in majestic Olympic stadiums and in unadorned hospital wards. At the very least, we can try to find God somewhere near us. Hopefully, within us.

God is eternally present to us—at the moment of conception and at the time of death, at the dawning of each day and at its closing.

God is present in our waking and in our sleeping, in our hopes and in our dreams. Though we might be indifferent and even forgetful, God remains constant—refusing to pull back, to withdraw divine love. Bending low, God embraces us in humble, compassionate love. God is the mysterious and often hidden presence in the ordinary events of life. If we would know God, we must take time to look for the unseen, to pay attention to the things of the heart.

Fresh out of language and cultural school in Rio de Janeiro, I am anxious to begin my missionary assignment in northeast Brazil. A glorious sunny day sets the stage for my first cat-echist training session. The village of Cabuçu, stretching for two kilometres along the beach, is a perfect setting. Perched on the side of a mountain, it provides a view of the ocean where palm trees, bending their branches in prayer, offer welcome shade. There is no better place to reflect on God and life than amid the splendours of nature.

Twenty-nine energetic youth responded to my plea for catechists. Ten of them are illiterate but keen listeners. The morning session begins with a Scripture reading—Jesus sending out his disciples in pairs. Following a time for silent reflection, I spend a half hour talking about teaching strate-gies. The volunteers eat it up like candy. Then off they go, two-by-two, to share ideas and prepare for their first class. Young and eager to learn, they are full of promise. A growing sense of confidence wells up inside as I watch them go. "This is God's work."

A full morning agenda culminates in a hearty rice and bean lunch. After a short siesta, the girls are ready to move on. The group sharing is spirited to say the least. After a refreshing swim in the Atlantic and a closing prayer, we are ready to call it a good day. Tired but filled with hope and more than a little confidence, we set off along the beach toward home. The young catechists take note of everything: a starfish here and a sand dollar there; swimmers and sunbathers; a team of fishermen pulling in their net. Everything provides fodder for conversation.

It doesn't take long for the catechists to spot the elderly man sitting on a rickety bench under a huge palm tree. He is staring out to sea. The girls are awestruck. No one sits that still. I recognize Pedro, a retired fisherman. He has a deeply wrinkled and dark brown, almost black face. It speaks of years of exposure to the sun, the wind, and the rain. Deep-set brown eyes reflect a peaceful but penetrating intensity.

In his declining years, Pedro spends hours silently looking at the vastness of the ocean. He knows that the still mind sees the deeper reality. Absorbed in thought, he doesn't seem to notice us. Maria, an eccentric and observant young woman, jumps to the occasion and quickly engages Pedro in conversation. I feel she is interrupting something sacred but I let it pass. "What are you doing here, old man?" she asks. "You just sit and stare at the great beyond. I don't get it."

Initially, Pedro sits in silence, his thoughts remaining with the sea. Finally, he turns and looks directly into Maria's youthful eyes. His reply is soft, almost inaudible: "I look at God and God looks at me. That's all. That's my prayer. Life is good. God is good."

God is the author of life, the origin of everything that is good and wholesome. God is the font of all love. God *is* love. Scripture gives us numerous images of God. All of them convey a profound connection, a deep union between God and all created things. Our whole biblical tradition centres on God's eternal relationship with the chosen people. God led them out of slavery in Egypt, guided them through the desert, and initiated an indissoluble covenant with them. The covenant was a blood bond, a deep connection designed to surpass time and space. God promised to remain faithful to the people and they were to be a community that gave witness to God's mercy and justice. They were to be a light to the world. And all the while, an entire nation just forgot about God.

One broken promise after another could not dissuade God. Repeated infidelities did not diminish God's love in any way. A magnificent and inspiring love story, the Bible points to God's eternal love that culminated in Jesus, the Son of God, who gave his life for the ransom of all. Even though humankind walked away from divine love, God sent Jesus to be our Redeemer. Jesus restored us to our original blessing. Then he sent the Spirit to draw the universe and humankind into the Creator's loving embrace.

The ancient Hebrew words "hesed" and "emet" were the faith community's attempt to define God. Hesed, meaning loving-kindness, gave God a personal identity. It described God in very human terms. Emet referred to the single-heartedness of God and described God as the righteous One. Capable of being utterly moved, God looks beyond our failures to the goodness that is deeper still. God hears our cries for help even when we lack the strength to voice our deepest hurts, fears, disappointments, feelings of rejection, confusion, and lack of direction.

Emet and hesed are ancient terms, Old Testament names for God. Jesus revealed God as "Abba," father, mother, shepherd, and friend. In Jesus, we meet a just and caring God who reaches out to the poor and the oppressed. We encounter a God of compassion who comforts the lonely and heals the sick. Jesus lifted up the fallen, ate with tax collectors and sinners, stood with the woman caught in adultery, and fed the hungry crowds. Jesus was a humble God, born of an unknown young woman in an obscure little town. He called lowly fishermen to discipleship. In the end, he was condemned like a common criminal and crucified between two thieves.

As the expression of God's love for humankind, Jesus looked beyond the surface to the depth of the soul. Because he saw the original goodness in all people, he was able to extend healing and mercy to the most hardened sinner. He revealed the forgiving heart of God and taught that love is greater than fear. It has the capacity to accept, to forgive, to set free.

Life gives us numerous opportunities to meet God "up close and personal," to discover our own unique insight into the heart and mind of God. Greater than we can ever imagine, God exceeds our wildest dreams and greatest assumptions. God comes to each of us in a very specific and personal way, calling us to confront reality and discover the potential for good in everything, most of all in ourselves.

God's love is our spiritual treasure, the gift that stretches our thinking, helps us remember the beauty of life, and feel the love that continues to envelop us. This gift is our spirituality. It helps us journey through life with our eyes on our ultimate goal. Amid missteps and miscues, we go from insight to insight and learn to discern life's general direction. It is always toward God, toward abundant life. Filled with the light and life of God, we gradually become bigger than we are. We grow to that wholeness of being, that holiness that is our destiny.

Awareness comes at any stage in life. To be aware is to delight in life and the Author of life. When we dwell lovingly in God's presence, we acknowledge and appreciate our original blessing. Going through life with our eyes wide open, we appreciate our relationships and refine our reactions to people and events. We learn to live with creative wholeness, to experience the full passion of our existence.

Children and youth are often blessed with a wisdom and insight beyond their years. Because they look with the eyes of the heart, they touch the very source of all life. They see goodness and try to emulate it. They see faith and stand in wonder and awe. It puts flesh on their concept of God and draws them into a loving relationship with the divine.

Josie is in grade five when she transfers to our school. Timid and unsure of herself, she is slow to make new friends. She feels awkward and uncomfortable, hesitant, and insecure in the classroom. Her greatest desire is to be like the other girls: popular, attractive, and academically successful. But her reading skills are well below grade level. Yet, deep down, she senses an innate potential for learning. Sheer determination and hard work help her overcome one obstacle at a time. Patience is her forte. She has ample opportunities to put it into practice. Over the span of two years she moves from caution and uncertainty to confidence and self-assurance. By grade seven, her welcoming smile speaks of unbounded joy and immense relief.

Josie turns thirteen on the last day of school. More than a little excited by the thought of moving on to grade seven, she celebrates the day with passion. It is much more than a class farewell party. It marks a huge milestone in her young life. Before the party ends, she steals away and comes bounding into my office. She is as calm as her beating heart will allow. She carries a fresh, green willow stick in her right hand. I wonder why. What is she thinking?

She places a warm hand on my shoulder. Then she reverently holds up the stick and bends it ever so slightly. Looking directly into my eyes, she declares: "I am giving you this willow stick because it reminds me of your faith. You can bend it but you cannot break it."

Time and time again, God breaks into our superficial and comfortable lives to gift us with an experience of profound insight and love. It may draw us into the beauty of nature. It may come in the hand extended in friendship. After long bouts of discouragement, it may be the light at the end of the tunnel. It may be the love and peace that flood our soul on First Communion Day or that sudden burst of energy that empowers us to reach out to someone in need during our youth. It may be an intensely quiet moment of stillness and peace that surrounds us in prayer or an incomprehensible feeling of intimacy with God before we fall asleep at night. Always, it leaves us with an amazing sense of interior stillness and peace. Slowly, ever so slowly, we get the message: God is forever a part of us, forever with us. We belong to God.

God's special gifts come when we stand most in need of them. Throughout life, we capture rare and precious glimpses of God. In reality, these moments of grace are truly exceptional in their intimacy and in the impact they have on our lives. In their intensity, they flood the soul with infinite light. They help us refine our image of God and stimulate our hearts to greater love and selfless service.

Through reflection and prayer, through the experience of living, we move beyond our childhood image of a Papa God, an all-powerful God who dwells far away in heaven. We abandon our youthful projection of an exacting Parent God—one who demands perfection at all cost, one we need to appease, one with whom we need to bargain and negotiate in order to "save" our souls. The almost forgotten God of early adulthood turns into the Soul Mate of our declining years. As our narrow sense of God and of life expands, we discover a whole new way of being. We know in our heart that all life is ultimately good.

The ability to reach out in love is absolute grace. We cannot grasp it like some hard-earned reward. It is simply there for us. Freely given, it must be freely received. When we are open and accepting, love cultivates our best qualities and draws forth all that is good and beautiful in us. But it also makes us vulnerable. When we love, we risk rejection, failure, denial, and even abandonment. But we also open our heart to the greatest opportunity of a lifetime—a chance to meet a "soul friend."

A soul friend identifies with your deepest dreams, knows your mind, understands your feelings of joy and frustration, adjusts to your moods, and still loves you. Such a friend rejoices in your presence and delights in who you are. The love of a friend expresses itself in complete and unquestioning loyalty even while it inspires you to grow. True love gives meaning and purpose to life. Animating and igniting the spirit, it calls you to be the best person you can be. It colours your days with vision and insight.

At age twenty-nine, Tonya is a mother of four. Her brown mulatto complexion is as smooth as papaya flesh. Sparkling brown eyes speak of warmth and intelligence. I am blessed to meet her on my first walk to the edge of Saubara, the fishing village where I live. The heat is unbearable and I am thirsty and tired. Before I notice her, Tonya calls out to me, "Edite, it is too hot to be out under this merciless sun. It's siesta time. Come and rest a while."

A practical woman, Tonya promptly offers me a glass of cold water to slake my thirst. The water is polluted. I know that, but it would be rude to refuse. Furthermore, the dryness in my throat cries out for relief. I notice from her tiny hut that Tonya is incredibly poor. I am about to learn that everything about her life is a struggle.

Tonya's husband, thirty years her senior, was a shoemaker. He chiselled away at pieces of wood to make a single pair of shoes every day. The shoes sold for eighty cruzeiros a pair, (the equivalent of a Canadian dollar). Not an extravagant amount to feed a family of six. When Ubaldo died, leaving her alone to raise four growing children, Tonya set her sights on meeting their needs rather than her own. Living life with a clear sense of purpose, she found her path and followed it with amazing fidelity.

A visionary at heart, Tonya is determined to keep her children in school. Habitually rising in the wee hours of the morning, she is at the ocean by five. Generally, she works six or seven hours digging shellfish out of the cool sand. A true entrepreneur, she turns her catch into tasty casseroles and sells them in the open market. Somehow, she is able to save enough money to pay for her children's tuition. Nothing is too much for her.

I go back to visit Tonya once a week and we become friends. We share a similar vision of God and of life, of goodness and compassion. Though our backgrounds are vastly different, we are both drawn to reach out to the most vulnerable. Each in our own way, we treasure life above everything else.

When Tonya learns that I trudge up a narrow, winding path on the edge of a mountain to deliver bread and powdered milk to the poor, she wants to help. She immediately frees up her Friday mornings. It's a costly sacrifice as it means digging up more shellfish on Thursdays to make up the deficit. It doesn't take long before she starts carrying small bags of shellfish to dole out to the poor women along our path. Each mother receives a portion of her dwindling supply. Insightful women are moved by her generosity. Her appearance is a dead give away: she is every inch as poor as they are.

One particular Friday, we find Alda, a mother of five, confined to bed. Not really a bed, just a single woven mat on the earth floor. Eyes sunken and weak. Body feverish and frail. There is a sense of tenderness about her. With no medical training, the only thing I can do is give her some of the worm medicine I carry in my bag. Alda's children dart in and out of the hut. All they have to wear are tattered shorts. No shoes. No hats to ward off the sun. They stand at the door, watching us intently.

While I mix some powdered milk and slice a loaf of bread, Tonya picks up the huge basin of dirty laundry at the back door. Off to the river she goes. The children watch me cautiously, but with great anticipation. Once they and their mother are fed, I hike further up the mountain to assist other families.

The scenarios are all too familiar. A sick mother. Starving children. The incessant stench of the open sewer. Endless, hopeless poverty! On my return, I find Tonya sitting in the dim light, holding Alda's hand. The clean clothes are piled neatly on a small table. The children, in fresh clean shorts, are playing in the street. We linger as long as the light of day allows before retracing our steps down the mountainside.

As usual, our conversation flows seamlessly. Topics range from Alda to Tonya's children, then back to the poor women who eke out a semblance of a living on the side of the mountain. As we plod further along, there is no need for words. A peaceful silence lies between us. My eyes start burning with tears. I steal a quick glance at my kindred spirit and notice that her eyes are also damp. Without realizing it, the destitute bring their own brand of holiness into our lives.

A full moon is edging its way across the horizon as we arrive back in Saubara. Tonya bursts into song: "I will follow the light high up into the mountain. It guides my feet and brings joy to my spirit. I will follow the light, the light of God." Her lyrics bring the connection between God and daily events into clearer focus.

Tonya and I take comfort and inspiration in each other's presence. She makes me a better person than I was before we met. Like so many of Brazil's poor, she faces her limitations with dignity and courage. In the fading light, I reach out for her hand and squeeze it. I thank her for being a true friend to her own people and to me. As I walk home alone, I marvel at the tremendous spiritual wealth I discover amid abject poverty in a vast and beautiful land.

Our spirituality is unique—an exclusive gift. It is the way we weave a personal tapestry of beauty and grandeur from the pieces of our life. It makes sense of our past, helps us live in the present, and enlightens and guides our path into the future. We are one of a kind. There is absolutely no one in the world that inherits the same combination of gifts and talents that we do. Responding openly and courageously to life's invitation, we unleash the wild and wonderful possibilities embedded in our soul. It is Providence's way of teaching us that we are precious in God's eyes, that we are profoundly beautiful on the inside. "O God, help me believe in myself—my inner truth, goodness, and beauty."

Spirituality summons us to take hold of our life, to trust our individuality. When we march to the tune of our own inner drum, we plumb the depths of who we are. We learn to appreciate the goodness and beauty that shine in on our lives in so many ways. We encounter the divine mystery in the concrete and daily experiences of life.

Spirituality is about our sincere yearning for intimacy and relationship. Like a magnetic force, it draws us deeper and deeper into God and into the centre of our being where body, mind, and spirit are intimately connected. There we see the order of all things and learn to let things unfold as they should. Trusting in the power of divine love, we let God mould us just as the potter shapes the clay. When we are soft and pliant in God's hands, we allow the Creator to cast us into a unique image of God. When we invest our time and energy into living life with passion and commitment, God brings creation to completion in us.

God's love is categorical and constant, steadfast and unfaltering. Frail though we are, God loves us still. We don't have to be perfect, unblemished, or absolutely holy to receive God's attention. Divine love is not dependent on our thoughts or actions or even our successes or failures. It is a totally free gift. God created us good and beautiful and delights in that creation. Beauty and imperfection are not mutually exclusive. They go together. When we respond to love, we unite our human efforts with divine grace—melding our life with the Spirit who guides us and loves us eternally.

In unconditional love, God accepts the fact that we are incomplete, less-than-perfect, saints in the making. God knows that we are filled with contradictory thoughts and confused feelings, and God loves us still. God is resolute and tenacious, forever inspiring us and leading us on. In unconditional acceptance, God sheds light on the goodness and grace that are a real and vital part of our true self.

When we walk in faith, the path becomes more transparent. We come to know and, subsequently, to fulfill our life's purpose. It is God who brings about the lifelong process of change and transformation.

Each of us, in our own imperfect but unique way, is destined to reflect a different face of God. People do different things with similar gifts. It's not so much what life gives you but what you do with your life that counts. You need to confront the whole of life, not just the easy things or whatever's the "rage" at the time. You can't cherry-pick your way through life. Life is full of surprises. There's something there for you in it all—the good, the bad, and the ugly. The wholesome person spends time getting into life rather than standing at the sidelines merely watching. In the end, life is an opportunity to be explored, a mystery to be cherished, not a problem to be solved.

No matter what our age or position, we are invited to grab hold of life, to seize it, to live each moment as though it were the only time we have. To live in the present moment is to experience the pure joy of being. These are sacred moments. Rare moments. We are inclined to dwell on past successes and failures. We fret and worry needlessly about the future. We are often so scattered and preoccupied that we miss the ordinary miracles taking place around us. We sweat the small stuff. Spirituality calls us to focus on the essential.

Spirituality is learning to love: being completely open, giving without counting the cost, trusting despite all odds. It is both a deliberate and a gratifying process. We learn love slowly, through grief and gratitude, successes and failures, ecstasies and frustrations, hopes and fears. An eternal gift with many, many layers, love is the work of a lifetime. Like a carefully wrapped gift, mature love takes a long, long time to open. But unwrap it we must or we will never reap its rewards.

Spirituality is fundamental to an authentic and fulfilled life. Beckoning us to take our life in our own hands, it teaches us to stand by our convictions despite dissenting voices. It defines who we are and serves as a moral guide throughout life. It is the incessant voice of conscience that urges us to dream our own dreams and to live by them. It fills us with the power to dig deep and draw forth the tenacity and strength we need to face the challenges of life.

Returning from school one afternoon, my fourteen-year-old nephew Tyler stops by a convenience store a few blocks from home. As he passes an old telephone booth, he spots a black leather wallet half buried in the snow. Naturally, he picks it up. Curiosity immediately gets the better of him. He opens it and takes a quick peek inside. To his utter amazement, it contains five hundred dollars. A huge amount of cash is lying in his hands. He lets his thoughts roam. He could buy a lot of things with that much money. But he knows it wouldn't be right. The money does not belong to him.

A recent driver's licence indicates that the wallet belongs to Henry Long. Now what? What is he to do? The more he thinks about it the more upsetting it becomes. He could be accused of stealing the wallet or taking some of the money. He needs time to think. So, he dashes home.

Not wearing his faith lightly, Tyler resolves to do the right thing. He finds Henry's name in the phone book and nervously dials the number. Shortly after receiving Tyler's call, Henry shows up at the front door. As Tyler hands over the wallet, Henry goes through it with a fine toothcomb. The money is all there. Embarrassed by his lack of trust, he hands Tyler a twenty-dollar reward. Tyler graciously declines. Astounded and more than a little relieved, Henry says: "You've had one exceptional upbringing, my boy. I wish there were more like you. Thank you."

How does a young teen find his inner law and obey it? What drives him to do the right and honourable thing? Surely, it is the light of conscience, an innate sense of right and wrong. Spirituality serves as an inner guide that gives direction and purpose to our lives. A powerful and intuitive capacity, it enables us to grow into the person we are destined to be. It takes us back to our roots, to the God who is consummate goodness and truth. It teaches us to define ourselves rather than be defined by others. It opens us to the Spirit who guides us.

Our spirituality sets the perimeters and defines the blueprint of who we are called to be. The rose is a rose from the time it is a seed to the time it dies. All the potential is there from the beginning. Unfortunately, most of us use only a small portion of our inherent gifts. We allow the seed, the potential for good, to lie dormant within. We lack the desire and the courage to let it grow and produce. Often, we are too indifferent to really care. Now and again, we resolve to change, to take hold of life, to grow into holiness and wholeness. But then we quickly drift back into our old ways. We forget that the human spirit needs room to soar. Still, God's love finds a way to transform us. When we respond to grace, we take on a semblance of God—a faint likeness, but an image of God, nonetheless!

Spirituality, an integral part of our conscious life, is hard to define because it is mysterious and illusive. We experience it as the energy that moves us and inspires us. We feel it in our awareness of the sacredness and interconnectedness of all life. It is an indispensable part of our dreams and aspirations, our endless searching and our perpetual longing to know ourselves. It is the spirit that animates us, the energy that moves us, the sensitivity that opens us to life and love, the passion that drives us. It is the inner light that guides us back into the heart of God. When we live in tune with the silent and mysterious presence of God, our life becomes a blessing to the world.

> **Deep within us all there is an amazing inner sanctuary of the soul, a holy place, a Divine Center, a speaking Voice, to which we may continuously return. Eternity is at our hearts, pressing upon our time-torn lives, warming us with intimations of an astounding destiny, calling us home unto itself.[6]**

Chapter 3: Love: The Essence of Spirituality

It is a warm, sunny August day. Tony and his young son Josh go fishing. The Yukon River, swift and deep, has countless dark undercurrents that snake along the bottom. Standing on the rocks, Tony and Josh cast out their lines. It is Josh's first experience. He is highly animated and full of expectation. If they are lucky, they'll take home four or five fresh grayling for supper. Suddenly, unexpectedly, the water swirls over the rock and pulls Josh into its dark embrace. Without hesitation, Tony jumps into the menacing waters to save his son. Barely able to reach Josh, he manages to grab hold of him and propel him toward safer waters. By chance, a strong, brawny stranger walking along the river witnesses the tragic scene. He immediately plunges into the water, grabs hold of Josh, and pulls him to safety. Unfortunately, there is no sign of Tony.

Several times a year, our Governor General awards great Canadians for bravery. Now and again, we hear stories about a family member or a friend hurrying to the rescue of a child in danger. Or a stranger happens to be in the right place at the right time and delivers a helpless victim from a threatening situation. Firefighters and police officers repeatedly put their own lives on the line to save others. Sometimes, these dauntless individuals are recognized for their gallantry. Often, however, their valiant deeds go unnoticed and unsung.

Every time I hear about deeds of bravery, I wonder what gives people such incredible fortitude and grit. What is hidden in the human spirit that has the power to evoke the best in us during times of crisis? What makes a person rise to the assistance of another even when it means putting his or her own life on the line? It has everything to do with spirituality and the power of God's love in the human soul.

The human heart is filled with desire. It is the energy that moves us and enables us to live this adventure we call life. Spirituality calls us to search for something More. The More of life is love. The object of our most profound desire is God and God *is* love. As God's eminent gift, love is the end of our longing. It is built into our dreams, our aspirations, our hopes, and desires. We all have an innate need, not only for God, but to experience in our flesh and in our soul the power of love. From the dawn of consciousness to the last breath we take, we are consumed with love. We need love. We pine for love. We seek love above everything else.

Love is the only thing that leads to understanding and peace, empathy and compassion, kinship and cooperation. It is the most profound and mysterious dimension of human destiny. It alone has the power to bring us into harmony with all things.

The word *love* is so casually bantered about and used so flippantly that it has lost its depth of meaning. We say: "I love my family. I love my job. I love my car. I love my country. I love the pure mountain air. I love my freedom. I love chocolate. I love hockey." Little wonder, then, that most of us miss the real meaning of love.

In its truest sense, love is a totally free and gratuitous gift from God. It gives us a new perspective and a decisive direction; it promises fulfillment and eternal life; it heals and restores our true grandeur. In the light of God's love, we reach a new horizon where our creative energy is channelled toward selflessness and consummate holiness. Gratuitous love is our response to God's overwhelming, unconditional, and faithful love.

The ancient Greeks used three words to define the dimensions of love: *eros, philia* (friendship), and *agape*. *Eros* referred to that love which arises spontaneously between two people. The Greeks considered it a divine power, a priceless gift that brings pleasure and happiness. Freud described it as erotic, sexual pleasure. We think of it as romantic love. But *eros* is much more than an intense physical sensation or a passionate desire. Neither planned nor controlled, it expresses itself as a wild, raw energy that becomes a powerful force for the spirit. Enduring in nature, it has the capacity to drive us, to lead us to commitment, and to make us aware of our superhuman abilities.

To the Greeks, *agape* was pure love, the love of the gods. An all-embracing and life-giving force, it was totally free and unfettered. The biblical understanding describes *agape* as the expression of God's faithful, abiding love for humankind. It is an outpouring of divine love that keeps on giving and giving. God's love creates us, remains with us through the gift of the Spirit, and will forever be a pure, simple, and unconditional blessing. Grounded in and shaped by faith, agape resolutely leads us back to the God in whom we live and move and have our being. As it nourishes and sustains, empowers and enlightens, it transforms us into a truer image of God.

Agape opens us to our true nature and makes us whole. But it is a lifelong journey, a never-ending exodus that takes us beyond self to a self-giving love. It leads us to accept without conditions, to forgive without limit, and to hope without confirmation. A universal love, *agape* reaches out to touch the lives of others. By its very nature, it focuses on the other. Genuine love ebbs and flows and mingles with the lives of others. Moving us beyond selfish interests, it brings people together in a relationship of fidelity, a connection that is mutually enriching and enlightening. Self-interest diminishes and gradually turns into concern and care for others. As love discovers the other, it expands and grows until it reaches perfection in the God who *is* love.

Love is a single reality, a unique gift with many dimensions. Eros is the fire in the soul, the energy of mind and body, and the vitality of spirit that comes from God and flows back to God. It is an amazingly dynamic gift. *Agape* teaches us how to pass on that gift. God is the example par excellence. In God, we see the passion of *eros*, for God is ardently in love with humankind. That is why God sent Jesus, the Word made flesh, to bring salvation to all. This is agape in its most radical form. Agape is God's faithful love, a love that is continuously poured out on humankind. A gratuitous gift of commitment, it empowers us to reach self-transcendence.

Eros is the inner drive that keeps us vibrant and alive, full of desire and longing. When it is formed and directed, disciplined and channelled in creative ways, it leads us beyond moral ambiguity to integrity of soul. We spend a lifetime integrating *eros* and *agape* into a prevailing desire to love fully and completely. Learning to love with all our heart, our mind, and our soul, we grow to the creative wholeness that is our destiny. When we are motivated and directed by love, we are open to life and all it holds. We are continually surprised and delighted by the goodness and beauty of living. Growth in love is always open-ended; love is never complete. There is always another dimension, another layer to uncover. Love calls us to go farther, to go deeper.

God, who is love, created us for love, invites us to love, holds us to love, and empowers us to love. God chose us before the foundation of the world, that we should be holy and blameless in love.[7] Whether we are conscious of it or not, love is the object of our quest, the end of our searching. To be human is to love. The essence of life is love. It is only through love that we discover our innate goodness. Love fills us with the desire to strive, to seek, and to find inner freedom. It inspires us to do the one thing necessary—to pour out our life for the sake of the other.

In the mid-eighties and into the early nineties, my friend Karen and I were the only two members of our Koinonia community living in Whitehorse. In response to a local need, we offered hospitality to young expectant couples from outlying areas. All of them lived in isolated communities or cabins in the wilderness. They had no access to a gynecologist, a general practitioner, or even a midwife. Since the roads were closed through the better part of the winter, expectant couples felt the need to be near a hospital well before their delivery date. Those who stayed with us became an integral part of our daily life. Walking with them through the last few weeks of pregnancy, we shared their anticipation and, eventually, their immense joy at the miracle of a new life.

November 1990. Bev, her husband Dan, and three-year-old son Greg have been with us for almost three weeks. The cold northern winds blow and the thermometer drops quickly. When it remains at minus thirty for several days, Dan gets more and more agitated. His thoughts turn to the prohibitive cost of heating their cabin. A good wood fire could keep it warm for more than thirty hours. Saturday morning father and son set out for home.

Sunday morning unleashes an unexpected and unusually wild winter storm. Karen calls Bev to get ready for church. A hint of regret in her voice, Bev replies, "I've gone into labour. Dan isn't here and there's no way to contact him."

Contractions intensify. Karen decides it's time to drive her to the hospital. No husband means no birthing partner. We can't leave her alone. I volunteer to stay. I hold her hand, wipe her brow, and encourage controlled breathing. As I watch Bev bear contraction after contraction, I can't imagine myself being that brave. She is definitely a survivor.

Relief spreads across Bev's face when she hears the unmistakable cry. "It's a girl," announces the gynecologist in a dramatic voice. Still, he seems to take forever examining the tiny infant. "When can I see her?" Bev asks. "I need to feel every muscle and count every finger. Why is it taking so long? Is there a problem?"

At long last, the nurse gently places the baby into her mother's outstretched arms. The little girl has a severe cleft palate. Bev struggles to contain her tears. The anguish mounts. I place a hand on her shoulder. There are no words to alleviate her sorrow. Bev sits in silence as she rocks her child. An hour later she begins to hum softly. Her sad melody gives

EMBRACING THE SPIRIT WITHIN

expression to a very painful moment. It is a moving scene—a young mother holding her deformed child. Empathy surfaces. Once again, I am intensely aware of an inner reality. This child will be deeply loved. She already is.

When Karen and I return to the hospital the next day, Dan is holding the infant. Bev is surprisingly upbeat. They name their daughter Amanda. Pragmatic by nature, Bev is already inquiring about possible surgery. "I know I am looking down the road," she admits. "But there has to be a way to correct that awful palate." The specialist hands her an impressive pile of medical journals. I know Bev will do whatever it takes to put Amanda on an equal footing with other children. Nothing will scuttle her resolve.

Two years later when Bev and Dan move south, we lose contact. The years fly by. Then, on a lovely July day, our door-bell rings. I am pleasantly surprised to find Dan standing there. The motorbike in the driveway suggests that he's come alone. Over several cups of coffee, we catch up on the events of the past sixteen years. As Dan begins talking, tears of sorrow well up in his eyes and begin to flow like a mighty river. Two short years ago Bev was diagnosed with a progressive form of breast cancer. It was too late. There was nothing medicine had to offer.

Ever the mother, Bev had all the right instincts. Amanda and Greg were much too young to be without their mother. But cancer has no respect for age or gender or circumstance. Bev put up a noble fight but lost the battle in May. As she lay dying, she exacted a simple promise from Dan. "I want you to visit those two sisters in the Yukon after I'm gone. Remember the peace we felt in their home all those years ago? You'll feel it again. Tell me you'll go back."

Karen and I spend several hours with Dan. It's the first time he's been able to cry since Bev's untimely death. Gradually the tears of deep sadness wash into tears of relief. There is a note of pride in his voice as he tells us about Amanda. He pulls out a picture taken on her sixteenth birthday and offers it to us. She's an amazing reflection of her mother. There isn't a trace of the cleft palate. Instead of wallowing in depression or chastising herself silently, Bev did what she had to do. She ful-filled her mission and gave her daughter a chance at a normal, happy life. No one could ask for more.

Wisdom, the love of God, is nurtured in the heart of the family. Parents pour themselves out for their children, willingly moving heaven and earth to protect their offspring. They sacrifice their time, their talents, and their own convenience for the sake of their children. Our first experience of the power of love takes place at home. There we learn the give and take of life. We grow in love by learning to share, to listen, to respect, and to care for each other. The one thing most of us can always count on is the love and loyalty of our family. The bonds of blood run deep. Family gives us roots, something to cling to. Genuine love gives us wings. It frees us to become fully ourselves. We need both in order to chart our life's journey, reach for our own star, and fulfill our unique destiny.

Love is always outgoing. It is not something we hold onto lest we lose it. Rather, it flows out into the world where it creates bonds of respect and acceptance, hope and expectation. To be like God, to love like God, is to move beyond personal wants and desires. It requires eyes that are wide open and perceptive. It develops an inner landscape, a heart open to every possibility. I must be the first to smile, to speak a kind word, to extend a helping hand, to be a shoulder for someone to lean on, and to champion the cause of the poor.

There is a fundamental connection between our "raison d'être" and our inherent desire to love. When God breathed the spirit of life into us, God gave us a share in divine life and called us to our special mission. Creation is incomplete, a work in progress. It is forever evolving. We are destined to be co-creators with God. When we learn to take the long view, we discover the pressing needs of our world. We strive to be people of peace, compassion, and justice. Our mission is to find kinder and gentler ways of being.

Long before I went to Brazil, the cardinal of Recife, Dom Helder Camara, fascinated me. I read everything I could lay my hands on about his life and work. I found his personal writings especially moving. A modern champion of social justice, he was renowned for his humble approach to life and his staunch commitment to the poor and oppressed. His life moved from ideas and words to meaningful action. As bishop and cardinal, he spent his time working for land reform and fair wages for the working class. Many referred to him as a walking sermon. His generosity knew no bounds. Looking beyond the surface, he saw new possibilities. He gave his Episcopal palace to a group of parishioners who turned it into a hostel for the poor and the homeless. He quietly moved into the sacristy, two bare rooms at the back of the cathedral.

As I begin my missionary work, my respect for Dom Helder and the way he lives grows exponentially. Most Brazilians have a strong opinion about him: the poor are exceptionally positive; the rich and powerful are extremely negative. Though they have never met him, the people in our villages speak highly of him. Naturally, I look for a chance to meet him.

During my first holiday I board an old, rickety bus to Recife. Seventy-three hours later, covered in fine dust, I disembark—tired, hungry, thirsty. It's a small price to pay to meet a truly great man. I get my bearings and walk in the direction of the cathedral. Across the street I spot an impressive building nestled in a treed area. A large sign identifies it as the Hostél Catølico. How convenient. I book myself in at the front desk and find a shower.

I rise at first light. Dom Helder's custom is to preside at Eucharist at 5:00 am and I want to be there. I have time for a quick walk around the downtown area. There is an undeniable smell of salt water and the sound of waves beating the shore a short distance away. Street vendors are already preparing for the business of the day. By 4:30 am, I am comfortably seated in the third row of the cathedral, a good vantage point. Eucharist is remarkably prayerful, though I spend most of it considering Dom Helder. I drink in his empirical dignity enhanced by his sparkling eyes and radiant smile.

At the conclusion of Eucharist, Dom Helder walks down the centre aisle. My eyes grow bright and I smile in blissful admiration. His manner speaks of gentleness and humility. Now directly in front of me, he extends his hand and introduces himself. "A small man with a huge heart," I think to myself. Placing a warm hand on my arm, he invites me to join him for breakfast. It is a surprising and powerful gesture.

I can hardly contain myself as I follow him to the sacristy. I am in for another surprise as we enter the two bare and simple rooms he calls home. Contentment and peace reign supreme.

He amazes me even further when he prepares our breakfast. I offer to help. Conversation flows freely. We laugh and cry together. We share common interests: life amidst the poor, the thousands of displaced families, the "favelas" (slums), and the disappearance of people with leadership capabilities. It is obvious that everyone in Dom Helder's world is precious to him. "Change is in the air," he says at the end. "It is time to replace the military government through fair and transparent elections." I know where he is going. I admire his balanced and sensitive approach.

Sometimes, God reveals the divine presence in the goodness and holiness of a person. On rare occasions, we are blessed to cross paths with a totally magnanimous heart. When I met Dom Helder Camara, I met a truly holy man. Everything about him left a lasting impression. I still think of him every time I read the beautiful passage from the prophet Micah: This is what the Lord God asks of you, only this: act justly, love tenderly, and walk humbly with your God.[8]

Just as our lives belong to God, so too does our love. Love begins in God and flows back to God. Divine love ebbs and flows into our lives in a never-ending stream. When we are attentive to that love, it becomes the bond that unites the human with the divine. It teaches us the truth about God, about life, and about ourselves. It helps us see things afresh, in their pristine beauty and eternal goodness. It beckons us to shine the gentle light of our love on the world around us.

We come into the world naked and alone. We are totally dependent on another. We need others to help us grow and mature. Even as we advance in wisdom and grace, we never become totally self-sufficient. We were created for love, for communion. We participate in each others' lives. Self-giving love expresses itself in community. Love grows and flourishes in the heart of community and moves us from individuality to communion—from my needs to our needs, from my desires to our desires.

To love is to respect, esteem, enrich, and bless those whose lives we touch. When we love, we learn to accept our differences and look on them as treasures. Acceptance is to see the potential in the other, to draw forth the best part. To love is to give the other space to grow. In sincere love, we become free enough to be ourselves. Love touches the real world. We love with our hands, our mind, and our heart. By caring for one another and carrying each others' burdens, we become the glue that holds the world together.

Teaching in a local Catholic high school, I serve as staff advisor to one of the house leagues, the House of Damascus. Our house is responsible for the Christmas dance, no small undertaking. It means five or six Saturdays at school. The senior pin, Cory, drives a hard bargain. But he puts his money where his mouth is. He never misses a Saturday, even though he is expected to babysit his six-year-old sister, Alicia. I like his even-tempered manner, his great sense of humour, and his strong work ethic.

The first Saturday, Cory casually walks in clutching Alicia's hand. He is strong and tall; she is slender, a wisp of a girl. Alicia is an extraordinary child—she has Down's syndrome, but Cory treats her like a princess. He doesn't dominate or manipulate; his gentle and patient manner alludes to a powerful bond between brother and sister. He has the grace to introduce Alicia to the group. All eyes widen, but everyone welcomes her warmly. There is a high degree of vulnerability there and everyone senses it.

Before long, the students are totally enamoured with Alicia and she with them. Someone gives her a huge paint-brush. Obviously thrilled, she sets about adding bold blotches of colour to an oversized dance poster. The girls spend time reading and singing to her. Hands clap and feet thump out the rhythm. The boys feed her junk food and take turns carrying her around on their shoulders. Wonky legs dangle freely; clear blue eyes speak of innocence. Youth has a gift for making the mundane special. Cory's sincere love for Alicia enhances her status in the eyes of his peers.

Love is the act of recognizing another as the temple of the Spirit. It is the most creative form of presence, a presence that calls for openness and attentiveness. Love is neither selective nor discriminatory. It reaches out to the other in freedom, no holes barred. To love is to be there for the other in good times and in bad, in sickness and in health, for richer, for poorer, until the end of time and into eternity.

People who are very poor still have a lot to give and the desire to give it never disappears. In Saubara, Brazil, everyone is poor. Many are so poor they do not have the means to bury their dead with dignity. The law is clear: the dead must be buried within twenty-four hours, little time for a family to come up with the exorbitant fee for a simple plot in the municipal graveyard. The alternative is the local potter's field, a roadside ditch. Naturally, people rally around the family of the deceased. There are the usual offerings of sympathy, the sharing of a meal, the building of a coffin, the preparation of the body, and the prayer vigil. Friends and neighbours also go door-to-door collecting money to pay for a burial plot.

It is a hot, hot Friday afternoon when Maria, Celeste, and I begin canvassing the south end of town. Taking a long view up the street, I spot Katita's house. A mud hut, like so many others, it consists of a single room with a dirt floor. Everything is bare, austere, old, and worn. All I've ever seen in her home is a small dark dresser, a table, two chairs, and several mats where Katita and her four children sleep. I hesitate calling at her hut today. I am uncomfortable asking for a donation from someone so incredibly poor. I voice my concern. Neither Maria nor Celeste agrees. Their vision is so far ahead of mine.

Katita welcomes us with open arms. She looks at me for a long time. Dark, determined eyes see right through me. Finally, she says: "I know why you are here. You are collecting money to bury Domingo. Why do you hesitate, Edite?" Without waiting for a reply, she walks over to her dresser and withdraws a small white handkerchief from the top drawer. Unrolling it, she carefully pulls out a hundred-cruzeiro bill and hands it to me. I am at a loss. What should I do? Accept the entire amount? I know she has been saving the money to buy a chicken for Sunday's supper. Again, she detects my reluctance: "Here. Please, please take it. God is good. God will provide something else before Sunday." The poor have a way of teaching us the real meaning of charity. I still regret not understanding love enough to respect Katita's dignity.

A totally free and uncomplicated gift, love reveals the inner mountain we all have to climb. Slowly and deliberately, it exposes our pretexts and washes away our defences. We need to get rid of the fantasies in our head before we are able to focus on the needs around us. Those who have it all are prone to flattery. Akin to the firefly that flickers here and there, they tell us what we want to hear. The poor, who have nothing to lose, call a spade a spade. Unwavering in their honesty, they cast a direct light on us and we see our pretences and inhibitions for what they are. Sincere and unpretentious, the poor teach us the art of humility and truth.

Happiness rises up out of our roots. Because it comes from God, love is patterned on God's love, a love that is faithful and unconditional. We all need love, more love that we deserve. The lowly and rejected also stand in need of love. Everyone has a claim on our love, especially those whom the world puts last. Love moves us beyond our comfort level to risk life and reputation as we reach out to those who appear undesirable.

In the movie *Dead Man Walking*, we meet Sister Helen Prejean. While she shies away from any direct involvement with politics and economics, she finds herself working in a New Orleans social housing project for black residents. Surprisingly, her life moves along rather smoothly, until the day she receives a strange invitation: would she serve as a pen pal to a death row inmate? It seems like an easy thing to do, certainly not very time consuming. What could be so hard about writing a few letters? Helen accepts the challenge. The correspondence flows back and forth. Then, one day, Matthew Poncelet's return letter contains another invitation: would Helen come to visit him in the penitentiary?

Helen has no experience with prisons and loathes the idea of going there. Still, she feels some mysterious pressure to do it, just once. As she drives up the long, winding driveway to the state prison in Louisiana, second thoughts drive out any semblance of calm. Fear and doubt cast a heavy mist in her unusually single-hearted soul. What is she thinking? What possible good could come of this? Yet, she continues on.

In the prison, Helen meets a terrified and troubled man. Beneath a rude, arrogant, and unrepentant façade, there is a deeply frightened soul. On death row, Matt has spent six years awaiting execution by lethal injection. He is a bewildered, sad, and angry man. Prison provides nothing but time—endless hours to think about his crime and its ensuing punishment. The tiny flame of hope burns lower and lower. Only death looms on the horizon. From Matt's vantage point, it is approaching with lightning speed. But he has his pride and he has no intention of sharing his deepest, darkest secrets with this woman, a nun at that.

It doesn't take Helen long to see behind the mask and discover the impenetrable anguish that engulfs this condemned man. In response to his flippant and often sarcastic comments, she reaches into her repertoire of scripture passages and quotes the one most pertinent for the moment. The sparring continues for weeks and months. Though Matt is pretentious, sexist, and racist, Helen is drawn to this lonely man. She is concerned, not only for his life, but for his dignity and his soul.

Helen has more to think about than Matt Poncelet. There are the bitter feelings expressed by the victims' families, fierce opposition from the public, and her own family's difficulty with her decision to continue visiting Matt. True to her Christian faith, she believes that only genuine forgiveness can wash away Matt's hatred and anger. At first, she wonders what role she is meant to play. As it becomes clearer, she pays a visit to each of the victims' families. Despite the jumble of emotions she sees there, she dares to speak of forgiveness. They take it as a cruel and insensitive insult to their children's memory.

Back at the prison, Matt's mixed messages bewilder Helen. Was it Matt or his partner, Carl Vitello, who committed the crime? Then, one day, Matt candidly admits that he killed the boy and raped the young girl. Helen struggles with the reality of it all. How could she possibly stand on the side of a murderer and a rapist? What is she doing to the victims' families?

In the end, she concludes that Matt stands in need of redemption. Despite mounting opposition, she initiates a new appeal for clemency: Matt will accept lifelong confinement in exchange for his life. Another dead end.

Helen's acceptance of Matt awakens a deep bond of friendship and love. Over the weeks and months, the tension drains away. The week before his execution, Matt chooses Helen as his spiritual mentor and guide. It proves to be an agonizing week for both of them. Matt struggles with his crime. How could he have done such a horrendous thing? How could he turn to God and dare to ask forgiveness? Looking beyond his guilt, Helen musters every ounce of inner strength to help him. Her deep faith arouses the latent spirituality inside Matt's troubled soul. The almost imperceptible light of faith is rekindled. For the first time in his entire life, Matt begins to see that he is not a totally bad person. There is a ray of light and goodness in him. He, too, is God's work of art.

Helen repeatedly places her hand on Matt's shoulder as she reads the consoling passage from Isaiah: "Do not fear, for I have redeemed you. I have called you by name; you are mine. When you pass through the waters, I will be with you; and through the rivers, they shall not overwhelm you; when you walk through fire you shall not be burned, and the flame shall not consume you."[9] Those consoling words lead Matt to come to terms with his pending death. He is not afraid to die and resolves to die with dignity.

Helen promises to be with Matt to the end—as he is led to the execution room, strapped into the chair, and given the lethal injection. She will be his strength. She makes only one request. She asks him to keep looking at her, to keep his eyes fixed on her. "I want you to see the face of love," she says. "The last thing you will see before you die will be the face of someone who loves you." Like the rest of us, Matt needs more love than he deserves.

While the human body is fashioned and formed in a relatively short period of time, the formation of the human soul is open-ended. It is shaped through every experience and every encounter. Everything has the potential to deepen and enrich us. Divine love is the powerful, consistent force that brings about this deepening, this spiritual growth. God is forever with us, calling us to let go of our pride and prejudice and open our deepest, inner self to the power of divine love. When we allow God to enter the sacred sanctuary of our soul, healing takes place. God accepts us and loves us definitively. And that makes all the difference.

Nothing worth knowing reveals its secrets easily. The beauty of love is not at the end of the road but in the journey itself. Love costs. God is for our growth as God is for our pruning. Like the thresher, love sifts us and grinds us to make us pure. In its blessed fire, love purifies and heals us. It is in the dark night of the soul that we discover the secrets of our own heart. It teaches us where our hearts ought to be. Through it all, love warms us with its gentleness, lifts us up when we fall, and carries us through the rough spots. And, in its sacred glow, love leads us to understand the dream God has for us.

Josef and Negar met at the University of Baghdad. He was a budding professor; she was a grad student. He was a Muslim; she, a Catholic. Both were bright, energetic, youthful, and charming individuals. Despite their best efforts, they fell deeply in love. Their love brought them to a crossroads, a painful quandary. How could they accept this beautiful gift of love? In Iraq, marriage between a Muslim and a Christian was totally out of the question. Even dating publicly resulted in communal punishment. The parties' families were openly criticized, ridiculed, embarrassed, and persecuted.

The decision to leave their homeland was not an easy one, but that was what their love required. Student visas in hand, Josef and Negar were filled with a nagging fear and a great deal of trepidation when they arrived in Canada. They faced an uncertain future in a foreign land. Their lives had been turned upside down.

Confusion and doubt are reflected in their eyes when I meet them at the airport in Calgary. She is leaning into him, almost afraid to look up. Love is supposed to cast out fear. But both are walking into a great unknown. Their eyes wander until they spot me with my welcome sign. I am supposed to give them some assurance that everything will be all right. I can't. I'm not all that sure that it will be. But I hide my doubts and insecurities.

I take them to the small apartment our committee rented for them. The accommodations are comfortable, certainly not luxurious. It has been a long day for them. After spending a few minutes answering their questions, I give them their own space. They have each other. I pray that their love will carry them through the coming months.

The next few weeks are weeks of overwhelming adjustments. The comforts of home are gone. Josef and Negar long to reach out and touch their families and friends. While the past recedes further and further into the shadows, the present looms larger than life. New images and hard reality take centre stage. They are forced to make many adjustments. The cold autumn winds allude to a deeper chill in their souls.

It is time to move on. Turning to the practical side of their new life, they face the task of job hunting. One frustrating day follows another. Being immigrants, and speaking "broken" English, makes it all the more difficult. Both are highly qualified, but a professional job for either one remains a distant dream. Eventually, Josef gets a job with a construction firm. Negar becomes a housekeeper in a local hotel.

A strange new life, with its unimagined challenges, brings them closer together. They take their love to a much higher level as they learn to share their convictions, their doubts, and life itself. Their love is tried and tested and proves itself strong.

It takes great courage to learn the art of loving. You don't simply fall in love and that is that. Like all growth, love demands many deaths to self. Love takes a long time growing. Magnanimous love reaches out beyond family and friends to the wider world. It seeks neither recognition nor reward. To love is to make the world a kinder place, not only for those whom we know but also for the stranger and the foreigner. Love moves out from the specific to the universal.

Love brings people together, shining its light on the dark spaces in our souls. It brings hope to a world that so often sees only emptiness and darkness. Forgiving injuries and healing wounds, love becomes an amazing force for unity. It opens us to the mystery of God. God's hopes become our hopes. God's desires become our desires. God's dream becomes our dream. And our life becomes God's.

> Love is patient; love is kind; love is not envious or boastful or arrogant or rude. It does not insist on its own way; it is not irritable or resentful; it does not rejoice in wrongdoing, but rejoices in the truth. It bears all things, believes all things, hopes all things, endures all things. Love never ends… Now faith, hope, and love abide, these three; and the greatest of these is love.[10]

Chapter 4: Spirituality:
The Mystery and the Challenge

It was early afternoon on the Sabbath. Jesus entered the synagogue to pray. He was about to sit down when he noticed a man with a withered hand. The suspicious eyes of the Pharisees were instantly fixed on Jesus. He knew what they were thinking. Their thoughts were completely unrelated to his. While they were preoccupied with the letter of the law, he focused on healing and mercy. While they were intent on maintaining their positions of power and control, he held out freedom and the fullness of life.

The man with the withered hand stood passively by. He didn't even bother to ask Jesus to heal him. Still, Jesus was moved with compassion and reached out to him. He invited the man to stretch out his hand. As the man did so, the hand was promptly healed. At once, he turned and left the synagogue without so much as a word of thanks to God. Jesus quietly sat down.

The Pharisees were furious. How dare Jesus cure someone on the Sabbath? Misconstruing his kindness, they spread an icy atmosphere throughout the synagogue. The environment, previously conducive to prayer, turned hostile and oppressive. Jesus had been through this before. Calmly and peacefully, he finished his prayer, left the synagogue, and went to the mountain to pray. Emotionally and spiritually drained, he renewed his inner spirit as he spent the entire night communing with God.[11]

Time and again, the experience of living lets all of us down. We become despondent and discouraged. With time, we become intuitively aware of the need to renew ourselves. Like Jesus, we need to find our own mountain, the place where we can be totally free, where we can be in touch with our soul. Some find comfort and inspiration on a mountaintop; others go to a sacred space or a place of worship; others turn to a memory of God—an experience that fortified and sustained them in the past. Some need an atmosphere of quiet stillness; others are renewed through music or art.

No matter what happens, the Spirit is always with us. When we live in harmony with its urgings, we recognize its fruits in us and in all people. The process evolves over the course of a lifetime. Very young children know that goodness adds to life. Youth take it a step further and develop the discipline inherent in ongoing friendship. Young adults find that loyalty to one's essence leads to inner peace and contentment. Seniors who have been true to the promptings of the Spirit reach a point of profound happiness and fulfillment in their declining years.

The example of others often inspires us to greater love. The movie *Pay It Forward*, released in 2000, portrays the "power of one."[12] It is the first day of school for a rambunctious grade seven social studies class. Their teacher, Eugene Simonet, is a scarred and troubled soul. Having suffered deeply, both emotionally and physically, he wants something different for his students. His goal is to challenge them to look past the sad and repetitious events of history, to stretch their thinking beyond the selfish and superficial ways of their world. During his first class, he draws their attention to the bonus assignment on the chalkboard. A most unusual task, it is to last the entire school year. It reads: "Think of an idea that could change the world and put it into action."

Trevor McKinney, the only son of a poverty-stricken single mother, immerses himself completely in the challenge. He conceives a truly novel idea—he will do a gratuitous act of kindness for three people. Rather than wait for someone to do him a favour so that he will feel the need to pay it back, he decides to "pay it forward." He anticipates that each of the people who receive his kindness will perform some unsolicited act of kindness for three more people. Trevor believes that when we "pay it forward," we set in motion an arithmetic progression: three acts of kindness lead to nine, nine lead to twenty-seven, then eighty-one, and so on. In this simple and relatively easy way, the entire world will eventually be coloured with kindness.

Trevor's sincere attempts produce mixed results. His first recipient is Gerry, a homeless man. At the young boy's invitation, Gerry enjoys an entire night in Trevor's home. But the very next day, while Trevor is at school, Gerry reverts to his old habits. Trevor goes searching for him and finds him in a well-known drug house. The curtains are closed and the door is locked. No amount of knocking or pleading produces any results. The addiction to drugs runs so deep it turns Gerry into a virtual prisoner. He is too weak to really change anything. Life on the street makes few demands on him and he can readily steal enough to buy the drugs he craves. With a heavy heart, Trevor goes home and puts an X through that name.

Trevor's second candidate is Mr. Simonet himself. Even at his tender age, Trevor senses that his teacher is an extremely lonely man. Perhaps there is a way to introduce him to another forlorn person and the two will find comfort in each other. Trevor honestly believes that a new relationship could prove to be mutually beneficial.

Trevor's mother, Arlene, isolates herself and lives a very solitary life. Repeatedly, Trevor beseeches her to do something about her abuse of alcohol. He is convinced that, if she really wants to, she can change her life. But her desire for self-improvement is simply not strong enough to lead to any lasting resolve. While she doesn't take a single, serious step toward recovery, Trevor refuses to give up on her. He contrives different ways of bringing her and Mr. Simonet together. When his alcoholic father re-enters the scene, however, the scheme backfires. Mr. Simonet feels more rejected, ridiculed, scorned, and utterly alone than he ever felt in his entire life.

Trevor's third candidate is a classmate. Adam, a small, asthmatic, and sickly boy, is easy prey for the schoolyard bullies, who find some strange delight in torturing him. The bigger boys in his class consistently take advantage of him; using intimidation, they coerce him into giving them his prized belongings. The first time Trevor chances upon a scene where the boys are punching and kicking Adam, he is too petrified to get involved. Instead of coming to Adam's rescue, he quietly and sadly backs away and rides home as quickly as he can.

The bullying becomes a malicious and ugly pattern. Every time Adam walks home alone, the bullies lie in wait for him. It doesn't take long before Trevor is given a second chance to intervene. Determined to rescue his classmate, he musters all his strength and inner resources to assist Adam. He gets off his bike, walks over, and confronts the bigger boys. His courageous act in defence of Adam produces tragic results. The bullies turn on Trevor and beat him so badly that he pays for his kind deed with his life. But Trevor does not die in vain. Through his audacity, a new movement takes root and spreads throughout the land. People across America begin performing spontaneous acts of kindness for others.

Spirituality challenges all of us to rise to the defence of the weak, to speak up for the timid, to intervene on behalf of the poor and oppressed. Generally, the results are inconclusive, sometimes barely visible. Though we may never see it, every sincere act of goodness, kindness, or compassion has a ripple effect. When we "pay it forward," we inspire people of good will to leave their mark of kindness and charity on the world. In the end, good always triumphs over evil.

If we are open, spirituality rouses our desire to set the world on fire with goodness and love. When we get in touch with it, it becomes a mighty force that opens us to see God in everything that happens to us. Spirituality moves us to take the high road, to follow the less travelled path. It is a steep and steady climb but God's grace is always sufficient for us. God doesn't ask for great and wonderful things, merely that we do little things extraordinarily well. We all have a tremendous source of energy, an amazing inner strength that enables us to overcome all obstacles.

Everyone longs to live an authentic life. Our deepest desire is to be fully alive in the Spirit, to be holy and wholesome. Mistakenly, we believe spirituality should consistently immerse us in light. We delude ourselves into thinking that personal growth and development is an automatic and easy process, one positive experience after another. To be human, to be fully alive, is to swim against the current, to take up the challenge, to face reality and deal with it as best we can.

Like a labyrinth, life takes us in many directions. We walk forever—to the centre of life and then back out. Sometimes, we retrace our steps until we come to a new unfolding. Our earthly pilgrimage is an intricate and complex mixture of consolations and desolations: successes and failures, good health and illness, peace and turmoil, welcoming environments and ugly situations. Everything has the potential to deepen us.

Always full of mystery and surprise, God continues to call us, shape us, renew us, and form us into an image of the divine. We need both positive and negative experiences to help us grow to our full potential. Anyone can bear "the beams of light and love." It takes discipline and courage, inner clarity and insight, constancy and perseverance, to walk through the dark valley of tears. All growth comes with a price. The good and truly noble life calls us to use our inner resources to bear the knocks, to confront the obstacles, to feel our way in the dark. As Thomas Merton said, it is not so much what happens to us, but the way we respond to each situation that is the test of our mettle. Every situation, event, and encounter has the potential to fashion us into God's holy people. Every experience has the power to deepen us.

Early in the Second World War, the concentration camps of Auschwitz and Dachau were already well established. The young psychiatrist Victor Frankl found himself on a transport truck destined for Auschwitz. On arrival, he stood in line with the common prisoners who awaited their fate. Young and naïve, he had not yet learned that his life, like everyone else's, was in the hands of the senior SS officer. An uncanny foreboding welled up inside as he observed how a silent wave to the right or to the left either gave a reprieve or condemned a prisoner to the gas chambers.

In the period following admission to Auschwitz, the original shock of the captives turned into self-deception. They deluded themselves into believing that somehow, someway, they would find reprieve at the last minute. When that didn't happen, they acquired an indifferent and unresponsive attitude. As the nights grew darker and the days filled them with fear and confusion, they learned to disengage their minds from the horror of their circumstance. Emotional detachment turned into a relative apathy and most of them died inside.

Over time, Frankl learned to blend in with the masses, to avoid unnecessary attention, to be one of the great army of unknown and unrecorded victims. Sometimes, he sought solace in the beauty of nature, the loveliness of a sunset, or the majesty of the Bavarian mountains. Every now and again, he found refuge in his daydreams. As he reminisced about happy and intimate times with his beloved wife, he remembered the power of her love and it kept him strong. He came to the conclusion that love is the highest goal, the essence of human life. No one comes to salvation except through love.

Frankl had ample opportunity to observe the way people respond to a traumatic situation. He concluded that all victims, in fact all of humankind, could be put into one of three classes. The first class was characterized by weakness. These captives had no energy, no inner resources, no dreams, no ambition, and no motivation. They were so fragile that the guards immediately waved them to the left, to the gas chambers.

The second class demonstrated a different kind of weakness. They were emotionally too insecure to see beyond their immediate needs. The SS used this weakness against them. These prisoners became informants. Unwittingly, they divulged the secrets of the camp in exchange for an extra piece of bread or a bigger portion of soup. The struggle for survival was so great that it blurred their vision.

The third class consisted of the steadfast and the strong. They faced the ups and downs of life with courage and determination. Tribulations made them more resilient. In Auschwitz, these prisoners were motivated by an inner source of strength that enabled them to assist and comfort others. Once Frankl realized that those who believe in something or someone beyond the self have a spiritual freedom that gives meaning to their lives, he volunteered to help care for the victims of typhus. It gave some meaning to the months and years he spent in Auschwitz.

In the period following his release, Frankl concluded that a prisoner had a choice to make: to turn life into a triumph of the spirit or to disregard the challenge and languish in self-pity. Those who survived stood out from the masses because they were able to determine their own attitude in the face of the most inhumane circumstances. Tapping into the power buried in their souls, they found a reason to live. Either they had a loved one to come home to, or they had some great project or work they needed to complete, or they believed in a higher Power. They became a living testament. They proved to their captors and to the world that "he who has a *why* to live for can bear almost any *how*."[13]

All of us fall into one of Frankl's three classes. Perhaps we move from one class to the other in the course of our lives. You long to be a good person, willing to stare the vicissitudes of life in the face and overcome them. You want to become increasingly more loving and more committed. But life also reveals another side of you. You are not consistently faithful to your dreams. You step up to the plate and then step back. Sometimes, you are too naïve to anticipate the hurdles that lie before you. When reality sets in, you need to draw from your inner resources to become a person for others. Selfless giving is not an overnight job. It takes a lifetime to refine and purify.

We all have the capacity to transcend the circumstances of our lives if we discover the guiding truth within. We always have a choice regardless of how despicable and abhorrent our predicament might be. The strong and the noble turn away from apathy and indifference because they know the power of God. They rise above the most difficult situation. It is not so much what we expect from life but what life expects from us that makes the difference. Spirituality empowers us to live and die for our ideals.

Underneath the surface, we all long to reflect the goodness and love of our original blessing. But desire alone is not enough. Sooner or later, goodness and light fade into darkness. We sin. We cave into human weakness. We indulge in the superficial and deceitful. We become self-centred and manipulative. But God doesn't leave us there. God calls us back into the barren wilderness of the desert where we confront our humanity. God throws us a lifeline in the person of Jesus. In his dying and rising, Jesus takes our sins on his own shoulders and washes us clean. Jesus set the healing process in motion. It is up to us to seize it, to take hold of it, and to let it bear fruit in our life. Redemption has the power to take us beyond our comfort zone and challenges us to make life-giving choices.

The book of Genesis presents two brothers, Esau and Jacob. We remember Esau as a victim; Jacob as a go-getter, one who pushed the margins. Malcontent with his place in the family tree, Jacob set out to supplant his elder brother. He did his homework. He saw that Esau was carefree and easy going, unable to think long-term, and he took full advantage of the situation. He offered his brother instant gratification with a simple pot of red lentil soup. In exchange, Esau sold his birthright to his younger brother. For Jacob, the price was right.

Jacob spent long days pondering his good fortune and devising an elaborate scheme to collect his "due." A master at deception, he prepared a meal for their blind father, Isaac. Pretending to be Esau, he asked for and received the traditional birthright blessing. The law was final. Once given, the birthright was irrevocable. Jacob's trickery had the desired result, but it came with an enormous price. When Esau discovered the betrayal, he threatened to murder his younger brother. Jacob immediately went into hiding. Under the cover of darkness, he travelled to Haran. His plan was to locate his uncle Laban, settle in with him, and find a suitable wife.

En route, Jacob came upon the shrine of Bethel. Recognizing the sacredness of the place, he stayed the night. In a dream, he envisioned a stairway going from earth to heaven. Amid the angels ascending and descending the ladder, he saw God standing over him. The promise was clear: "I will give to you and your descendants the land on which you are lying… I will keep you safe wherever you go."[14]

Jacob had an eye for beauty. When he encountered Laban's lovely daughter, Rachel, at a well, a surge of passion flooded over him. Rachel was the woman of his dreams. Still a fugitive and obviously penniless, he offered Laban seven years of labour in exchange for Rachel's hand in marriage. But the master of deception faced his own betrayal. The wedding night was exceptionally dark and Laban used it to his advantage. Unsuspectingly, Jacob married the elder daughter, Leah. Still longing for what wasn't his, Jacob remained attracted to the unavailable Rachel. Consequently, he worked another seven years to win her hand.

Jacob's craftiness never left him. Over time, he made sure the tables were turned on Laban. He asked permission to return to the land of his father. He needed a small herd of sheep and goats to provide for his family along the journey and offered to take the dark sheep and speckled goats. They would be no great loss to Laban. But, while Laban was occupied with the annual shearing of the sheep, Jacob took his family and the best of the flock and fled.

Jacob lived on the edge for most of his life. He continually found a way to skirt the rules. Still, he was not without a conscience. In God's own time, Jacob was moved to seek forgiveness from his brother. With the hope of appeasing Esau, he sent messengers to carry gifts and arrange a meeting with his brother. When Esau thwarted Jacob's plan and marched forward with a small army, Jacob decided to cut his losses. Dividing his camp, he sent his wives, children, and possessions across the river and remained with his men to face Esau.

Alone at night, Jacob had another dream. This time a supernatural being, an angel of God, attacked him. It was a wake-up call. Jacob wrestled with the angel of his real fears throughout the night. Exactly who won remains ambiguous. The angel wounded Jacob then asked to be released. Once again, Jacob demanded a blessing. The blessing he received changed him forever. "I have seen God face to face, and yet my life is preserved."[15] The conniving, manipulative man became a person of honour and integrity and lived a life worthy of his calling.

Like Jacob, we all have our strengths and our weaknesses. Like him, we are called to transcend the circumstances of life. We are not called to use his questionable methods, but we are to take our life into our own hands. Rich in spiritual traditions that serve as guides, we are to accept the love that sometimes pushes us beyond our habitual way of seeing things. Love takes us to a place where life is different. The journey to new insight broadens our understanding of life and faith and essential values.

One of my favourite stories is *The Little Tern*. It is an enchanting, simple story that contains a decidedly powerful message. For some unknown reason, the little tern lost his ability to fly; at least he thought he did. Confined to the shore, he discovered new and different friends: a falling star, a little purple flower growing in the sand, and a small ghost crab. From them, he learned that true friendship takes a long time growing. Since none of his friends knew what it was like to glide through the air, they opened his eyes to the opportunities available along the shore. They taught him to look beyond his own limited expectations.

The tern valued all his friendships, especially with the crab that always had time to listen to his story. The crab concluded that the tern had not lost his ability to fly but merely misplaced it. Once the tern realized that all his appendages were intact and there was nothing missing on the outside, like wings and feathers and tail, he started looking on the inside at his attitude and beliefs.[16]

Some time later, as he walked along the shore, he suddenly observed his shadow beside him. He noticed that his feathers and wings were truly magnificent. Spontaneously, he raised and stretched them out to their full length. Then he slowly began to glide over the shore's edge. He had learned to let life take its natural course.

Handicaps are blessings in disguise. They gift us with a new way of looking at life—from the inside. When we walk boldly and courageously into the heart of God, we become aware of the magic and the mystery of love. Our handicaps don't loom as large as they did in the beginning. We find a way to use them to enrich the lives of others. The more we listen to the heartbeat of God within us and in all of creation, the more we discover and cherish our true identity. We are made with love. The missing pieces draw forth the best in us. They help us become who we are destined to be. They show us that everything is gift, and everything leads to love.

It is the last day of school and my thoughts turn to Jordan. Behind a tough exterior there is a decidedly sensitive heart. I hear him before I see him. He never makes a quiet entry. A bold knock on the door announces his presence. Happiness is written all over his face as he hands me a colourful, handmade thank-you card. He doesn't like art, so this is a stretch. It moves me to the core.

The past seven years have been shaky. Initially, there were more downs than ups. In kindergarten, Jordan's emotions ran like a roller coaster. A prisoner of his own anger, he was sullen, friendless, and hostile. Impossibly stubborn, he couldn't afford to let others into his confused inner space and would lash out at the nearest victim. Aggressive reactions kept other students on edge. Relationships developed slowly, amid much pain and a lot of counselling. It took a long time before Jordan bought into an anger management program. It helped him face his inner demons.

Today Jordan breathes in the scent of success. I like it. In a rapid succession of words and pointed gestures, he shares the reason for his contentment. "I finally figured you out," he proclaims triumphantly. "Remember all those times I was sent to the office. You just let me sit and sit. Most of the time, I practically shouted to get your attention. You'd pretend you didn't hear me," he states rather emphatically.

"Of course I remember," I admit.

"I know now why you did it. You gave me time to cool down before I got in your face and stretched the problem into a bigger one." Still beaming with satisfaction, he gives me a quick hug and adds, "Thanks." I smile to myself as I wonder how much he's figured himself out along the way.

The spiritual life is a journey, not a destination. Its richness, its potential for growth, lies in the journey itself. The whole of life is an evolution—a process of cleansing and purifying, stretching and expanding, enriching and uplifting. Everything in us strains forward. In each circumstance, as in the totality of life, the journey consistently beckons us to holiness, to life, and to God. It offers us countless opportunities and tremendous challenges. How we meet them and work through them depends on our approach. When we look out into the distance and see beyond the surface of things, we discover God's all-encompassing presence. In spiritual freedom, we see both the journey and its end as the gift God holds out to us.

> I am a part of all that I have met;
> Yet all experience is an arch wherethrough
> Gleams that untraveled world whose margin fades
> Forever and forever when I love.
> How dull it is to pause, to make and end,
> To rust unburnished, not to shine in use!
> As though to breathe were life! Life piled on life
> Were all too little, and of one to me
> Little remains; but every hour saved
> From that eternal silence, something more,
> A bringer of new things; and vile it were
> For some three suns to store and hoard myself,
> And this gray spirit yearning in desire
> To follow knowledge like a sinking star,
> Beyond the utmost bound of human thought…

Though much is taken, much abides; and though
We are not now that strength which in old days
Moved earth and heaven, that which we are, we are—
One equal temper of heroic hearts,
Made weak by time and fate, but strong in will
To strive, to seek, to find, and not to yield.[17]

Part 2

Spirituality: Celebrating Our Original Blessing

Chisel in hand stood a sculptor boy
  With his marble block before him,
And his eyes lit up with a smile of joy,
  As an angel-dream passed o'er him.

He carved the dream on that shapeless stone,
  With many a sharp incision;
With heaven's own light the sculpture shone,—
  He'd caught that angel-vision.

Children of life are we, as we stand
  With our lives uncarved before us,
Waiting the hour when, at God's command,
  Our life-dream shall pass o'er us.

If we carve it then on the yielding stone,
  With many a sharp incision,
Its heavenly beauty shall be our own,—
  Our lives, that angel-vision.
                    —George Washington Doane

Chapter 5: Created and Loved by God

One day in time, God peered out into the empty darkness. And God was inspired to create—to fashion something vital and dynamic, something truly splendid and magnificent. It would be a thing of beauty that would last forever. God's decision was a monumental one that would reverberate through time and back into eternity.

Quietly and joyously, God set to work and created a masterpiece of unparalleled majesty, grandeur, and loveliness. Then God paused and looked at the universe in all its glory: the expansive sky with the heavenly aura cast by the two great lights, the rugged mountains with their peaks reaching to the heavens, the vibrancy of the trees and plants with their fruits and flowers, the profusion of fish in the sea and fauna roaming the land. God was impressed and pleased with every creature. As God listened to the gentle song and watched the dance of creation, God said, "It is good."

Then God rested and declared the day holy. The next day, as God walked the earth, God noticed that something was missing. So, the maternal side of God began to imagine an infinite number of possibilities. Intuitively, God conceived a truly awesome image. God took some earth and fashioned the most exquisite creatures and breathed life and love into them. Woman and man were truly magnificent, sensuous, and breathtaking in body and soul. Charged with spirit and life, created in God's image and likeness, they were blessed with powers akin to God. They could think, feel, love, and be loved. They were gifted with a remarkable capacity to experience God's infinite love and to respond in love.

Overwhelmed with delight, God embraced and welcomed woman and man. God invited them to behold the created world in all its goodness and beauty. And God made an eternal promise: You are precious to me and I love you. I call you by your name and you are mine. I hold you gently in the palm of my hand. I will never forget you. I will not abandon you. And God blessed woman and man in their earthiness and filled them with a passion for life. Planting the seed of love within them, God said, "I created you to share life with me. I love you and cherish you. Walk in beauty. Walk in love."

God looked on woman and man with unsurpassed love and undying appreciation. Once again, God proclaimed: "It is good. It is very, very good!" Woman and man looked at each other with affection and satisfaction. A sincere desire to image God's love and peace welled up in their hearts. With an eye fixed on the future, God longed to see woman and man grow into a sense of their potential for holiness. God was already dreaming big dreams. Creation was just the beginning. Far from complete, it would be ongoing, and woman and man would share in the process. They would be co-creators with God.

God had great faith in woman and man. God loved them and trusted them. God shared the divine vision with them: "I entrust you with the earth and everything on it. Reverence it, care for it, and nurture it, and it will nourish and sustain you. My dream is that human life goes on and on. I bless you with the miraculous gift of fertility. Be fruitful and multiply, and fill the earth." Authorized to bring new life into the world, woman and man felt fulfilled and happy. God held true to the divine promise and new people began to inhabit the earth.[18]

So began woman and man's journey into awareness. They took pleasure in their relationship with each other. They appreciated the sacredness of the earth and valued their connection with all created things. Invigorated by love and aware of their own innate goodness, they were filled with a sense of belonging, of dignity, and of being loved. Instinctively, their creative energy was set in motion. As they walked the garden of Earth, they cultivated the plants and enjoyed their beauty. They learned to rely on the animals for food. Life was good.

Woman and man looked on everything as a gift. While the earth did not belong to them, it was there for them. There was a higher Power at work in the universe and it made them dependent on it. The mystery of God that surrounded them was more beautiful than anything they could imagine. God loved them into life and presented them with a sacred treasure: one that would sustain them, fill them with joy, and be a source of blessing for generations to come. Their relationship with the earth grew into a deep mutual bond.

All the earth asked of them was that they walk gently upon the land, that they respect her cycles of growth and rest, and that they protect all of creation. They were blessed with a tremendous capacity to enjoy creation, to savour life in all its facets, and to relate to each other in love.

It is a pleasant July day and the sun is slowly climbing across the azure firmament. Karen and I respond to nature's invitation to drink in her loveliness and enjoy the sounds of life around us. The Millennium Trail along the Yukon River is vibrant with every shade of green. A sea of deep magenta fireweed adds an impressive splash of colour. Bird songs herald the presence of a variety of winged creatures.

Ever keen and observant, Karen is the first to spot the exquisite little creature. Soft, rose-coloured wings offset the lime-green body of a hummingbird. Diminutive and elegant, it flits from flower to flower. Altogether absorbed in its task, it takes little note of us. We, on the other hand, are enamoured by its charm.

Karen carefully takes a sprig of fireweed, moves further down the trail, and crouches down. On bended knee, she remains as still as a statue. I am sceptical: that tiny bird will never approach a grown woman. I am wrong. Undaunted, the hummingbird flies up to Karen and pushes its long, pointy beak gently into the fireweed. Karen is ecstatic as she feels the fluttering of its wings on her hand. She remains transfixed as it carefully draws the nectar from each blossom. In her innate grandeur, nature reveals the face of God to all who take the time to look and see.

Humankind stands at the pinnacle of creation. We are the work of God's hands, the "brainchild" of God's dream. We come into the world as blessing—full of beauty, light, goodness, and love. We are born with love and for love. Before every human being comes a retinue of angels announcing, "make way for an image of the Holy One. Blessed be God."[19] Most cultures have a maxim related to the birth of a child. They speak of the tremendous potential of the human soul, the infinite possibilities of the human spirit, and the divine element that brings forth new life. It is in our nature to respect and cherish life from its conception.

It is a dark, cold December night. A howling wind whistles through the fireplace, adding a steely background to our evening prayer. The lone Advent candle casts its gentle warmth about the room. The phone rings, breaking through the stillness of the night. I recognize Nikki's voice immediately. I detect a strange mixture of emotions: part bliss, part confusion; part joy, part trepidation; full of hope one minute, full of apprehension the next. An element of expectation surfaces as she shares the news of her pregnancy. "Why the disquiet?" I wonder.

Nikki really wants to have this baby, but she doesn't trust the reactions of family and friends. She will be peppered with questions. She can handle that. She is more concerned about the negative comments that will surely come. Some will say she is being reckless and irresponsible. She gives that a second thought. Others will focus on the challenges that come with being a single parent. Still others will plead for the well-being of the child. Assuming that a single mother can't provide a secure home environment, they will advise a speedy termination of the pregnancy.

Nikki is fully aware of the pending obstacles and asks for our support. She knows that a few friends will become revolving doors. However, the majority will be supportive and loyal, true as unfiltered light. They will need time to get their minds around the new reality. Nikki needs someone to stand by her now. Morally, we stand on the side of life. Emotionally, we will be there for a friend. We promise to support her and her baby. We are either for or against life. The choice seems so obvious.

Nikki has a flair for life. A baby will cramp her style. She knows that, but the anticipated joy outweighs all the sacrifice. She already loves the child in her womb. Her focus is shifting—from self to child.

Sleepless nights and worrisome days come and go. Time marches on. The mother-to-be has nine short months to ready herself. Nikki's anticipation grows by leaps and bounds. Every little movement within her womb stimulates the growth of love. Physical and practical preparations go hand-in-hand with emotional and spiritual formation. Everything is a non-verbal commitment, a promise to be a good mother. God entrusted Nikki with the awesome gift of a new life. She will do her best to merit that trust.

Immediately after Analee's birth, Nikki beams with happiness. She is astounded that something so precious and beautiful came out of her body. Grace and beauty rest in her arms. Ten little fingers; ten little toes. Everything about Analee is perfect. The miracle and the mystery of a new life have burst upon the human stage. Nikki basks in joy and expectation. She utters a prayer of thanksgiving and asks God to guide her in the days and months and years to come.

God's creative energy knows no bounds. It conceives each of us as exceptional. At birth, we are all an untapped source of blessing. God calls us by name and imprints our essence upon us. We come in different shapes and sizes, a variety of dispositions and inclinations, distinct gifts and talents. Arriving on the scene at a given time and in a given place, we bring our unique vantage point. Life is an astonishing and challenging pilgrimage and each of us has a special role to play. Life is a journey of becoming, an invitation to let God make grace and life abound in us. Life is our sacred pilgrimage back into the heart of God.

Everything that happens to us is our teacher. It behooves us to let life teach us. When we stand before God naked and unashamed, with open hands and open heart, we experience the power of God's faithful love. As life unfolds, God confirms our trust and invites us to greater freedom. When we respond in trust, we learn to define ourselves from within, in the light of our principles and values. We discover the new possibilities that are within our reach. God trusts us with our moment in history. We need to trust our original blessing.

Life is a study in contrasts. On the one hand, we experience unimaginable goodness and love. On the other, we encounter blanket darkness and intermittent shadows. Some darkness naturally falls into everyone's life. There are disappointments, setbacks, obstacles, hindrances, sickness, and disease. As life calls us to face the many deaths along the way, it invites us to look on the world with the eyes of faith. All things change and pass away. Just as we cannot hold on to the happiest moment, so we are incapable of wishing away the darker times. Life is made up of diverse and, sometimes, incomprehensible experiences.

Like nature, life gives us mixed messages. A long litany differentiates one human journey from the other. In a world that is divided, distorted, and disfigured, some of us live sheltered lives. Others live in places of endemic violence and perpetual war. People would like to rearrange their lives but never get the chance. The strong can direct their energies. The weak are dependent on others. Created and loved by God, we journey through life in different ways. I have the luxury of time: time to go to school, to reflect and pray, and to think about my giftedness and how it calls me to reach out to others. I take a lot of things for granted.

Those who are impoverished and marginalized have few prospects for the future. Brazil's street kids are the forgotten children of our world. Most of them are orphaned at a young age. They lack the guidance of a significant adult in their young lives. Left to fend for themselves, they turn their thoughts to survival. They learn to cope with hostility and abuse on the dark, cold streets. Instinct teaches them how to deal with sickness and disease, how to fend for themselves, and how to hide from the military police. Life is an enormous challenge for them.

1975. The sun is already high in the sky as I arrive in the bustling city of Salvador. Driving along a side street, I search for a place to park near the downtown core. The crowded, bustling city has outgrown the narrow cobblestone streets of slave days. Parking is at a premium.

Long before I spot their familiar faces, the street kids spy me. They point to a space on Conquisto Street. "Rather tight," I think as I give it a try. It works. As soon as I get out of the car, I am greeted by a group of smiling faces. Everyone has something to tell me. A brown, rough-skinned hand reaches out for my keys. Gildo assures me that he and his gang will take charge of my car. After spending a few minutes talking to the boys, I give them the bread and milk I brought for them. Then I set out to complete my long list of errands.

Patience is an important skill for street kids. They can spend an entire day guarding cars. There isn't much else to do. So they look for every opportunity to be of service or to earn a few cruzeiros. The boys I know struggle to earn enough to buy a little food for the day. When that is impossible, they resort to begging or stealing. Usually, it is bread from a local bakery.

Between ten and fourteen years of age, they hang out together. Living on the street is a silent witness to deep personal loss. These kids have no family, no home, and no security. They are poorly and skimpily dressed. Most of them have never had a chance to go to school or to learn a trade. They have no toys, no books, and no extras. They pick up the things other people throw away.

The streets of Salvador are always full of excitement and turmoil. Shopping is a wearisome task. Dusk is already setting in when I finally return to my car. The little gang is waiting for me. As they stood watch over my car, they washed it inside and out. The ritual is always the same. I ask them how their day went. They admit that not a single person stopped to give them as much as a cruzeiro or even a morsel of food. The bread and milk I gave them that morning is long gone.

They are hungry. They beam with satisfaction as I give them the large bowl of rice and beans I purchased for them. I thank them for taking care of my car and quietly squeeze a hundred cruzeiro bill into each pair of hands. It isn't much, but it is all I can afford at this time. As I drive off, I ask God to protect these boys and the thousands of street kids throughout my beloved Brazil.

Life on the street exacts an incalculable price. But it holds the boys together. It makes them aware of their interconnectedness. They forge deep bonds of friendship. Among themselves, they share a tremendous sense of love and loyalty. They are a sacred gift to each other, a lifeline that gives them something to cling to. They, too, were born in blessing. I don't pretend to understand it. But the memory of something powerful and mysterious remains with me.

As fall approaches in the Yukon, the swans wing their way south for the winter. They are kind enough to sound their trumpets as they fly, alerting us earthlings to a wondrous natural phenomenon. They invite us to turn our gaze upward. It is intriguing to see the natural formation of a flock in flight. The pattern keeps shifting. The same few swans are not at the forefront for any great length of time. Knowing how taxing it can be to break the wind and create the lift for the entire flock, the swans at the back rhythmically stretch their wings and rush to the front. A new configuration takes hold and the followers become leaders for a while.

We too are called to share the burden of leadership for a span of time. We don't always appreciate our noble calling. Sometimes, we have nothing new to bring to the task. We build our lives on the same assumptions, erroneous as they might be. From time to time, we need to change our perspective in order to see the obvious. When we keep looking at something from the same viewpoint, we restrict our thinking, constrict our potential, and muddy our vision. We lose objectivity and fail to discover what is beneath the surface. To be completely open-minded, we must learn to look beyond the superficial and to observe the inner reality.

The school year is taking shape. I spend mid-morning in the kindergarten classroom on Tuesdays. My objective is to assist students in writers' workshop. The expectation is that each child begins with an idea, visualizes it, and illustrates it through the medium of art. Finally, the children are to write their stories. I like being part of the process. It provides insight into their individual minds and hearts.

I quietly draw up a chair at Craig's table. A sullen and angry child, he finds it difficult to reveal anything about himself. There is a secret place inside where he stores everything personal—opinions, feelings, experiences, and insights. Intrusive questions annoy him. Art and writing run dangerously close to self-revelation. No wonder he rebels against them. He already has the avoidance techniques down to an art. Playing a solitary game or engaging in small talk with the children at his table works as long as no adult takes note.

Today, Craig takes little time to think about a story. Details can be frightening. I observe in silence. He quickly grabs a black crayon and expresses his irritation by scribbling bold and heavy lines across the entire page. Handing his book to me, he announces, "Done."

I remind him that his teacher wants him to use at least three colours. Silently, but very deliberately, he takes a red crayon and adds a series of large acrimonious lines to the page. Again, he passes his book back to me and declares, "Done. Now are you satisfied?" It seems a bit over the top to remind him of the assigned task.

I give him a penetrating look. It works, in a way. Certainly not the way I was expecting. He angrily seizes a purple crayon and takes his irritation to another level as he hisses under his breath. Then he spreads his third colour across the page. Triumphantly, victoriously, he claps his hands together and proclaims, "Done. Done. Done at last." Bewildered and a bit disconcerted, I struggle for an appropriate response. There's a fine line between tolerating obstinate behaviour and coming across as negative and discouraging. I feel caught between a rock and a hard place.

As though he senses my dilemma, Marcel comes to my rescue. Casually picking up Craig's "masterpiece," he affirms: "Wow! What a beautiful tornado." Five-year-old Marcel instinctively observed what I failed to perceive.

We are all created and loved by God. No one has a prerogative on love. No one is superior to love. If we believe God's creative act dispenses goodness and love to us, we must rightly assume that our sisters and brothers throughout the world share similar gifts. Everyone inherits an original blessing. No one is left out and no one is passed over. At birth, we are all an untapped source of blessing. We carry within us all the goodness and energy we need to fulfill our destiny. Life is a journey of becoming. We walk on the edge of mystery every day. Human life is a sacred pilgrimage, a journey of revelation, an awakening. We discover the deeper dimensions of mystery when we receive each other and allow our lives to weave into one another. To be fully alive is to be present to the mystery of God, of life, of self, and of others.

The gospel of Luke describes two opposite ways of being present to another. "A woman in the city, who was a sinner, having learned that [Jesus] was eating in the Pharisee's house, brought in an alabaster jar of ointment. She stood behind him at his feet, weeping, and began to bathe his feet with her tears and to dry them with her hair. Then she continued kissing his feet and anointing them with ointment."[20] The woman demonstrated a powerful, passionate presence. She loved deeply and expressed that love in action.

The Pharisee, on the other hand, stood back and observed. His stance was distant and aloof. He offered Jesus no human kindness, not so much as a bowl of water to soak his tired feet. He was irritated by the woman's approach and he showed it. Perhaps, it pointed out his personal inadequacies. He muttered to himself, "If this man were a prophet, he would have known who and what kind of woman this is who is touching him—that she is a sinner."[21] Preoccupied with dark thoughts, he spent his time judging rather than welcoming, categorizing rather than accepting.

Everything has the power to move and inspire us. When we are sensitive and aware, truly present to the other, we see things with the "eyes of the heart." Spirituality does not take away all mystery. It merely shines the light of faith on life's miraculous little things and on the situations we cannot understand. Faith tells us that everything is full of the mystery of God.

When we are young, we look at life with great expectation. We know no bounds. Because we feel we can do almost anything, we are not afraid to try. There are no limits to our enthusiasm. Consequently, we work hard and make our unique contribution to the world. We are respected and admired. When we age and retire, life changes considerably. In many ways, we are no longer needed. We become invisible. Our own values change. We learn to use the luxury of time to deepen our inner spirit, to "grow our soul" in a new way. Spiritual growth reaches its ultimate perfection in heaven.

The journey to death begins at birth. Life has a subtle way of preparing us for it. Struggle and loss, disappointment and failure, weakness and dependence, obedience and submission pave the way. The moment of death, however, is more than loss, disappearance, and letting go. It is the moment of truth, the moment of fulfillment. It is to arrive at the end of our earthly pilgrimage, realizing that we have come full circle. We have come home. It takes faith to recognize it as our starting point. In death, we find ourselves back in the heart of God.

1979. The rainy season has settled in. The day promises to be a hot and humid one. I rise early to spend the first light communing with God. The streets are still quiet, except for a few fishermen walking down to the sea. Sitting alone at the well, I suddenly feel an icy wind across my shoulders. I hear the squeaking of the gate and look up. Ilza hesitates before walking over to me. She doesn't want to disturb my prayer, but her message can't wait. Our mutual friend Lika is dying. She is asking for me. I leave immediately and walk rapidly down the street. I anticipate meeting God in a dark, dingy hut a mere five doors from my home.

Lika is a striking woman with a beautiful soul. Recently, her physical attractiveness has been deteriorating. Old at forty, her body is bent, her legs are weak, and her hair is streaked with grey. Over the years, she walked past my house every day on her way to the mandioca fields and we got to be good friends. At the end of the workday, she was always tired and hungry. It didn't take much coaxing to get her to stop in for a glass of "vitamina," a concoction of avocado, milk, and honey. Lika loved it.

Sharing food gave us a chance to talk about life in general and our lives in particular. Potentially a reflective giant, she understood life. She was sensitive to her reality and lived within her means. Poverty and hard physical work led her to spiritual growth and freedom. She was candid and sincere and demonstrated a remarkable sense of humour. Now and again, I recall the first time I fell into the open sewer. It was Lika who helped me see the absurdity of my predicament.

From the beginning, Lika struck me as a woman full of purpose. She knew what she wanted and went after it. Until recently. A cancerous tumour has taken hold of her body and sapped her of energy. Now it is my turn to visit her. She enjoys the "vitamina" until she finds it too difficult to swallow. Miles from a medical centre, she doesn't have access to chemotherapy or radiation. Even painkillers would be a luxury in Saubara. When I offer the last bottle I have, she immediately suggests that Nilda needs them more than she does. In constant pain, Lika never complains. Concerned only for her daughter Ivonize and her grandchildren, she wishes she could do more for them. She has always been a spark of light to them.

As I enter Lika's tiny hut, I think about the inevitable pattern of life. The Paschal Mystery repeats itself all over again. Life and death are juxtaposed with each other. As earthly life fades, eternal life dawns. A dying person is drawn into a timeless world. Death is one's final and sublime self-surrender.

I would like to stave off Lika's pending death. My reasons are purely selfish. My dear friend is in the final throes of dying. Touching base with her inner depth, she is at peace—serene, fearless, and free. She knows she is going home.

I kneel down on the earth next to her mat. I pray aloud. Familiar prayers we've prayed together many times. She is too weak to join in. Her face becomes more and more luminous. Holiness is completely unselfconscious. After a long silence, Lika shifts slightly. I bend low to hear what she has to say.

In a soft, raspy voice she says: "Edite, I've always loved that blue dress you are wearing. If I may ask, could you bury me in it?" Love explodes inside. "How can she honour me so?" I bless my dear friend, kiss her gently, and take my leave.

Home I go. Off comes the dress and into the soapy water. I carefully hang it over the well to dry. The intense heat of the sun does its thing and the dress is dry within the hour. Carrying it reverently, I turn my steps back toward Lika's hut. Ilza is already approaching and I know that my dear friend is gone. I cling to the memory of a truly brave soul. It is a rare blessing to meet someone so remarkably unafraid in the face of death. Those who are not afraid to die are not afraid to live.

I feel privileged to help prepare Lika's body for burial. She looks regal in my blue dress. Peace reigns in her hut and in the street. Neighbours bring flowers and stand in reverence before a woman of great substance. The next day, I lead the prayers at her funeral. That night, as I look up at the stars, I choose the brightest one and remember my amazing friend.

All of life is a declaration about God. Creation is a holy gift. Everything around us speaks of the divine, the transcendent. All has the potential to deepen and enrich us. We walk in a universe that beckons us to go further, to go deeper. Each of us is a unique and special story. The challenge is to let our personal story unfold. The love poured into our soul gives us a starting point, a sense of identity. While it makes us aware of the best and the worst in us, it sheds a penetrating light on our blessing. We carry a treasure in earthen vessels, so that others might see the extraordinary power of God. This treasure is our original blessing, our bequest. It calls us to trust our inherent goodness and to trust the God who loved us into life.

We all have deeply entrenched spiritual roots. They are not intended to hold us down or restrict us in any way. Rather, they are the gifts that set us free. They are the wings that empower us to become who God calls us to be. Life is the Creator's gift to each of us. What we do with our life is our gift to the world.

> *Do you know what you are?*
> *You are a manuscript of a divine letter.*
> *You are a mirror reflecting a noble face.*
> *This universe is not outside of you.*
> *Look inside yourself;*
> *everything that you want,*
> *you are already that.*[22]

Chapter 6: Nature and Grace

The confident young mother strides into my office, two little boys in tow. I can hardly keep myself from staring. The boys are, indeed, identical twins. The similarities couldn't be greater—the same golden hair, deep blue eyes, freckled faces, broad grins, and matching body build. Both boys suffer from asthma and are allergic to cats, dust, and milk products. It will be a challenge to distinguish Dave from Dan and vice versa. The kindergarten year is almost over before I discover that Dave has a larger freckle that sits dead-centre on his nose. At least now I know who is requesting a special favour.

Over the years, I discover that the similarities go much deeper than external appearances. Dave and Dan are equally gifted in solving mathematical problems, writing intricate story plots, spinning a good tale, and hitting a baseball. Both love music and both play the clarinet. They can play each other's parts in school musicals. And, when one is in trouble, he knows how to pretend to be his innocent brother. It takes a very keen eye to tell the difference.

The boys share the same roots and common genes, but they are also very different. While they appear to get along together, an element of alienation crops up from time to time. Few people detect the terrible competition and fierce jealousy that festers beneath the surface.

By nature, Dave is carefree and easy going. He surrounds himself with music and dancing and celebrating. He spends his time with friends who demand little. He finds routines wearisome and is constantly seeking the novel and the new. Pain and frustration are an integral part of his journey toward maturity. His learning curve into adulthood is an abrupt and precipitous one.

Dan thrives on fidelity and hard work. He believes he can earn approval and love by doing the right thing, being in the right place, and living up to others' expectations. He cannot understand his brother and his need for adventure. In Dan's mind, beauty and loyalty are the ultimate perfection and leave little room for the slightest flaw. Oblivious of his own scars, he can be highly critical of his brother.

In the act of creating, parents transmit a unique combination of their own original blessings to their offspring. It is an awesome phenomenon. Our DNA, established at conception, is entirely unique and personal. It is God's special gift to us. Our intellectual abilities, attitudes, approach to life, and responses to situations and circumstances may resemble those of our parents, but deep down there is a decided difference. Heredity defines our unique blend of gifts and talents and establishes the frontiers of our destiny. It is an exclusive blessing.

We are given all the potential we need to walk the journey of life with dignity, grandeur, and grace. All God asks is that we accept our inherent nature as good and beautiful, that we allow it to evolve and grow, that we uncover who we were created to be, that we consistently walk toward wholeness. If we want to appreciate the treasure we hold, we have to dig deep. The essence of who we are goes well beyond our physical appearance and mental capacity. I remember a young teacher telling me about his photographic mind and his exceptional cognitive ability. I couldn't help wondering where he stood in terms of emotional, social, and spiritual intelligence. Our human gifts go deeper than the things we can hear and see and touch.

Our most fundamental blessing is our spirituality, our passion for life. It is the energy that drives us and inspires us. An essential and exceptional gift, it speaks of the lavishness of God's love. It gives us the power and the inclination to be people of integrity, uprightness, and fairness. We are ordained and chosen to be people for others.

Spirituality opens the eyes of the soul to the goodness and beauty around us. People of integrity and generosity inspire and energize us by the way they live their lives. While they may not be aware of it, they have the power to bring out the best in us. They help us discover our own spiritual capacity. Different spiritual aptitudes tend to seek their own kind. We find our comfort zone with people who are on the same wavelength, people who have similar drives and ideals.

I am approaching my thirteenth birthday. A time of raging hormones, an awakening interest in boys, and an incessant need for adventure. I find dusting and restocking shelves in our family's general store pedestrian and tedious. It's my job every Wednesday after school. Annoyance always wells up in my chest. I'd rather be hanging out with my friends. Because of my love and respect for my Dad, I hold my contrary feelings in check and remember how hard he works to put food on the table. I often see tiredness in his eyes but he doesn't complain. I try to be like him. Most of the time, I'm afraid, the results are quite mixed.

Today is a relatively quiet day. Customers arrive sporadically. It doesn't make for a lot of excitement. I give my mind permission to roam. I recall last Friday's family dance. How I love to dance! After the dance, a few men got into a street fight. I was proud of the way Dad helped break it up.

The store's bell chimes as Mr. Whyte walks in. I look over my shoulder and detect a note of sadness in his manner. My curiosity is aroused and I need to find out what's going on. Not particularly good at observing things from afar, I creep a little closer. If I keep my head down, they won't notice me monitoring their conversation. "My crop was hailed out—every single acre. All I can do is plough it under," Mr. Whyte says bitterly.

Dad knows the feeling. Farming a section of land himself, he empathizes. My heart fills with compassion toward the Whytes. How will a family of seven survive the winter with no grain to sell?

A thoughtful look settles in Dad's eyes. He sometimes makes decisions based on gut feelings. After a long pause, he makes an offer: "Why don't you charge the things you need for the time being and we'll see how things turn out next year?" My eyes widen with incredulity. It's an unbelievably generous offer. Relief spreads across Mr. Whyte's face. He shakes Dad's hand to clinch the deal. Tears well up in my eyes and I quickly turn back to my dusting.

Farmers are always talking about next year—the next seeding, the next rainy season, the next harvest. Things seem to look better down the road. Dad was like that. He understood Mr. Whyte's predicament and spontaneously came to the rescue. It certainly wasn't the first time he bailed someone out. It seemed to be second nature to him. On that special day so long ago, my esteem for Dad grew by leaps and bounds. I resolved then and there that I would become as kind and caring as he was. I must admit that the results have been multifarious. However, I believe the potential is in my genes. Heredity and environment go together like two peas in a pod. Both are part of my spiritual endowment, my original blessing.

The first time I accompanied Karen to her family home, her mother was working at the hospital. Bea entertained us well into the night with hospital stories. I marvelled at her sensitivity and her obvious love for the sick. She spoke the language of the heart. Years later, I wondered how much Bea's kind and gentle ways with the sick influenced Karen's decision to go into nursing school.

Karen's reputation as a maternity and pediatric nurse was stellar. More comfortable in a stance of giving rather than receiving, she was an extraordinary caregiver. Diligent. Zealous. Dedicated. Sometimes, she was called back to the hospital in the middle of the night to "special nurse" an injured child or a mother who was having a difficult labour. There was never a moment's hesitation. Duty called and she responded wholeheartedly.

July 1982. My writing task begs a place of peaceful quiet. Since Karen is at the hospital most of the day, I decide to take her up on the offer to use her home for my work. She rises early and is at the hospital by 7:00 am. I sit down to a second cup of coffee. This morning any thought of writing retreats into the background. It's one of those off days. I feel the need to recapture my inner peace. Then the thoughts will surely come.

The ringing of the phone breaks the silence. I'm not expecting a call but I push aside the temptation to ignore it. Recognizing Karen's voice, I know instinctively that something is awry. She sounds deeply moved as she gives me the short version of a highway accident that claimed the life of a local teenager. Ronnie, the eldest son in a family of five, was heading back to town shortly after midnight. There was no way he could avoid the semi coming around a sharp curve on the wrong side of the road. It cost him his life.

Typically taking a utilitarian approach, Karen maps out directions to Ronnie's home. "Not so fast," I think. "I don't know the family." I have reservations. "Of what use can I be, a total stranger? They don't know me and I don't want to intrude on a very private and painful moment in their lives."

But Karen can be very persuasive. Without skipping a beat and with a prophetic tone in her voice she advises: "Just be yourself. They need a gentle presence. You will know what to do." Benevolence comes naturally to her. She assumes I will do the right thing. How can I refuse?

Ten minutes later I am ringing the doorbell at Ronnie's house. When I introduce myself as Karen's friend, I receive a hero's welcome. Ronnie's mother, Jane, holds me close for a long time. Finally, she admits, "We need someone to help us through this. Any friend of Karen's is a friend of ours." After spending most of my waking hours over the next three days comforting and consoling the grieving family, I have no regrets. I try to catch my breath, as I get dressed for the funeral.

After the last rose is carefully placed on the casket, Karen and I walk home together. Emotionally exhausted, we sit down to a cup of tea. We laugh and cry together. Karen is director of nursing at the local hospital. Patients come from every stratum. I know there must be a story somewhere in there. I ask about her week. She laughs as she talks about three-year-old Henry, a victim of a motorbike accident. Her tone betrays her feelings for this precious and needy patient.

Earlier in the day, Henry rang for Karen. When she arrived in his room, he grabbed her hand and led her into the adjoining bathroom and carefully pulled her directly in front of the toilet. Looking up at her, he broke into a soft grin. Karen was puzzled but remained patient. Henry proceeded to stand on her shoes and faced the toilet so he could "do his thing." Unabashed, he announced, "I like to pee into the toilet like a man." After completing his task, he whispered, "Thank you, Karen. I love you."

Original blessing gives us all the raw materials we need to fulfill God's dream for us. We were created with a beautiful purpose: to warm the world with our smile, to lighten the burdens of life with our laughter, to animate the world with our love, and to share our gifts with those whose lives we touch. By divine decree, we are assigned a special task, something only we can realize. It is an integral part of our nature. It becomes our code of honour. God calls us to shape life, not merely endure it. Life's circumstances have the power to draw forth the best in us. There are certain things that animate the imagination, arouse the spirit, and propel us heart and soul into the journey of life.

I am seventeen when our school principal is hospitalized for six weeks. Small prairie towns don't have the luxury of supply teachers. From grade eight on, I have been serving as a substitute whenever a primary teacher is sick. But this scenario is different. This is high school.

The whole town is in an uproar. Grades eleven and twelve students face departmental exams at the end of the year. They can't afford to be without instruction for an extended period of time. Ideas are tossed about like baseballs. Some are drastic; others sound rational, perhaps even plausible. Within two days, parents call for a meeting with the vice-principal, Ms. Eaton. They desperately need to come up with a solution. Students are not invited to the meeting. In my absence, parents devise a plan that hinges directly on me. The consensus is that I will take over the class. Even Mom and Dad concur.

After the meeting, Ms. Eaton pitches the proposal to me. I am stunned into silence. "What are they thinking? I'm no miracle worker." I voice my reservations: "Grade Ten wouldn't be a problem. I've been through that. Grade eleven? Well, I could learn as we go. But I draw the line at Grade twelve chemistry and physics. That would be reaching for the moon."

Ms. Eaton looks at me, her brown eyes warm and encouraging. She counters my objection by playing on my feelings for my brother in Grade twelve. "I think you could do it. We could solve the harder problems together." She's a good talker. I'll hand her that. I find myself moving from a definite *no* to a weak *maybe* and finally a *yes*. God willing, my decision is the right one. I like to keep my word.

Life shapes us, often on the run. In the wee hours of the morning, I am still replaying my new enterprise over and over in my mind. The pride I felt at being asked is replaced by fear of failure. But I've already given my word. I can't go back on that. In the end, it's my strength of mind that wins the day. I'll have to trust my innate gifts and work hard at sharing my understanding and skills with my colleagues. I'll be honest about the things I don't know. We have to work through those together.

We hit a few road bumps along the way. The six boys in Grade ten are full of mischief. They use protractors as prods and shove them into my thighs as I move from desk to desk. Ouch. Once the mathematical instruments are carefully stowed in the fume cabinet, the boys search for other things to distract themselves. I learn early on never to relax my vigilance. The older students are incredibly cooperative. They prove to be resourceful as we work together on science problems. Gradually, my tension melts away.

Departmental exam results arrive in August. Everyone is a winner. Tangible success speaks for itself. My stubborn determination coupled with a high degree of cooperation from the other students proved to be a great combination. A very humbling victory for me! I learned a lot about human nature, teenage moods, and my ability to interact positively with my peers. Six weeks chalked up solid teaching experience and set me on the path to education for life.

Just as creation reveals its Maker, so it sometimes conceals the essential goodness and perfection of God. Every now and again, nature appears to defy its own laws. Now and again, we encounter its apparent contradictions and discrepancies. Life is not always what it seems to be. The most optimistic among us stumble upon the wearisome and burdensome aspects of life. Alongside its blessings, nature presents us with afflictions, handicaps, and disadvantages. These often place heavy burdens on those around us. It is then that grace comes into play and provides strength for the journey. Grace builds on nature; it does not supplant it. Nature provides the raw material and grace gives us the courage to trust what we have received.

> Baby Melanie comes into the world like every other child, kicking and screaming. She is an absolute delight to her parents. In the beginning, she seems to be like other children. Over time, however, the differences become more glaring. While her body grows in infinitesimal steps, her organs develop at a much slower pace. Mom and Dad wait patiently as surgery after surgery proves ineffectual. At age two and a half, Melanie is unable to hold up her tiny head or feed herself, much less walk or talk. By all external appearances, she is a burden to her family. At the deeper level, she is pure gift.
>
> Though Melanie is unaware of it, she draws forth the best in people. Friends and neighbours who help out provide times of respite to her parents. In turn, the opportunity to care for her expands the hearts of those who give of their time and talents to serve her needs. The loving support she receives from her extended family and her community is a witness to the power of nature and grace working together. In many ways, it restores the observer's faith in humanity.

Our innate, essential qualities make up our character. When we discover who we really are, we automatically reach out in love and service to others. All genuine service begins with a sense of our inherent gifts and talents. Every good gift, every blessing, is for community. It is to be shared. The God who loved us into life summons us to fulfill our particular role in bringing creation to completion. Our unique destiny is tied up in our potential and reveals itself through the circumstances of life. We have to be aware of our interior strengths and innate weaknesses in order to give our life a decisive direction.

Self-knowledge helps us expand our understanding of the inner world. It is the first step toward the realization of who we are and who we might become. The spiritual life reveals its secrets slowly. Multi-layered and multi-faceted, it presents itself incrementally. It's like peeling an onion—we loosen and unfold one stratum at a time. It requires careful handling. Sometimes, there are tears.

To be holy is to know the truth and to hold onto it, as we would clasp a precious gem. The memories of our original blessing may fade, but they never entirely disappear. They were imprinted on our soul long before we were born. Like yeast, they well up inside us, enriching and filling our lives. Memory is an essential ingredient in self-knowledge. It puts us in touch with our ideals and gives direction to our lives.

Shedding its light on the composite person that I am, self-understanding helps me interpret the way I view the world and respond to it: "Do I see the glass half full or half empty? Do I look at life and see stars or do I behold the mud and the muck? Am I carefree and easygoing or inclined to focus on tasks to be accomplished?" Beyond my natural disposition, self-understanding illuminates the way I respond to others and to the circumstances of life: "Am I a people pleaser? Too timid to take on the challenges that worm their way into life? Am I a fighter, a survivor, a pacifist, or somewhere in between?"

Sweeping in its scope, self-knowledge exposes both our tremendous possibilities and blessings alongside our compulsions and constraints. Both personal and spiritual growth depend on the way we navigate through our gifts and weaknesses. Sometimes we see life, as it were, through a rear-view mirror. Hindsight is always 20-20. It exposes our needs and desires as well as our fears and anxieties. Discovering our usual behaviour patterns, we broaden and deepen our understanding of self.

Some recent models of personality are derived from the Jewish mystical tradition of Kabbalah and the German insight of the Enneagram.[23] They describe both convergent and divergent aspects of the human psyche. They categorize the feelings, actions, and normal relationships of different people and group similarities as personality types or "gestalten." While no two people are identical, there are some commonalities we share with others.

According to these models, discovering our "type" helps us understand the way personal feelings lead to action and foster relationships. It helps us appreciate our image of God, our unique behavioural patterns, and our perception of life. Original blessing and personal weakness form the building blocks of one's personality. The way we stack them up determines the kind of person we become. To follow God's dream for us means becoming aware of the source of energy in our soul. Spiritual energy arises from one of three centres: the gut, the head, and the heart.[24]

Like everything else about us, our centre of energy is part of our original blessing. What inspires, excites, enraptures, inflames, and animates us is our personal spirituality, our deepest passion. It defines us and describes the ways we are different from everyone else. When we hold it to the light, examine it, and explore its possibilities, we enter its depth. We come to know who we are deep down in our soul. When we understand the power of our original blessing, we behold its eternal promise.

We are born with our own innate gifts, our personal temperament, and our essential outlook on life. Each of us is an invaluable and indispensable part of creation. Every person has a unique role to play. We are all capable and worthwhile. Disciples sent on a mission, we are entrusted with our personal blessing so that we might fulfill our higher purpose. When we fall short, the world is a little poorer. When we succeed, life takes us beyond ourselves to compassionate love. We can be whatever we want to be if we understand our original blessing and follow our own heart.

There is in each of us more beauty and goodness
than the human eye can perceive;
There is in each of us more goodness and kindness
than the earthly heart can know.
There is in each of us more compassion and love
than we dare dream possible.
There is in each of us what God sees and appreciates,
knows and understands, loves and cherishes.
There is in each of us a penchant for greatness,
a distinctive capacity,
a promise,
and an abundance of grace that awaits us—
longing to be explored and developed.
There is each of us an original blessing,
conceived in the mind and heart of God,
that we might become all that God destined us to be
from the beginning.

Chapter 7: Family, Community, Geography

After spending forty days and forty nights in the silence and solitude of the desert, Jesus was filled with the power of the Spirit. His desert experience put him in touch with his humanity. He came to the realization that to be fully human is to be vulnerable, obedient to one's destiny, and open to the will of God. Now he understood that human life limits one's control of everything, even life itself. "[Jesus], though he was in the form of God, did not regard equality with God as something to be exploited, but emptied himself... and being found in human form, he humbled himself and became obedient to the point of death—even death on a cross."[25] Refusing to cling to the power of God, he learned to appreciate the precarious reality of human life.

As he walked out of the desert, Jesus knew his time had come. He had a clear sense of his life's mission. By the sea, in city squares, and in the synagogues, he was to show God's love. He healed the sick and comforted those in distress. He called people to repentance and conversion. While the crowds pressed in on him throughout the day, he spent the night in solitude and prayer. There he renewed his inner strength and prepared for the events of the coming day. One night, he came to the realization that if this mission was to continue after him, he needed help.

Early one morning, Jesus walked slowly along the Sea of Galilee. His eyes were fixed on two brothers who were fishermen. Quietly but deliberately, he walked up to Simon and Andrew. Looking directly into their eyes, he said, "Follow me and I will make you fishers for people." Immediately, and without hesitation, the two brothers left their nets and followed him. A little further along the shore, Jesus spotted two other brothers, James and John. Busily mending their nets, they hardly noticed the threesome approaching them. Jesus called to them and invited them to walk with him. Like Simon and Andrew, James and John were irresistibly drawn to every word that Jesus uttered. They, too, left the very things their livelihood depended on. Instinctively, they followed Jesus, became his closest disciples, and learned to share in his mission.[26]

The groundwork was complete and a new ministry surfaced on the human stage. In his wisdom, Jesus knew it was necessary to prepare others to share and eventually assume his mission. He needed companions to walk with him, to listen to him, to become familiar with his values and ideals, and, sometimes, to comfort and reassure him. Like the rest of us, Jesus needed others.

Companions on the journey of life, we are gifts to each other. One person fills out what is lacking in the other. We are not the whole or even the centre of things. We are all part of something bigger than ourselves. It is in family and in community that we find ourselves and grow to our full potential. Jesus spent his entire public life creating community. His vision was open, inclusive, welcoming, and accepting.

We are born into a particular family, a specific community, and in a distinct geographical place. After the initial shock of entering into the world of light, we quickly grow to feel at home in it. When we are very young, if we are fortunate, we trust our surroundings and feel secure. Our parents offer us constant care and loving attention while they demand nothing in return. Initially, there are no restrictions, no reservations, no stipulations, and no conditions. Ideally, there is only love. Life is simply good—something to be relished to the utmost.

Unfortunately, the reality of life is that some children receive very little parenting. Yet, in many cases, they find the inner strength to "raise themselves" while others seem to flounder most of their lives. The difference is puzzling. I think it has a lot to do with a child being independent enough to embrace the Spirit within. Grace compensates for what is missing in family life.

As children grow older, the serene and peaceful existence of childhood slowly but surely begins to evaporate. The situations of life shift and evolve. We are no longer the centre of the universe. Our serene and comfortable world expands to include others. Ordinary family living begins to limit our choices. Parents set boundaries and siblings cramp our free-spirited outlook on life. We become aware of brothers and sisters who rightly, and naturally, demand their share of affection and attention. They rush in to voice their needs, their wants, and their desires. Sometimes, as they reach out to us, we see it as an invasion of our time and space. It is hard to let go, to move out of the limelight, to let others glory in their share of attention.

The gift of life is much more than restrictions and limitations. When we are young, no matter how hard we try, we are incapable of understanding the wondrous mystery that is our life. We need to live life, encounter its joys and sorrows, as well as its trials and tribulations, before we are ready to grasp the wisdom of the human spirit. Our status in our family and community opens up new prospects and unsolicited challenges. Gradually, we come to appreciate and value the love and friendship of our siblings. Then we move out and welcome strangers into our secure nuclear world. We begin to realize the importance of community. People, both young and old, open our minds and teach us to look beyond the mundane and the superficial. We discover the joy of sharing the simple pleasures of life.

Slowly but surely, the need to adapt creeps into our young lives. Sometimes, conflicts and struggles arise. Unconsciously, we search for some coping mechanism. We strive to protect our inner self, to remain true to our original blessing. At the same time, we realize that life itself is in motion. The road to transformation is spread out before us. With a great deal of parental prodding and guidance, we learn to clean up after ourselves, put things back where they belong, share our things, and live in peace and harmony. We realize the marvellous effect of three tiny words: "I am sorry." And: "I love you."

Growth necessarily involves leaving the old ways behind. To grow is to surrender to new and diverse possibilities. We no longer have everything we want when we want it and how we want it. Change is an inevitable part of life. As long as we cling to the familiar, we shut out the promise of growth and expansion. Over time, we learn to contain our thoughts, protect our feelings, and respond to life in a more measured and restrained way. A new and different sense of self emerges. But this too is part of our original blessing. Our environment, our family, and our community are priceless gifts. They have the potential to advance our growth, enrich our lives, and to make us more compassionate people.

Our roots encompass both heredity and environment. Heredity is our original blessing. Environment is an extension of that blessing. To acknowledge our personal history is to recognize and celebrate our true self. It is not a question of being better or worse off than another. It is a question of developing our budding gifts and making our own unique contribution to the world. Spiritual growth arises from an awareness of where we come from and what we are called to do with our lives. It beckons us to look deeply into our family, community, and culture to unearth what is both uplifting and liberating in them. Conversion begins with who we are, not who we wish we were. It is to accept our roots with gratitude and thanksgiving.

There is nothing particularly glamorous about growing up in a small prairie town. But it was home for me. The constancy of daily life was a given. Predictability fostered security. A wholesome, healthy lifestyle kept my feet planted firmly on the ground. Everything contributed to my cumulative wisdom: my family, my favourite teacher, the annoying kid living next door, the curious neighbour across the street, the postmaster, the station keeper, and the priest. All worked together to produce a rich harvest in me.

It is Halloween night, two months after my eighth birthday. Highly animated and anxious to get into our costumes, we hurry through supper. I get into my fairy dress and Mom starts painting my face. When everyone is dressed and painted, the five of us trudge off into the night. A mélange of stars creates a mass of light in the sky. Behind them, dark clouds are rolling in. A prairie wind adds mystique to an annual adventure. As usual, we stick together. Winding through town, we shoot west then south, knocking on doors. Neighbours know us by name and are generous with their treats. Everyone, except Mrs. Panther. Because she is consistently grouchy, we've come up with some unflattering nicknames for her. Tonight, "witch" fits the bill.

Her house is in darkness, except for the shattered light coming from a kitchen candle. We crowd around the back door and knock loudly. No response. After three tries, we add several piercing whistles. Still nothing. I feel a rift developing as two of my siblings mutter something about calling it a night. I am not one to be defeated. Standing on tiptoe, I stretch my long body tall enough to peer in through the kitchen window. "She is sitting by her old wood stove," I announce.

Together we decide that she ought to pay the price for her rudeness. You can't break through layers of tradition without some consequence. We will teach her a lesson she won't easily forget. Clouds thicken and intensify the darkness. Only a wedge of sky remains open. Nature is giving us a cover. We run through her precious garden, intentionally tramping on her carrots. Then we help ourselves to several large ones. A shameful deed and we know it.

Mom is a brilliant detective. We can't be coming home with carrots in our baskets. The few we are able to munch down are delectable, fresh, and sweet. We stash the remainder in a hole behind the garage. We swear each other to secrecy before entering the house.

The following day is magical. At school, an extravagant exchange of treats naturally leads into a hilarious comparison of success stories. Childhood is, indeed, a carefree and happy time. Later, I wonder why none of us dared mention the episode with Mrs. Panther. Feelings of guilt, no doubt.

Our exuberance comes to a precipitous end when we arrive home after school. Mom's face is rosy and flushed as she glares intently at each of us. Something is wrong. Obviously irritated and embarrassed, she is not in a happy mood and it is written all over her face. We fall over ourselves trying to hide behind each other. Wasting little time with niceties, Mom cuts directly to the chase: "Did you stop at Mrs. Panther's last night? Was she handing out treats?" I keep my eyes riveted to the floor. Mom has an uncanny way of seeing through falsehood.

It is well nigh impossible to lie to mothers. They have a creepy way of discovering the truth. We are well aware of this. I don't know why but we stubbornly stick to our story: "We didn't bother going to Mrs. Panther's because she hates kids." Mom touches my nose. I hate that. She says it feels warm, a sure sign that I am not being forthright. Does that kind of wisdom come just from being a mother?

Our combined efforts to dissuade Mom from her mission are fruitless. Defeated and humiliated, we follow her to Mrs. Panther's. Five little people know what they have to do. In mumbled, almost incoherent voices, we blurt out our apology. I don't have the heart to look into Mrs. Panther's eyes. I can see her victorious grin in my mind's eye and that is enough for me.

To know our history is to know our true blessing. Our outlook, attitude, and passion for life germinate and grow in the heart of the place we call home. A deepening of faith cannot be bought or sold or bartered. It is developed slowly and in the community that is our family. We become who we are destined to be in the context of family and community, in the give and take of life, in contact with others. We walk the journey of life on a never-ending search to discover who we are and to know our rightful place in the universe.

Our place in the family tree plays a unique role in bringing our inherent personality to the fore. My sister Jean is the oldest girl in our family. By nature, she is a caregiver, a protector, and a good steward. Circumstances placed a heavy burden on her young shoulders. They gave her an intuitive sense of what needed to be done. Somehow, she was able to pick up on the countless demands a large family put on Mom and responded graciously and generously. She spent a great deal of her childhood and youth nurturing the physical and spiritual needs of her younger siblings. Life shaped her into an incredibly competent woman.

> From age four, I loved harvest time. More than anything, I remember the smell of grain—the aroma of soil and seed and dust. It settled in my nose and seemed to stay forever. Ripe grain, awash with gold, announced: "Here I am ready for the picking." The stalks stood straight and tall even as they waved gently in the breeze.
>
> Harvest time tests the endurance of both my mother and my elder sister. Watching Mom pack a lunch early in the morning, we anticipate a day in the fields. My siblings and I know we will have long hours of free time. Most of it is spent chasing each other up and down the long rows of cut grain.
>
> We walk to the field together. Today, the oats has already been bound into huge sheaves. Disappointment wells up inside. We will have to crouch down on our bellies in order to hide from each other.
>
> As soon as we arrive in the field, Mom carefully spreads a blanket on the ground. After instructing Jean to watch over us and call for her if there is any sign of trouble, she slips on her work gloves. A solitary figure, she walks further into the field. I watch her as she stacks the heavy sheaves into peaked stooks. She knows how to lean them into each other so they remain standing together. I marvel at the art and I wonder where she learned to do that. It has to be backbreaking work for a short woman like my mother.
>
> Jean keeps us busy and safe for the entire morning. Around noon, Mom walks back toward us. Her face is flushed from the wind and sun. Thirsty and hungry, she wastes little time opening the huge picnic basket. Egg salad on whole wheat bread, chunks of dill pickles, apples, and home-baked oatmeal cookies are common fare. Mom eats quickly, compliments Jean for a good job babysitting, and sets off down the field again. A shy smile of satisfaction spreads across Jean's face. My admiration for my big sister ascends a notch or two every time.

When circumstances call on you to assume adult responsibility as a child, your antenna becomes refined. You naturally tune in to the needs of others. As Jean grew older, her amazing generosity continued to expand. An astonishingly sensitive and responsive person, she left an enduring impact. From as far back as I can remember, she's been an anchor of support amid the storms of life. She seems to know how to make my stumbling blocks appear smaller—less ominous and stressful.

As a young woman, Jean embraced the teaching profession. I was not surprised when she got involved in drama. She directed high school plays for many years. Drama gave her direct contact with students in a casual and reassuring environment. The stage was a safe place for her students. There they were able to act out their joys and aspirations, as well as their disappointments, frustrations, and humiliations. Life turned Jean into a good listener and a compassionate person. Her kind approach endeared her to her students.

Everyone's life is a beautiful tapestry where the past, present, and future are entwined. The threads of our past keep weaving themselves forward. While we may be completely unaware of it, the fabric of our original blessing continues to take shape. When we enter attentively into the depths of each moment, we learn to appreciate what we find there. We see how we are like our siblings and how we are different. When we reflect on the community of our childhood and youth, we uncover the values that held people together. As the rings of a tree are shaped by each year's sun and rain and storms, so each one's life is fashioned and moulded by those who walk the journey with us.

Just as our family is in a class of its own, an unsurpassing gift, so too is our community. We all need to belong, to be part of something. We get together in community for multiple reasons: personal growth, a higher good, a specific cause, or a common goal. Sometimes, geography plays a role in bringing us together. No matter what the reason or the circumstance, community binds people to each other. When we share our resources, everyone stands to gain. Just as we note each others' unique gifts, we also confront each others' weaknesses. Community helps us grow our soul.

Growing up in a small town had its advantages and its stumbling blocks. Whether I liked it or not, my life was an open book. Everyone seemed to know my every move. There was an invisible bond of solidarity among mothers. They spontaneously shared their observations and condemnations. I had a hundred mothers—reassuring in many ways, frustrating in others. It was only as I grew older that I learned to appreciate the common wisdom behind Guidance 101 for Mothers.

The Oxford dictionary indicates that the word "gossip" once meant someone akin to a godparent. Kathleen Norris, the author of *Dakota: A Spiritual Geography*, gives an insightful interpretation when she speaks about "holy gossip." Listening to people's stories is, indeed, holy gossip. It makes us more accepting and supportive. It calls us to reach out to our sisters and brothers in need. When we hear of the elderly woman who faced illness and death with invincible courage, we are inspired to appreciate life in all its circumstances. Another's conversion involuntarily leads to gratitude.

My parents were common-sense people who lived life on a human scale. Hence, they were often called upon to perform ostensibly impossible tasks. Raising nine children, they didn't have time to delve into great theological discussions or debates. But they were deeply aware of God and passed that grace on to us. I learned the power of prayer by kneeling with my family on the kitchen floor as we prayed for the sick, the dying, the troubled, and the suicidal. Mom and Dad knew intuitively what was right and good. I owe my sense of decency, kindness, and nobility to them. Affirming our strengths and giving us a healthy dose of reality when we strayed, they taught us to be people for others.

> I am eleven years old. A wild storm is raging across the prairies. It is bitterly cold and blustering as the snow pelts down relentlessly. The sky looks moody and leaden as we run home from school. On a night like this, people huddle together in the warmth of their homes. No one ventures out. The roads in and out of town are closed.
>
> Shortly after eight, the phone rings. It is Bill, a local farmer who lives three miles out of town on a lone, country road. Bill's wife Bridget is in labour and Bill is in panic mode. More than anything, he needs to hear a comforting and reassuring voice.

But he also needs someone to come to his rescue. Mom has no training or experience as a midwife. When she relays the saga to Dad, we know she plans to help.

Without hesitation, they bundle up and inform us of the gravity of Bridget's situation. Dad starts up the little Ferguson tractor and they set off together into the dark, chilly night. Instinctively, we kneel on the kitchen floor and begin to pray. God simply has to protect Mom and Dad and the unborn baby. Time drags on and on, and still there is no sign of Mom and Dad's return. Eventually, we drift off to sleep.

On hearing Mom in the kitchen the next morning, I whisper a prayer of gratitude. No one else could have brought them home safely in such a merciless storm. Full of a million questions, we burst into the kitchen. Mom's radiant smile says it all—the baby is okay. Mom talks about the initial fear she felt as she walked into the farmhouse. She describes her sense of relief on safely delivering the infant. "It was like holding two pounds of butter in my hands," she says. "The baby is so tiny and fragile."

In rapt attention, we listen to the rest of the story. After dropping Mom off at the farmhouse, Dad returned to an isolated railroad crossing two miles away. He kept the tractor lights burning bright so the section foreman and the doctor would know where to find him. By the time Dad came back to the farmhouse with the doctor, Mom had already washed and dressed the little girl. The doctor suggested she wrap her in layers of warm blankets and put her in a shoebox. And that's exactly what Mom did. Then she carefully placed the box in a large basket amid a small duvet. Dad drove the doctor and his precious cargo back to the railroad crossing. The tiny, squirmy infant traveled twenty-two miles by section wagon to the nearest hospital. She spent the next six weeks in an incubator. A survivor, she already knew how to hold her own.

Seventeen years later, a petite and attractive young woman walks into my Christian Ethics class. Somehow, she looks familiar to me. Then I remember. I introduce myself to Iris. We talk about her background. Yes, we have a common origin. She spent her childhood on the outskirts of the prairie town I call home. She knows the story of my mother serving as midwife that cold winter night years ago. She already knew how Dad drove the doctor and her to the railway crossing. We smile knowingly at each other. Once again, I remember that magical, mystical, and miraculous night and I give thanks.

Nature, no matter where we live, is an expression of the divine. Every place has its own character and challenges. The basic principle for survival and happiness is to be open to one's surroundings and to like what one finds there. For the outsider, the prairie landscape appears desolate and empty. The casual traveller describes it as mile after mile of nothing—boring emptiness. For the prairie girl, it is tranquility and peace, expansive skies, and flaxen sunsets. I can still hear the gentle summer breezes whispering, *God is near.* I recall the rainbows that stretched from one end of the horizon to the other and announced the end of a summer storm. Solitude often hung in the air and took hold of my soul. It pared down my pretences and reminded me of the sacredness of the place.

We all dream dreams—earthy and sensual, evocative and inspiring, puzzling and disturbing. At eighteen, I had big dreams. Determined to chart my course into the future, I struggled to know my secret gift. The key to my vocation was in there somehow. I loved kids and was always good with them. Babysitting, tutoring colleagues, and serving as supply teacher at age fourteen gave some direction to my search. I would definitely work with children. But tugging at my heart was an incessant desire I couldn't suppress. I read about missionaries, watched documentaries on missionary work, and dreamed of doing great things for God and the poor.

My journey to the mission field was a long time coming. I taught in various schools in Saskatchewan for ten years. I loved every class I taught, but the allure of the missions was never far away. Over and over again, my longing spilled into my dreams. There was nothing definite, just a series of night visions where I saw myself surrounded by hundreds of dark women with their children in tow. Always, there was a dilapidated old church in the background. One day, things changed. My religious community planned to open a mission in

Brazil and asked for volunteers. I promptly enlisted. At long last, my dream was coming to fruition.

The twelve-hour flight from New York to Rio de Janeiro takes us through the night. The morning sun is coming alive as the plane circles the city. The view from my tiny window is out of this world. Luscious, emerald-covered mountains embrace the ancient city. On the opposite side, sandy beaches stretch as far as the eye can see. And overlooking it all is the monumental statue Cristo de Corcovado, luminous and mystic in its pristine beauty. What is there not to like? This is Brazil, the land of my dreams. I sit in silent awe before its dazzling splendour.

Following baggage claim and customs check, I walk out into the blinding light and instantaneous sultry, oppressive heat. It takes hold of me with an iron grip and refuses to let go. The long bus trip through downtown and into the suburb of Santa Terésa sets off a few warning signals. Brazil is decidedly a country of contrasts: unimaginable grandeur and tragic squalor, imposing mansions and crude hovels. There are people of every size, shape, description, and colour. Some are impeccably dressed, others in faded rags.

I expect people of the tropics to be different somehow, and Brazilians certainly fulfill my prophecy. They appear to be capricious and unconventional. Scantily clad, smelling of sweat, loud and boisterous, they jostle with each other to maintain a semblance of order on the bus. Though I can't understand a single sentence, I find the language musical and exotic. Picking me out as a foreigner, several try to strike up a conversation. I can't keep up. Suddenly, seven years of university appear to be quite useless. A hint of dis-ease bubbles to the surface. I quickly suppress it. I'll deal with it by and by.

Cultural and language school ushers in a new wave of unforeseen challenges. Sixty students represent thirty-seven countries. An awesome opportunity—invigorating and tiring at the same time. My language group consists of Lorenzo, Toshiro, Kohiti, and myself. Our common language is the Portuguese we are trying to master. Superficial communication skills sometimes lead to confusion and frustration. We discover that in a hurry. The cafeteria menu takes some personal adjusting. Rice and black bean sauce today, black beans and rice tomorrow. And Sunday dinner is more of the same.

It's week three. Full moon. My group gathers on the balcony to take in the dramatic view. A thirty-eight-metre-high statue, crowning the mountain of Corcovado, adds a burst of sparkling light to the night sky. Arms raised in blessing over the city, the "Cristo" is impressive in its bearing. I am ecstatic when Antonio arrives on the balcony and offers to drive us to Corcovado. Beyond the parking lot, it's a half hour's steep climb to the base of the statue. Lost in my own thoughts, I think of it as a pilgrimage. The quiet splendour of this night secures itself to my soul.

Week four. The cultural coordinator, Antonio, and his team urge us to embark on weekend immersions in Brazilian communities. The only way to get to know Brazil, they suggest, is to leave the security of Santa Teresa and live in a homey Brazilian setting. They count on our initiative to scout out plausible locales.

It's time for the plunge into the immersion experience. Lorenzo and I are partners. He is a draft dodger who describes himself as rootless and restless; I am a demure young teacher who feels naïve and shaky in her new setting. Thursday afternoon, we start walking south. The earlier evening visit to Corcovado had revealed a *favela,* one of Rio's biggest slums, not far from Santa Terésa. Hoping to spend our initial weekend there, we decide it's time to make the necessary arrangements.

We walk endlessly in the punishing heat. The stroll takes us past tall scarlet poinsettia trees, majestic jacaranda, verdant cacti, and sweet-smelling olive groves. Suddenly, the most revolting, reeking smell comes drifting through the still air and hangs there. "Where are we going?" Then I see it. Not fifty feet ahead is an open sewer. The sun glistens on little puddles of water here and there. Naked brown bodies jump across the muck. Black pigs wallow in it. Little children walk through it. Young boys pee in it. Mothers call their children to get out of it.

Endless rows of mud huts stretch down both sides of the sewer. Ragged clothes are laid out to dry on sandy areas between the huts. Constructed of mud and old cardboard, the lean-tos are dull in hue. Here and there, I spot a splash of vibrant colour: fuchsia cattleya orchids, orange poppy papaver, yellow begonia, pink hibiscus, and green tobacco plants. The favela provides a strange point of convergence: the elegant and the ugly, the young and the old, the strong and the weak. Nothing, absolutely nothing, prepared me for this.

There doesn't appear to be anything romantic about being here. Not at all like my dreams. What was I thinking? Why am I here? Either stubbornness or some inner strength drives me as I slowly place one foot in front of the other. Lorenzo motors ahead and I dutifully follow. We are a strange sight: too fair, too well dressed, and obviously disoriented. Children study us in stunned silence as we literally stumble into the favela.

We immediately meet a gracious, outgoing young couple. Like everyone else, Duca and Cézar are poorly clad. They welcome us and offer to show us around. I am not sure I want to see more, but common courtesy puts its demands on the spirit. They listen intently as we present the purpose of our visit. Of course we can join them for the weekend. The favela is planning a Bible study. We will be a fascinating addition.

As per Cézar's instructions, we set off for the favela early Saturday morning. It promises to be a blistering day. We take no food, no bottled water, no toiletries, but one change of clothing. Bibles in hand, we jump over the open sewer and arrive at the designated meeting place. The scene is striking. Drums beat incessantly as a large crowd swarms around an opening between the rows of huts. Young and old are dancing the samba. A festive feeling prevails.

The warm-up to the morning session is animated and rowdy. Many are speaking; few listening. As people settle, Matthew's version of the beatitudes is proclaimed. Opinions are freely shared and freely received. I take delight in the affability and energy I see all around. Neophytes in our adoptive language, Lorenzo and I both struggle to share our insights. People are too polite to laugh or request elaboration. Indiscernibly, I come around and begin to look forward to an instructive weekend. The beginning of conversion? Who knows?

Lunch is announced with considerable fanfare. Out of nowhere a large pot of rice and beans appears in the centre of the circle. Plates and cutlery have not yet arrived. Brazilians are never in a hurry, so I practice waiting. Then, to my utter dismay, I see people digging into the pot and eating with their hands. Organized chaos! Repugnance settles in my stomach. What am I to do in this situation? I feel my sense of dignity evaporating.

Duca, amazingly observant and entirely forthright, asks if there is anything I need. Pressure mounts inside. The awkward situation focuses my energy inward. My high ideals said nothing about a complete lack of sanitation or the unnecessary risk of disease. On the other hand, I cannot let details assume enormous proportions in the present circumstance. If I hope to survive as a missionary, I will have to go through a steep learning curve. I resolve to start now. There is no time to catch my breath and rearrange my dreams. My romantic notion of missionary service flies into the muggy air. I will learn one step at a time. I have to. God help me. I squeeze my eyes shut tight and dig into the pot like everyone else. It isn't all that bad. I passed my first test at being a Brazilian. But, as a blind uncertainty continues to spill deeper into my soul, I realize that the race is far from over. I have miles and miles to go.

As the light of day begins to withdraw, I have a foreboding of another torturous hurdle. Tiredness takes over and I begin to wonder about sleeping arrangements. Cézar escorts us into the tiny backyard where a few candles have been strategically placed. Duca brings out two long woven mats. There are no pillows and no blankets. The thin mats will serve as our beds. A basin of water sits on an old stump. Lorenzo and I swish enough water over our faces to rinse off the grime of the day. We settle down on our respective mats and try to sleep.

The sound of snoring coming from Lorenzo within the first five minutes indicates a remarkable ability to adapt. I am not like that. Under different circumstances, I would anticipate spending a night under the tropical stars. But this is a first for me. The filthy black pig keeps wriggling its wet nose into my face. The scrawny grey hens pluck at my feet. The stench of the open sewer burns its way deeper and deeper into my nostrils. Once again, I feel trapped by my insecurities.

The last candle flickers out and night settles in. I look up at the dark sky. It is littered with stars. A half moon casts its glow on the palms, the patches of moist grey sand, and Duca's miniature mud hut. A lone owl hoots somewhere in the distance. Instinctively, my eyes focus on Rio's beacon of hope, Cristo de Corcovado. The floodlights project a burnished warmth on the magnificent statue.

A remarkable change begins to take over my soul. Some irresistible power stirs within. I have no words to explain it, but my dream and my present reality no longer appear to be all that far apart. My once restless spirit settles and a pervading peace descends. Seldom have I felt so close to my Maker. I am content in God's hands and I know that all things work together for those who love. Convergence is both mysterious and uplifting.

Six months later, I arrive in the fishing villages where I am to live and work. Cultural shock, chapter two. At least Santa Terésa had running water and flush toilets. There is nothing akin to that here. The water is polluted, food is scarce, open sewers run down every street, and bats and rats roam freely in and out of the hut that is my home. I feel caught in a net that is pulling itself tightly around me. The demon of darkness and insecurity surfaces once more. A nightly wrestling with the "angel" appears to be my lot.

We all play our personal game of hide-and-seek. Life here is not the way I conjectured. If there was any hint of this reality at cultural school, I either missed it or pushed it down into my subconscious. Now, my benign façade is crumbling. I am at an intersection. I either accept the package deal or walk away and return to my comfortable life in Canada. Rio expanded my vision and exposed me to the goodness and generosity of the Brazilian people. As I recall those life-altering experiences, the inconveniences of my present circumstance appear insignificant. I resolve, yet again, to be the missionary I longed to be.

My third weekend in my "home" village conveniently falls at fiesta time. Gathering in the town square, the entire village is alive with activity. Drums beat and brown bodies sway and dance to the music. Children fall asleep in their parents' arms and still the music goes on. Cararrü (chopped, fried animal intestines smothered in onions) enhances the staple rice and black bean supper. Cooked shellfish are wrapped in banana leaves and roasted over an open fire. A noisy group of teenage boys carries a huge cobra on a stick. Roasting it over the fire adds a smoky flavour. The flesh is akin to rubber and sits in my stomach like a piece of lead. I wash it down with Cerveja and join in the samba. I am convinced that no one can party like the poor.

A year later, a bit of missionary wisdom is rubbing off on me. Initiation into Brazilian ways repeatedly compels me to face my inner shadow. It forces me to separate present circumstances from my preconceptions. Somehow, I see myself growing into a very different person—more open, more respectful, and more compassionate. Gradually, I am learning to let go of my rigid assumptions and expectations, my comfort and personal security. The growing pains are far from easy. But my Brazilian friends gently chip away at my inhibitions, and I learn to break out of the prison of my own thoughts and ideas.

God is ever the generous giver. In a relatively short period of time, I fell ardently in love with Brazil and its people. In my own self-centred way, I originally thought I had a lot to offer the poor. They taught me infinitely more than I could ever imagine. Pride has a way of duping us. It took me the better part of a year to see that. Reality surpassed my dream and filled my heart with an overpowering sense of gratitude.

Every place has its own mystique, its own depth, and its own appeal. Growing up on the prairies played a role in the kind of person I became. Its cold winters developed a certain strength of character. Living along the northeast coast of Brazil added another dimension. Life was as precarious on the open sea as on a road trip during a prairie winter storm. Each was a submission to the elements. Each called for a blind trust in Providence.

Happiness is not measured by material possessions or worldly achievements but by a life well-lived. Panning my memories, I am overcome with enormous gratitude. Throughout my missionary experience, reality eclipsed my dream. I learned to disentangle from my false gods—cleanliness, convenience, material riches, and control over every circumstance. In their place, I discovered the God of abundant life. Many supposedly important things were relegated into the background. I learned to vanquish my fears and restraints.

No matter where we live, life is full of "the good, the bad, and the ugly." How we face it determines the kind of person we become. Dreams and reality are different somehow. But when we look beneath the surface, we unveil the deep connections. The superficial falls away and we are left with what is essential. As we grow in wisdom and understanding, we begin to unwrap the precious gift of our life.

How quietly God breathes forth abundant life.
I am conceived in love; I am from love.
I am from family; I am from community.
Everything serves to fashion my soul
into the vessel of God's eternal grace.

How eagerly life takes hold of me.
I am from humble beginnings, from prairie stock.
I am from feasts and sacred festivals,
where everything speaks of love and growth
and endless possibilities.

How slow I am to understand.
I am formed out of the earth and its fruits.
I am from the winds that whistle through the land
and the sun that sheds its light upon the day.
I am a child of the universe—a child of God.

Chapter 8: Woman and Man

The sun feels warm on my back as I walk home from school in mid-April. At seventeen, I love the longer days because they announce the renewing cycle of life. Spring is resurrection time, nature's sacred awakening—a testimony to new life. I search eagerly for the first crocus. A shrub of pussy willows feels soft and fuzzy to the touch. I spy tiny sprays of green that have edged their way through the last remnants of snow. I admire the unwinding of several lovely lavender crocus petals. A festive feeling pervades the countryside. New life puts a fresh spin on everything.

Following my usual path through town, I see the church steeple to my right. The sight of the large steel cross thrusts me into the realm of the sacred. Once again, I come face to face with God's piercing question: "Where are you going, my love?" I still struggle with my answer. The naked truth is that I don't know. So many paths stretch out before me. It's hard to know which one to choose.

Faith has always been front and centre in my life. I feel close to God and love explaining life's mysteries to children. I spend time with the elderly, listening to their stories of faith and doubt. I train altar servers and lead prayers in church. It seems like quite a lot to me. Still, there's always a nagging doubt—is God asking more?

I find myself ascending the church steps. I open the front door. I haven't paid God a personal visit in weeks. Today is a good time to renew acquaintances. My eyes are immediately drawn to a new poster that graces the entrance. It is a large, inviting picture of Jesus. I stand in silence, staring intently at the icon. Then my eyes move down to the inscription: "Come, follow me." I instinctively look away.

There is something about it that I don't want to face. I'd like to leave the church, but the poster attracts me like a magnet. Before I know it, I am scrutinizing it again. It seems to hold some special message. I feel I've been reasonably faithful to God. "Why isn't that enough?" I wonder. Aware of my unrest, I walk up the centre aisle and sit in the front pew. I need a safe place for honest reflection.

The invitation has unsettled me. I need time to think and pray. I have known for a long time that I will go into education. Some degree of involvement in the church would mesh well with a teaching career. But now I feel that God is definitely asking for more. The poster with its poignant invitation adds to my disquiet. In the Catholic Church, only men are ordained priests. "Aye, there's the rub." I am a woman and that lets me off the hook. Or does it? I don't want to be a nun and that's that. End of story.

After what seems like forever, I look up at the life-size crucifix over the altar. Placing my head in my hands, I cry out: "Look, God, you know me through and through. You know I'd do anything for you. If you had made me a boy, I would gladly be a priest in your church. But, since you made me a girl, I will be a 'nobody' in your church." It's no great epiphany, but that poster's blessed invitation hangs around my soul. Finally, when I can't take any more, I make the sign of the cross, get up, and quietly walk out of the church.

I revisited that poster and my reaction to it many times in the ensuing months and years. The inner journey to self-discovery opens out and encompasses both sexuality and spirituality. When we look beyond our physical differences, we discover the broader dimensions of the human heart. In the soul, the divergence fades into the background. God calls us all to love and service. Once we admit that, a whole new world of possibilities emerges. Over the years, I've discovered countless ways that women can serve in the church. The church can only be enriched when it accepts and promotes the beauty and power of women and men ministering together.

The Catholic philosopher Jean Vanier wrote, "The difference between man and woman is a radical and fundamental one which permeates the depths of their consciousness and affects all human behaviour."[27] In our physical existence, we are sexual beings and, as such, women and men are incredibly different. We see things differently; we think and feel and act differently. But we are more complex than that. No one is exclusively "masculine" just as no one is completely "feminine." Understanding both the "masculine" and the "feminine," leads us to greater insight into the human psyche.

Oriental philosophers describe our differences in terms of "yin" and "yang." Yin represents feminine energy. Generally, women are open, attentive, tolerant, intuitive, imaginative, sensitive, nurturing, and deeply tender. Artistic and creative by nature, we are given to reflection and contemplation. Because we tend to be more subjective and look at the big picture, we make allowance for various shades of grey.

Yang refers to male energy. By and large, men are directed, focused, task-oriented, productive, logical, resolute, organized, and challenging. Highly motivated, they are achievers as well as thinkers. More disposed to view a situation objectively, they see things as either black or white. They have little tolerance for the seemingly vague and undefined.

Women are able to roll with the spontaneous and unstructured. We are inclined to adapt to changing circumstances. Men value order and clarity. Their need to be prepared and ready for every possibility makes them critical of anything that is indistinct and circuitous. They do not take kindly to curve balls. Masculine energy focuses on one aspect of reality at a time. Female energy is holistic and embraces the world.

Women hold friendships in high esteem. Oriented toward others, we are prepared to "nest" and create a home. Oftentimes, we act as the "glue" that holds the family and the community together. Our original blessing lies in our appreciation of the figurative, the symbolic, and the affective world. We are comfortable with the body and its cycles. Women move toward their centre, to matters of the heart. Men look outward. They enjoy constructing and assembling. The original blessing in men is in the area of the mind and its ability to observe, define, and name reality.

Left-brain and right-brain theory presents another way of viewing "masculine" and "feminine" strengths, or innate gifts for serving God. Some philosophers present masculine qualities as being closely aligned with the left hemisphere of the brain and feminine powers flowing from the right hemisphere. In reality, the human brain has dual capabilities. The left hemisphere enables both men and women to move outward to invent, produce, strengthen, sustain, refine, and rectify. Endowing us with the ability to view situations in a logical way, it makes us heedful and circumspect.

The right hemisphere, more closely aligned with what we have learned to call feminine qualities, empowers men and women to move inward to the realm of feelings and emotions, values and ideals. It blesses us with a capacity to perceive with the heart. Nurturing, loving, and supportive traits arise in the right hemisphere. Just as it draws us to receptivity and creativity, the right hemisphere opens us to thoughtful reflection.

Each hemisphere gathers in sensory information. While the left analyzes, counts, plans, and verbalizes, the right recalls, imagines, dreams, and creates new possibilities. Society pushes us to give greater prominence to the left hemisphere. Spirituality cries out for right brain "thinking." The truly wise admit that we need both. Left-brain thinking requires the intuitive gift before it can arrive at untainted insight and pure wisdom.

Women and men are distinct. It's a matter of some dispute as to how much our point of view arises out of socialization and how much is innate. We arrive at generalizations through our limited experience. Our mind-set has a lot to do with the way we observe people and situations. Reality teaches us that both men and women are blessed with a passion for life. It makes us cognizant of the contributions different people make in all areas of life—the emotional, physical, intellectual, creative, artistic, and spiritual.

Family, community, and society help us establish attitudes and patterns of behaviour. Most children carry these into adulthood. In many cultures, the biological differences in girls and boys play a central role in determining educational opportunities and prospects for the future. The result is a terrible disparity between women and men throughout the course of their lives. In the Brazil of the 1970s, sexism was very much alive. I recall many encounters with its repulsive head. It gave men an illusion of being in control. It paralyzed women.

I was shocked to see intelligent, competent women accepting infidelity on the part of their male partners while they remained unwavering in their loyalty. I could neither understand nor appreciate it. I had a hard time watching women cower before their men. It often appeared incongruous to my rational mind. Yet, when I shared my views, it was the women who told me that I was thinking like a Canadian. In their opinion, I needed to accept the Brazilian way down to the finest detail. "Just close your eyes, Edite, and let things be." I saw it as a collective weakness, a cultural attitude. Despite their own inner light, these women accepted the circumstance of life and tried to make the best of it.

It is Holy Saturday night and the Saubara town square is abuzz with activity. The custom is to celebrate the eve of the resurrection as a community. A few prominent men build an effigy of Judas and raise it on high over an open fire. Everyone gathers to see who will be chosen as the "Judas" for the year. The effigy is set aflame and the individual becomes a laughing stock for months to come.

At the stroke of midnight, Gustavo ascends a series of steps and announces the awaited verdict. The 1977 Judas is my neighbour Sebastião. I am horrified. "How can this be?" I wonder. As I walk home an hour later, Sebastião catches up with me. He feels he has some explaining to do. Everyone knows that he has a second "wife" at the west end of town and they accept that. The problem is that he has never shared this information with his wife Eugénia.

I get the point. It isn't that he has been unfaithful to his wife, but that he is deceptive about it, that matters. There is an obvious duality in moral standards. "Paradigm shifts take a long time coming," I tell myself.

Seeing is more than observing. It has the potential to lead us to perception and insight. Naturally, it involves both the left and right hemisphere of the brain, both "masculine" and "feminine" energy. Seeing one aspect of reality, the dominant male moves quickly, arrives at decisive conclusions, and enforces decisions in a strong-minded way. With an eye for the big picture, the dominant female sees underlying patterns and relationships. Reactions are thoughtful, sensitive, and passionate. When we allow the masculine and feminine to work together, we see new possibilities and discover creative solutions to the problems of our world.

The human person is more than hormones and biological functions. Created in the image and likeness of God, we are thinking, feeling beings. Both masculine and feminine energy runs through all our veins. Part of who we are is intimately connected with our sexuality and our orientation toward life. Each of us is a beautiful, complex, and mysterious blend of male and female qualities. The world is poorer when it fails to look beyond the surface and discover the complexities within the human spirit.

Our sexuality, like everything else about us, is part of our original blessing. The road to wholeness follows the path of integration. We need both our masculine and feminine energy working in harmony with each other to become fully human. The head without some heart leads to a cold and calculating life. The heart without the head lives in the realm of imagination and nothing concrete gets done. The visionary needs the doer and the man of action requires a healthy dose of intuitive feminine potency. The gospel is clear in its understanding of salvation. It is about partnerships and sharing, not control and domination. The ideal can be found in a respectful sharing of leadership and power.

The integrated person is able to move beyond the raw logic of facts and figures to perceive the inner workings of the Spirit. For most of us, this calls for a paradigm shift. Society holds up power, prestige, and possessions as the only things that matter. It values the "masculine" qualities of strength, certitude, single-mindedness, and independence. But in the global village there is a mounting call to carry each others' burdens, to care for the weak and the vulnerable, and to guide children and youth to right living. The potential to accomplish both lies in our original blessing.

A well-balanced life meshes flexibility with audacity. It turns our aggressive behaviours into assertive responses to situations. When we let go of our positions of power, we begin to see the necessity for change and adaptation. There is more to our lives than the things we produce. Created for relationship and community, every person has a unique contribution to make. Family and community function most effectively when they respect and employ the multiple qualities of their members. A healthy community makes room for the intuitive, sensing, feeling, and thinking personalities in its midst. All serve to enrich the group.

Love and understanding tear down the walls that separate us. They create the fertile soil where the delicate soul can emerge and blossom. Faith assures us that each of us is born with a higher purpose—something to live for, something to give to the community and the world. Scripture provides inspiring examples of women and men who used their gifts for the good of others. Great prophets, prophetesses, priests, and leaders relied on both their masculine and feminine gifts to fulfill their God-given missions.

Moses is a case in point. He learned as an infant that the world could be a fearful place for both men and women. Born in Egypt of a Hebrew mother during a time when Pharaoh was executing Israeli male infants, he was saved by Pharaoh's daughter, who raised him as her own. His mother served as his nursemaid and made sure he was aware of his Hebrew heritage. However, circumstances dictated that his origin be kept secret. The legacy that turned him into a champion of the underdog remained lodged inside awaiting the opportune moment.

As a young man, Moses witnessed an Egyptian taskmaster beating a Hebrew slave. It infuriated him. Spontaneously, he rose to the challenge and came to the rescue. It was a courageous but dangerous reaction. Fearing for his life, Moses fled into Midian, where he eventually married Zipporah, daughter of the priest Jethro.

The people of Midian were unaware of Moses' past. Hence, they respected and trusted the young shepherd. Herding sheep was a humble task. It provided little opportunity for rocking the boat. Life was safe and comfortable. Moses liked it that way and planned to live out his days in this faraway place. It would have worked, except that God had other plans.

One memorable day, God showed up unexpectedly. It was a deeply moving and mysterious encounter. Moses could neither describe nor understand God's presence. Even so, it left him a changed man. The burning bush may have been a natural phenomenon at that time of year. In the Sinai Peninsula, brilliant red flowers graced many country bushes and their pollen could give the impression of a burning bush. But Moses, who was comfortable with signs and symbols, saw it as an indication of the divine Presence.

When God asked Moses to go back to Egypt in order to save his own people, he hesitated. He enjoyed his well-ordered life and hoped to keep it that way. In Egypt, he was still a hunted man. He had no desire to go back to the scene of his crime. He voiced his concern and made sure God understood that it would be asking too much. Still, God persisted: "I send you to Pharaoh to bring my people out of Egypt." Moses' anxiety level soared a notch or two. Desperate to find a way out, he set his mind to convincing God to choose someone else. "I am of lowly stature, definitely not an orator," he argued. God elected him for the job anyway. Moses finally gave God his word and never looked back.[28]

A most unlikely leader, Moses accepted his role as the instrument of God for the people. He moved into his mission with a strong sense of duty and undying commitment. Somehow, he found his voice as he stood before Pharaoh. The end result was freedom for his people. It was not a freedom that came easily. The people wandered through the desert for forty years. They complained loud and long. Sometimes, they turned their backs on God and worshipped idols. From time to time, Moses lost his patience with them although he never wavered in his loyalty to God or turned from his task of taking the people's concerns to God.

The once frightened and introverted Moses became the tangible symbol of God's presence among the people. His "masculine" strength kept him loyal to the task. Once he moved beyond his self-interests, he became an authentic and faithful teacher of the Torah and a courageous leader. His "feminine" tenderness assured the people of God's enduring love and protection. The God who remained ever faithful to the covenant was a forgiving God. Moses presented a God who loves unconditionally, demands a high moral code, and leads people to their destiny.

Looking at Moses superficially, we wonder why God chose such an insecure man to be such an important instrument. Moses had no great ambitions, no dreams beyond his small world. Yet, when God called him and appointed him priest, prophet, and leader, his feminine energy empowered him to see the big picture. He dedicated himself to the role despite strong personal reservations. His openness to God and his reliance on others led him to a wisdom few people ever realize. Because he did not act alone, but included his brother Aaron in many aspects of his work, he was able to carry on despite insurmountable obstacles. It took both his masculine and feminine energy to do that.

The book of Ruth is actually the account of two women: Ruth and her mother-in-law, Naomi. The tragic death of Naomi's two sons followed closely upon the death of her husband. The two women found themselves widows dealing with limited resources in a hostile country. At the same time, a famine took hold in Moab and left them destitute. Naomi decided to return to her native land. Ruth's love and respect for her mother-in-law inspired her to travel with her. A Moabite, Ruth left her past and all that was familiar and secure. Dutifully, she accompanied Naomi to Bethlehem. She knew full well that she would be an ethnic outsider, a refugee, a widow, and a woman alone, scorned as one who worshipped a foreign god. Her "masculine" logic and strength of character saw her through.

From the moment she stepped foot in Bethlehem, Ruth resolved to confront the world on its own terms. She steadfastly made her own way, neither expecting nor asking for favours. Entitled by Jewish law to the leftovers in the field, she sought justice and worked as a gleaner to support herself and Naomi. She challenged the ancient Israelites who viewed her with suspicion as she worked in a field belonging to Boaz, one of Naomi's kinfolk. He was an older, well-established, and honourable Jew. It did not take him long to recognize both Ruth's diligence and her youthful beauty and charm. He summarily took her into his inner circle. Eventually, the old man and the young woman made a covenant between them. Their marriage union was blessed with offspring. Their son Obed became the grandfather of the great King David. It was through Ruth, the foreigner, and not from her Israelite relatives that the genealogy of Jesus derived.

Ruth learned loving kindness from her own god and saw that same kindness in Naomi's God. Everything Ruth did, she did for love of her mother-in-law and for love of Naomi's God. On the road to Bethlehem, she made a promise she was determined to keep. It was a deeply "feminine" commitment: "Where you go, I will go; where you lodge, I will lodge; your people shall be my people and your God my God."[29] Little did Ruth know that her fidelity would become a blessing in her life and in the lives of future generations.

In her femininity, Ruth was attentive to the needs of Naomi, aware of Boaz' interest and care for her, and open to the events and circumstances of life. She dug into her masculine strength as she refused to shrink from the arduous challenges that life held out to her. People who move beyond ritual and tradition are able to grapple with life itself.

Languages and images combine to reflect our understanding of self, our sense of life and all that is human, our perception of community, and our awareness of God. It follows, then, that our spiritual language must reflect both the feminine and masculine energy of the human spirit. Nowhere in the Bible is the feminine more visible than in the Book of Wisdom. There is a powerful dimension of God that is best expressed in the feminine imagery of wisdom. "For wisdom, the fashioner of all things, taught me… Because of her pureness she pervades and penetrates all things. For she is the breath of the power of God… and an image of God's goodness."[30]

It takes time, patience, and openness to appreciate our original blessing. Individually, we are complex beings. Members of the human family, we are also interconnected. Life is not clear-cut and simple. Ambiguities abound. We all face hard choices—decisions that impinge on the lives of others. Over time, we learn to look for a discernible pattern. Invariably, it incorporates our blessings and our limitations. To be fully alive is to look beneath the surface of things and identify both the "masculine" and "feminine" potential that is our legacy.

Responsive to grace, we meet life head on and attain the equilibrium and stability that are our spiritual possession. The healthy life is a balanced life, a life wherein we use both our masculine and feminine energy to the full. Spirituality is about recognizing that energy, harnessing it, and disciplining it. When we know how to access and contain that energy, we learn to use it for the fulfillment of our life's purpose. The end result is a creative, practical, and integrated life.

O God of abundant life,
mother and father of us all,
you who live in the depths of all life,
you created me as the temple of your Spirit.
You give me the wisdom to know myself
and the strength to be who you call me to be.
Open my eyes to the promise of my original blessing,
to look beneath the surface,
appreciating my innate potential--
my call to love and to serve.
Give me the insight
to recognize the gifts of others.
Give me the courage to mend what is broken
and the compassion and gentleness
to touch my heart and all the world with love.
Amen.

Part 3

Spirituality: Acknowledging Our Original Sin

I know the way you can get
When you have not had a drink of Love:

Your face hardens,
Your sweet muscles cramp.
Children become concerned
About a strange look that appears in your eyes
Which even begins to worry your own mirror
And nose.

Squirrels and birds sense your sadness
And call an important conference in a tall tree.
They decide which secret code to chant
To help your mind and soul.

Even angels fear that brand of madness
That arrays itself against the world
And throws sharp stones and spears into
The innocent
And into one's self.

O I know the way you can get

If you have not been drinking Love:

You might rip apart
Every sentence your friends and teachers say,
Looking for hidden clauses.

You might weigh every word on a scale
Like a dead fish.

You might pull out a ruler to measure
From every angle in your darkness
The beautiful dimensions of a heart you once
Trusted.

I know the way you can get
If you have not had a drink from Love's
Hands.

That is why all the Great Ones speak of
The vital need
To keep remembering God,
So you will come to know and see Him
As being so Playful
And Wanting,
Just wanting to help.

That is why Hafiz says:
Bring your cup near me.

For I am a Sweet Old Vagabond
With an Infinite Leaking Barrel
Of Light and Laughter and Truth
That the Beloved has tied to my back.

Dear one,
Indeed, please bring your heart near me.
For all I care about
Is quenching your thirst for freedom!

All a Sane man can ever care about
Is giving Love!

—*Shams-ud-din Muhammed Hafiz*

Chapter 9: Fallibility

The creation of woman and man was God's ultimate accomplishment. Given powers like God, these creatures were awesome in every way. God had a fantastic plan for them. God's dream was magnificent and beyond anything they could ever imagine. Their life's mission was to reflect God's love and life and peace. They were destined to grow to that wholeness and holiness of being that God most deeply desired for them.

In the beginning, woman and man spent their days tasting, touching, feeling, smelling, hearing, observing, and enjoying the beauty of God's creation. They were completely satisfied. They were in love with each other and with life. It did not take long, however, before melancholy set in. Woman and man began to question their role in the garden of delight. They wanted to know all things, to be masters of the garden, and the centre of the universe. In truth, they set their hearts on being like God. Their dark thoughts turned to darker deeds. And so, the first sin came into the unspoiled world of love and light.

The darkness of sin and selfishness soon spread across the earth. But it could not envelop it because God was watching. God's creative energy went back to work. And God conceived a truly novel idea: "I will send my own son, Jesus. He will be a light that darkness cannot overcome. And he will walk the earth and share the people's struggle and feel their pain. He will redeem them from their sin. He will pay the price of unconditional love and the people will receive the fullness of their God. They will have life and have it abundantly."

So, Jesus came as the Word among us and taught us the way of love—accepting, healing, forgiving, recreating, and liberating. Jesus was the Way, the Truth, and the Life. Yet, despite his kind and gentle ways, he was rejected, convicted, and crucified. But, from the anguish of his death, new life sprang forth. His incomprehensible gift of self turned the page of history. The pain of death gave rise to the pangs of birth. And, once again, God said, "It is good."

Henceforth and forever, woman and man are forgiven and healed. Redeemed and released from sin, they are given a second chance. Notwithstanding their sin, they are destined to be bearers of the light. And when they walk the journey of life with integrity and humility, they are empowered to live in harmony with each other and every living thing. Then, all the yearnings of creation are fulfilled.

The inconceivable and awesome gift of Jesus makes us ask: Will woman and man and their descendants immerse themselves in the waters of life and reach out to the redemption Jesus won for them? Or will they go down the road of selfishness and sin? The answer is all too familiar. Even to this day, we all vacillate between grace and sin, redemption and selfishness. We jump into the water, then, when we begin to sink we turn back. Our desire to live rightly is not strong enough and we falter over and over again. There is a decided tension in human life. Darkness replaces light and the light eventually returns to dispel the darkness. Where there is fullness and abundance, a barren emptiness creeps in for a time. Still, grace reminds us that we have the power to stop the pendulum and take hold of our life.

Goodness and light pull us in one direction while ominous shadows draw us into confusion and unrest. We see beauty and righteousness all around us, but the ugliness of self-indulgence and greed is not far behind. There are curious and inexplicable discrepancies in the human spirit. We waver between good and evil. "I do not understand my own actions. For I do not do what I want, but I do the very thing I hate… Now if I do what I do not want, it is no longer I that do it, but sin that dwells within me."[31]

It is a dreary day in the northeast corner of Brazil. Typical of the rainy season, clouds burst open and pour down interminable rain. Everything is grey and gloomy for three or four days on end. Rain or no rain, I must make a trip to Salvador today. On the early morning bus, I make a mental note of the many errands I have to run. My priority is to cash the quarterly five hundred dollar cheque from Canada. It will keep our mission going for the next three months.

Darkness is already descending when I am ready to go home. The torrential rain has not let go of its grip on the city. Thankfully, I spot a city bus that will take me to the bus depot. There is no time to tarry. Hanging on to my bags, I dash down the street. The bus is about to pull away when I manage to get one foot on the first step. I hang on for dear life. The heavy rain soaks through my clothes to my skin. Chilled and drenched, I am happy to have made it this far.

Little by little, as people get off the bus, I worm my way onto the bus. Every seat is occupied. Live chickens peck at my feet. The smell of damp feathers fills the air. I clutch my bags and hug my purse to my chest. At long last, soaked and tired, I arrive at the bus depot.

Relief surges through me as I enter the depot to purchase my ticket. On opening my purse, I discover it completely empty. The money is gone. "How can this be?" I ask myself. Caution aside, a thief discovered a weakness and moved in for the kill. Someone quietly and carefully slit my shoulder bag and withdrew its entire contents. I was too preoccupied hanging on to even notice. I want to sit down and cry, but what good would that do? A terrible aching void inundates my soul as I beg a few pesos from a stranger and call a missionary friend for help.

The four-hour bus trip to our fishing villages is a sobering one. Many thoughts race through my mind. My cash supply is all gone. How could a Brazilian do this to my mission? It makes a cruel mockery of my missionary intentions. After a long and painful hour, my thoughts take an about-turn. Who is the guilty party here? Is it not the political and social system that turns a blind eye to the plight of millions living in abject poverty? The destitute will do anything to survive.

Even with our best efforts to seed the world with love, we turn in on ourselves. The propensity to selfishness seems to be deeply entrenched. Over and over again, our time, energy, and talents become instruments of separation rather than unity. Selfishness invariably leads to divisions and misunderstandings. Life becomes barren and unfulfilled. We are incomprehensible mysteries even to ourselves.

What is original sin? Essentially, it is an inherent weakness in the heart and soul of every person, the root cause of confusion and indifference. It holds the soul prisoner as it destroys the human spirit and distorts its inner passion for life. Blurring our vision, it distorts our thinking and makes us unpredictable. It clouds our judgement and weakens our will. Because of its continual presence, we are unsure of our spiritual potential. God is always there, reaching out to us in unconditional love. We don't understand that kind of love and create our own image of God. We put limits on God's eternal love. Forgiveness is God's way of assuring us that there is nothing we can do that makes us unworthy of love. Because we don't quite believe it, we hold out on God. The spiritual treasure that is our original blessing grows faint, sometimes invisible.

Sin is whatever destroys love—any thought, word, or deed that makes it difficult or impossible for us to love. It affects our relationships with God, with self, and with others. Sin ignores God's gratuitous gifts. It puts limitations on our original blessing. Afraid of being criticized and rejected, we ignore and even repress our blessing. We expect too little. The packaging frightens us; the gift is too precious. We do not take the time to unwrap it, examine it, and assess its worth. We guard it as a priceless jewel, something to be looked at but seldom used. Like the woman in Jesus' parable, we take our invaluable treasure and bury it in the field, somewhere deep down inside. Little do we realize that when we brush aside our original blessing, we deprive the world of its riches.

Northeast Brazil is in the midst of the summer's heat. I decide to drive to the village on the north end of the mission. As I approach Itapema, I see Dora frantically waving her arms to stop me. Nilda, obviously in the last stages of pregnancy, is standing at her side. Dora asks if I could get her daughter to the municipal hospital in Santo Amaro. The baby is breeched and there is nothing the midwife can do. Noting the look of anguish on Nilda's face, I offer to drive her. I fully expect Dora to accompany us. But she waves me on the minute Nilda is in the car.

I've never delivered a baby and feel uneasy. I drive as fast as the road conditions allow and, yet, the fifty-kilometre trip seems to go on forever. Nilda is a petite sixteen-year-old beauty. I want to give her some assurance, but I don't know what to say. She voices her concern about not having any money and no medical insurance. Then it dawns on me, neither do I. I left in such a hurry that I didn't think of going home for my purse. I pray that we will make it to the hospital on time.

By nine thirty, we walk in the front door of the hospital. As I look at Nilda, I can't help but see the beads of perspiration covering her brow. She is nervous, and with good reason. The hospital smells of disinfectant. It nauseates her and she clings to my arm for support. The receptionist asks about the purpose of our visit and immediately wants to see a medical insurance card. I shake my head. We have nothing. At that moment, a young doctor, Paulo, appears on the scene. But he, too, feels we need some insurance. I can't get my mind around this. Nilda needs to be seen. There is no time to waste. I explain the situation as quickly as I can. I believe there is only one thing to do.

Paulo looks at me in a stunned manner. He is not about to offer any assistance. I stare intently into his dark brown eyes and put on my most appealing expression. Then, I surprise myself as I say: "My charity was to bring Nilda to receive the help she needs. And your charity begins right now." I squeeze Nilda's arm and give her a quick wink as I announce, "Some things in life have to be free. It all goes with the territory." I turn and walk quickly out the front door. I learn later that Nilda gave birth to a little boy. Mom and baby are doing fine.

The impossible is often a door to something profound and beautiful. We never know where it will lead until we give it a try. Often, we are too insecure to trust our better instincts, to give hope a chance. Afraid of being criticized or rejected, we ignore and even repress our original blessing. Light surrounds us but, when push comes to shove, we choose darkness. A vague insecurity drives us and we miss countless opportunities for good. Our fearful, fractious approach is the result of original sin. Born into an impure and contaminated world, we coast along the surface quite afraid of the depth.

Original sin is about attachments, addictions, compulsions, hang-ups, and the need to cover up human weakness. It is human to flaunt our successes and gloss over our failures. From the beginning to the end of life, we are immersed in a world tarnished by inflated egos. We meet powerful, influential people whose vision is much too narrow and we cave in to their way of thinking. We give them permission to define us. We allow our own illusions to serve as our guide. We can't see the forest for the trees. Sin blinds us and we become indifferent to the needs of others. Instead of doing our part, we merely sit on our hands. We pass judgment, condemn, dismiss, and discount others.

The term "original sin" is confusing and disconcerting. We know where it came from. We were definitely not the first to commit it. Somewhere in human history our first ancestors did that. And they passed on its effects to all generations. Try as we might, we cannot take hold of it and eradicate it. It seems to go hand in hand with life itself. There is no evading it. Like our shadow, it follows us everywhere. For some reason, God lets it simply be alongside our original blessing. The why and the wherefore remain shrouded in mystery.

Both grace and sin abound in everyone's life. To be human is to live with the light and the darkness. The spiritual journey, fraught with sin and blessing, takes us through ecstasy and growth as well as darkness and pain. Real growth necessarily includes some painful moments. The twists and turns of life show us that we do not create our own path to wholeness. God works in and through others—sometimes through their weakness. I recall a heart-rending experience I witnessed in the life of a student. It helped me realize that the great mystery of God, of love, and of life is revealed to us over time and sometimes amid unbearable pain.

The first time Sylvie walks into my Christian Ethics class, I like her. Bright and attractive on the outside, she is lovely inside. A high moral standard lies beneath a calm and casual manner. Her remarkable ability to express her ideas and perceptions are a good omen. Sure-footed, disciplined, highly energetic, and keenly interested in what others have to say, she is popular with girls and boys alike. But they learn early on that no one tells her how to live her life. Involvement in extracurricular activities rounds out her academic success. One could say she has it all. And she does, until the month after her seventeenth birthday. I am about to discover the reason for her unexpected melancholy.

Arriving at school early on a Friday morning, I walk casually down the semi-lit hall. Sylvie is at her locker. "A bit early for a student to be in the school," I think. As I draw closer, I detect a puzzling transparency reflected in her unusually pale face. Her eyes are fluid as though she's been crying. She turns abruptly and nearly falls into my arms. As I escort her to the medical room, I apologize that the school nurse is not available on Fridays. Sylvie replies, "That's good. I really don't want to see a nurse."

I make a few inquiries about her parents. She replies, "My parents are my problem. I am in serous trouble. I need help. No one here can know about my situation."

I give her my word: "Your secret is safe with me."

On the edge of exhaustion, Sylvie sits down on the bed. A bit more relaxed, she pours out her troubles. Her deeply ingrained discipline makes her blush to the roots of her hair as she blurts out: "I'm pregnant." I see the fear creeping into her soft blue eyes. "I definitely want to have this baby," she whispers, then adds, "I am up against incredible odds, mostly my Mom and Dad."

I admire her single-minded intent. She is standing on a precipitous cliff. She absolutely believes she has the moral responsibility to protect her unborn child. She desperately needs support and it is highly unlikely that her parents will come around. I respect her firm decision, but I know it will exact a high price. I promise to assist her any way I can.

Honest to the point of bluntness, she describes a gruelling meeting with her parents, family doctor, a psychiatrist, and an abortion doctor. Her voice is strained and weak as she says, "It was like court. They were the jury; I, the criminal. I've never felt so small, so trapped, and so alone." When I put a reassuring arm around her shoulder, she admits, "I know I should never have become pregnant. But I did. It's done and I will live with the consequences."

I pledge to stand by her and her decision. I assure her that she made the right moral choice. But I caution that it won't be an easy journey. Her tired face looks up at me as she pleads, "I desperately need your help, Sister E. I need someone to stand up for me against my parents and the brick wall they've built between us. Thank you."

I look at Sylvie for a long moment before I ask, "Are you up for another difficult meeting? I think we should confront your parents together."

Her blue eyes brighten and she responds immediately, "Yes. Yes. As soon as possible. Monday works for me." Concerned for her emotional well-being, I think it best that the idea comes from me. She hugs me tightly when I offer to arrange the meeting. I have never met the Winters, but my money's on Sylvie.

Sylvie's parents, Jason and Shannon, arrive after school on Monday. They talk incessantly, mostly about their jobs and how hard they've worked to build up their reputations. They stand on the pinnacle of success. The tension in the room escalates the minute Sylvie walks in. Jason and Shannon have run out of escape talk. This is the moment of truth. I take charge of the situation immediately by informing them that I am on Sylvie's side. Questioning looks. Stunned silence. They need time to absorb this information. What did they expect from me?

After an elongated and painful moment, Jason speaks for both of them: "How can you take her side? Sylvie will bring unimaginable shame on us." I get the impression that he has an inflated opinion of their family reputation.

Shannon's dark eyes drop down as she jumps in: "We only want her to have a solid education and a real chance at a good life. She is so young. How will she manage to look after an infant and continue her schooling? It is virtually impossible." Somewhere deep down, she seems to feel genuine concern for her daughter. But it's a different kind of solicitude, not the kind Sylvie needs right now. I ask myself, How do you move people away from the innate need to defend their turf? It is like cutting through thick ice.

My thoughts steamroll ahead. Birthright is the answer. When I mention it, Jason and Shannon become suddenly conciliatory. Of course they attach a condition to their consent. Nothing seems to come easy with them. "Sylvie, you must give the child up for adoption immediately after its birth," Jason says with an authoritative air. My heart is in my mouth and I gasp audibly. I want to object. An innocent child is the second victim here. Sylvie sits in a trance, staring off into space. Then, in a sad and despondent voice, she announces her acquiescence. She agrees to all the terms set out by her parents. Jason and Shannon walk out in silence without so much as a kind gesture toward their hurting daughter.

I find a suitable home across the city. Sylvie is content to live with strangers, complete grade eleven by correspondence, and silently move away from her friends. I don't like the clandestine arrangement, but there is no other option. Sylvie's underlying goal is to safeguard the life of her child. Commendable fortitude. Months later, she takes one look at the little girl with the spun gold hair and the turquoise blue eyes. Then the tears flow in an interminable stream. Planting a passionate kiss on the infant's cheek, she hands her over to social services.

At the end of the school year, I set off for Brazil where I serve as a missionary. My thoughts turn to Sylvie over and over again. It saddens me to think I might never see her again.

On my return to the prairies five years later, I take a casual walk downtown. It is part of my efforts to reclaim my Canadian roots. Out of nowhere, I hear a familiar voice calling my name. I recognize Sylvie's strong voice and spot her on the other side of the street. We meet over a long, long coffee. Two years ago she married Phil, the father of her baby. Now she is trying to become pregnant again. Her parting words say it all: "I have to keep believing that God is good."

The Bible is full of stories that boggle the mind. Amid countless heroes and saints, we find conniving, scheming, spiteful people. In the novel, *East of Eden*, the philosopher farmer Samuel Hamilton makes a candid admission: "Two stories haunted us and followed us from the beginning… the story of original sin and the story of Cain and Abel. And I don't understand then at all, but I feel them in myself."[32] The stories that confounded Hamilton trouble us today. Through the ages, thinkers and sages, kings and lords, serving women and ordinary men, have tried to make sense of them.

Scripture's stories describe the people's attempt to comprehend life and its contradictions. Indisputably written thousands of years after the events, they reflect the deep faith of a people. Repeatedly touched by a God who protected and cared for them, a God who forgave and understood them, they developed a profound sense of God. But they were not immune to sin and treachery and cruelty. Love and hate, goodness and cruelty, mercy and revenge, light and darkness, were present in their community just as they are in ours.

In Genesis, the original temptation began as a casual conversation between the woman, the man, and the serpent, a symbol of fertility. The conniving creature set out to fill their heads with half-truths: you will be happier than you have ever been; you will be filled with the knowledge and power of God; you will be like God. In a subtle way, it suggested that God was keeping something magnificent from them. The trap was set. It didn't take long before woman and man looked regretfully at the forbidden fruit. It appeared delicious and inviting. What harm could there be in tasting it? So, they picked it and ate.

This first act of disobedience ushered in a series of consequences. The woman and man immediately saw themselves naked. It had nothing to do with a lack of clothing and everything to do with guilt and shame. They needed a cover-up. An uneven fear took hold of them. Having over-stepped the imposed limits, they didn't know how to face God. When God called out to them, they panicked and hid behind a tree. It didn't work. God was unrelenting. The response of the man was to blame the woman. And the woman, in turn, blamed the serpent. An all too familiar prototype!

Every story of sin simulates the sequence of the first sin. I find it in my personal sin and in the sin around me. Caught in a mean or petty act, my automatic reaction is to shift the blame to someone else or some peculiar circumstance. The blame game has been popular through the ages. We all make mistakes but don't come clean. It is never our fault. Just as we are pulled toward selfishness, so we are inclined to come up with excuses. We always seem to find a boulder to keep us out of sight. Any place where we can hide, regroup, and carry on with the pretence will do.

It is a beautiful spring day. As I walk to school, I take in the sights and sounds: trees are pregnant with tiny buds; robins sing as they flit through the air. The renewing pattern of life always lifts my spirit. I listen for the welcome laughter of children at play. I am still enjoying the reverie when three girls start walking with me. Solemn expressions tell me that something is amiss.

On her way home from school, Barb observed two class-mates, Randy and Jon, sneaking around behind the corner store—forbidden territory for students. Curiosity got the better of her and she stood behind a tree. Randy picked up a can of spray paint. Standing before a wall that was already covered in an ugly collage of colours, the boys took turns spraying arches of heavy black lines across the mottled design. No one would ever know, at least so they thought. Barb stole away before they saw her.

Confident that their graffiti trick passed by unobserved, they smile innocently when I call them to the office. Randy has the audacity to say, "Please make this quick. We don't want to miss the soccer game." I am not amused, but I let his impertinence pass. Jon, always in the line of fire, is the first to catch on. This isn't a friendly visit to the office. Their thoughts race ahead and the boys exchange silent glances. The jocular atmosphere has turned sour. Their eyes turn to the floor as they struggle with their deception. When I paint a picture of what supposedly transpired behind the corner store, a sullen silence wraps itself around them. Neither is prepared to answer my questions. At this point I feel I am the prosecutor, not yet the judge.

I wait patiently for some explanation. Finally, Randy blurts out, "It was Jon. The spray can was just lying there. He picked it up and made the mess. Honest. I just watched." Fear drives out all sense of loyalty. Caught, the boys play the blame game for all it is worth. Vehemently denying Randy's story, Jon puts the blame squarely on his friend's shoulders. We walk to the store together to view the damage. At the grotesque sight, I let out a deep sigh. It has the desired effect. Hesitantly, falteringly, the boys finally relate the whole story.

The scene replays itself when their parents arrive. Both boys want to save face at all cost. They scuttle along until they run out of steam. Eventually, they realize they have come to the end of their rope. The story comes into clearer focus. They go so far as to admit their guilt to the store's manager and willingly accept the community work Sam suggests.

Three years later, a new student enrols in the school. Zak's mischievous nature knows no bounds and often progresses to hurtful pranks. Prone to defacing property and taking things from younger children, he often brags about his conquests. He is in Jon's class. Jon has learned his lesson well. Not wanting to be drawn into trouble again, he asks for some community work he can do after school. It is a way of saying he has better things to do than follow Zak down a path of destruction. As long as he is unavailable, Zak has no hold on him.

The story of Cain and Abel exemplifies the deep connection between blessing and sin. While Abel walked with God, Cain busied himself tilling the soil. Both were loved and blessed from the beginning. At some point, things changed for Cain and he lost his self-confidence. Jealousy raged inside. Weak and despondent, he was ripe for a fall. One afternoon, he tricked his brother into going for a long walk. Far removed from any watchful eye, he turned into a heartless murderer. Like the first woman and man, Cain was called to task. Embarrassed and humiliated when God asked for an explanation, his only response was: "Am I my brother's keeper?"

The story leaves many unanswered questions. While it illustrates humanity's inclination to selfishness and sin, it points out God's never-ending love of the sinner. Following his sinful act, Cain was overcome with fear—fear of self and of others. Despite his heinous crime, he remained under God's protection. In fact, God set his seal upon him and protected him.[33]

The pattern of sin entrenches itself in all of us. Personal sin, communal sin, and corporate sin proliferate across the global village. Sadly, the result often affects the lives of innocent people. For many, life is lived in the dark tunnel of oppression and abuse, dependency and poverty. There is an inequality that appears impossible to eradicate. Opportunities for change are available for people of means, not for the underprivileged. A desire to be like everyone else lures some of the most needy into a life of crime and deceit. It doesn't bring happiness. It never can.

The courthouse stands overlooking the river. A massive and impressive building, it is an icon of justice. Now and again, one wonders, "Justice for whom?" Courtroom trials are full of drama. Posturing, the correct costume, and good eye contact are designed to present the "right" image and to lessen the sentence.

I meet Ester through the church and we become friends. She invites me to her home on numerous occasions. I feel comfortable there. Desiring the best for her family, Ester left the reserve and moved into the city. She refused to marry the father of her five children because she couldn't afford to lose her Indian status card. Her partner, Pete, mostly worked at casual jobs. The pay wasn't great, but it paid for the essentials. They rented a small house on the wrong side of the tracks. But it was home.

Late one night, I receive a mysterious phone call. "Can you come over for an hour or so?" Ester pleads. I set out at once. I feel my heart tightening as I walk in the door. The younger children are crying; Drew, the eldest, stands with his back to the door, staring at the wood stove. Ester swallows hard before she pours out her heart. Drew was caught robbing a local drug store. The crime took place ten months ago. The family only heard about it because Drew is scheduled in court tomorrow morning. The information is sketchy, not much to go on. I offer to accompany them to the trial before they feel the need to ask. Ester and Pete are humiliated enough already.

Ester looks weary as we walk into the courthouse. A legal aid lawyer, Matthew, is waiting for Drew. The meeting lasts all of ten minutes. In a system where days can begin with schedules already too full, time is of the essence. Matthew directs us into the courtroom where we talk in hushed tones until the judge arrives. I notice that Drew is wearing jeans and a casual T-shirt. It doesn't present an impressive image in this situation. But it is too late now.

Drew's friend Joey is called to the stand first. He is also charged with breaking and entering with the intent to steal. Dressed in a dark suit and tie, hair neatly combed, and with Mom and Dad at his side, Joey is full of confidence. He strides boldly to the stand. Dark eyes look directly at the judge. His lawyer emphasizes the fact that he is back in high school and is working part-time. Joey receives a lecture, a fine, and fifty hours of community service. He grins broadly as he walks past us and out of the room.

Ester shifts uneasily. Can the outcome be that easy for her son? Her eyes are full of questions as she looks at me. Having no guarantees, I shrug my shoulders. Ester can hardly keep her jaw from quivering. I bless myself inconspicuously. Drew walks to the stand with a nervous step. Consumed by fear, he keeps his eyes cast down. His posture speaks of panic.

It is the prosecutor's time to speak. He paints Drew as a drifter, the son of a single mother, no father, uneducated, and jobless. Tears begin seeping out of Ester's eyes. Pete's energy is depleted, but he puts his arm around his partner and braces himself for the worst. Drew receives a sentence of six months. He cannot even look at his parents as police officers lead him away.

We carry our shadow with us through the ups and downs of life. Despite our conscious and unconscious efforts to gloss over the unresolved and underlying issues within, reality finds a way of exposing us. Sooner or later, all things come to light. We can't keep hiding behind our façade. The truth leaks out of us. We can either become a floundering ship awash at sea or we can turn to the one who has the power to mend and heal and restore. When we refuse to acknowledge our sin, we give it free reign. When we let God's healing grace wash over us, we are redeemed. The choice is in our hands.

Human life is full of inconsistencies. Sin and blessing appear to intermingle. Humanity is fractured and fragmented. We all have reason to carry our heads low. Miscues, mistakes, and selfishness surface in everyone's life. We can rub our wounds until they are raw, we can gather our arms full of guilt and carry it around with us incessantly, but we don't have to. False guilt is part of original sin. When we fail to rise above it, we create all kinds of masks to fool those around us. And all the while we are crying out for help.

Healthy guilt is a wake-up call. A messenger of truth, it shines its light on the darkness in our soul. Piercing through our self-deception and exposing our illusions for what they are, it raises disturbing questions. It calls us to drop our erroneous thinking and take the necessary steps to authentic conversion. Because honest guilt leads us to reparation, it holds out a promise of spiritual growth. It fills us with the desire to apologize for the unkind word and for the gossip that's torn people apart; to repay others for the things we've taken from them; to pray for those whom we've judged harshly; to take an extra step to preserve the earth whose resources we've used in a selfish, thoughtless way.

God's clemency is unqualified. Divine absolution is definitive. God never leaves us alone to our fate, our disgrace, or our culpability. The rivers of disappointment may take us into murky waters, but they do not have the power to keep us there. Grace repeatedly draws us back into the magnanimous heart of God. It helps us believe that "in all things God works for the good of those who love."[31] Life is our teacher. Honest reflection exposes our guilt for what it is. Admission of sin is the first step toward reconciliation and healing.

Love bade me welcome; yet my soul drew back,
Guilty of dust and sin.
But quick-eyed Love, observing me grow slack
From my first entrance in,
Drew nearer to me, sweetly questioning
If I lacked anything.

"A guest," I answered, "worthy to be here;"
Love said, "You shall be he."
"I the unkind, ungrateful? Ah my dear,
I cannot look on Thee."
Love took my hand, and smiling did reply,
"Who made the eyes but I?"

"Truth Lord, but I have marred them: let my shame
Go where it doth deserve."
"And know you not," says Love, "who bore the blame?"
"My dear, then I will serve."
"You must sit down," says Love, "and taste My meat."
So I did sit and eat.[35]

Chapter 10: Centres of Energy

One Sabbath day, the son of a rabbi went to pray at another rabbi's synagogue. On his return, his father asked him, "Well, did you learn anything new?" The son replied, "I certainly did!" His rabbinical pride somewhat hurt, the father continued nevertheless, "So, what do they teach over there?" "Love your enemy!" came the answer. The father explained eagerly, "Why, they preach the same thing as I do. How can you say you learned something new?" His son explained, "They taught me to love the enemy that lives within me, the one I am so desperately trying to fight."[36]

The human soul is marked by an inexplicable divergence. There are seemingly hostile forces at work in us. We are contradictions even to ourselves. Every one of us is sometimes saint, sometimes sinner. Original blessing and original sin abound in all our lives. We spend the better part of a lifetime trying to uproot the enemy within. Like the darnel in the parable of the grain and the weeds, our shadow often resembles good deeds.[37] Because the roots of the wheat and the weeds intertwine, early separation is well nigh impossible. Jesus advises tolerance and patience until the harvest. Wisdom counsels us not to dismiss our shadow too quickly. It can be a stepping-stone to holiness.

On the surface, original blessing and original sin appear to be complete opposites. The blessing is all light, the sin ominous darkness. In reality, one is closely related to the other. We find this same dichotomy reflected in nature. A tree grows in two directions at the same time. While it sends roots deep into the darkness of the earth, its branches reach higher and higher toward the light. The seed plants itself in the black earth where it germinates and stretches up to the light. To become fully alive, we must drink deeply from life's endless fountain of light and love, even as we endure the struggles and pain that are an integral part of it. As we journey through the shadows, we are continually "re-fired" and refined.

"You were taught to… be renewed in the spirit of your minds, and to clothe yourselves with the new self, created according to the likeness of God in true righteousness and holiness."[38] The first stirrings of conscious awareness set the spiritual journey in motion. They awaken us to the mystery of God and of self. Time and again, we remember our childhood and the ways we reacted to circumstances, the ways we dealt with the world around us. Over the years, our initiatives and responses either became more entrenched or we found a way to change directions.

While family relationships influence our patterns of behaviour, heredity establishes our personality type. Just as we come in different shapes and sizes, so we approach life in different ways. Some of us are great intellectuals; others are dreamers. Some are soft-spoken and gentle; others are loud and abrasive. Some put on a pretence of strength and control; others reflect a commanding inner force. Some are independent; others lean on their family and their friends. Some have a need to be noticed; others are humble and content. Our special gifts and singular needs define the kind of person we become.

Creation is unfolding. In the divine plan, we are part of that evolution. God invites us to grow and mature, to purify and refine our inner self. It is the work of a lifetime. God's creative power helps give shape to our life. Becoming is about seizing life and all that it holds out to us, trusting our instincts. Life is not one path, but many paths. The world lies open before us. Countless untapped resources are at our beck and call. How we use them is a matter of personal choice. It helps to know and understand the way we usually deal with life. The way to redemption and healing follows the path of self-understanding.

One of the billions of people who walk this earth, I know where I came from and where I hope to be, but not necessarily how I will get there. I struggle with the basic life questions but I approach them in my own way. While I am rich in potential and unlimited in opportunities, I am also handicapped by weakness and sin. My journey through life is riddled with grace and sin: reaching out and drawing back, opening up and shutting down. Even while I accept spiritual healing, I live life on my own terms. I strive to find my own inner balance.

There is a critical divergence in human life. The human desire to be complete is innate. But life is full of gaps. It is the holes in the lace that give it an aesthetic beauty. Most of us have a hard time accepting the disparity within us. While we understand that life is tentative and limited, we crave certainty. But spiritual growth is about living with imperfection and incompleteness. It involves an acknowledgement of our inner reality. We are all inadequate, unfinished, and restricted in some way. The Spirit helps us discover our personal deficiencies. The miracle of redemption is that we are somehow able to give up our false image of self and start becoming who we are destined to be.

Before we do anything at all about the "sin" in our lives, we need to recognize the roots of our spiritual makeup. Adaptation and growth are based on self-knowledge and self-understanding. For all our differences, there is a commonality we share with other groups of people. As noted in chapter six, every personality type gets its energy from one of three centres: the gut, the head, and the heart.

Gut people relate to the world by instinct. Their energy is expressed as: zeal, passion, focus, and directness. They are the world's idealists, peacemakers, and defenders of the weak and vulnerable. In a world of bigotry, prejudice, inequality, and cruelty, they feel the need to set things right. Their path is the path of desire. For some, the unrelenting desire to seek perfection and righteousness comes first, last, and in between. With the best of intentions, gut people do what they feel is necessary to return the world to its original beauty and virtue. Their inner critic warns against weakness, mediocrity, hypocrisy, and pretence. Hence, their stance tends to be inflexible and unyielding.

The real world, biased and unfair, displays numerous shades of grey. Because gut people see only black and white, they are generally unwilling to compromise. They are inclined to check out when they think something is not worthy of their time. Their path to inner freedom is through the truth. "Lord, grant me the serenity to accept the things I cannot change, the courage to change the things I can, and the wisdom to know the difference."[39]

In the novel *East of Eden*, by John Steinbeck, we meet twin boys, Aaron and Caleb. The only thing they have in common is that both are undirected and unnoticed as they are growing up. Their mother abandoned them immediately after their birth. Alone and devastated, their father, Adam, virtually ignores them. Both boys spend their childhood and youth seeking his exclusive love and undivided attention.

Aaron is the golden-haired boy who draws love from every side. People are attracted to his shy and delicate disposition. Gentle by nature, he spends hours observing the complicated life of the tiniest creatures. Nature's mysteries hold him spellbound for hours on end. Cal, on the other hand, struggles all his life with internal enemies. He can be cold, cruel, and calculating; he is deeply jealous of his brother. His incessant need to keep Aaron off balance is often couched in deception, which puts an uneasy distance between them. When Aaron builds a fortress to protect himself, Cal's envy intensifies.

Ever the idealist, Aaron needs to rearrange life, to put things right. He cannot accept the fact that his mother walked out on him when he was an infant, so he buys into the lie that she is dead. No matter who suggests otherwise, he will not, and probably cannot, wrap his mind around it. Something has to go, either his mother or his world, so he pushes his mother back into death.

Aaron stands firmly by his beliefs and convictions. Once he sets his path, he follows it tenaciously. Totally incapable of conceiving a harsh and cruel world, he sets out to make things perfect. He cannot handle the enduring human battle between good and evil. In his surreal world, denial is his game. He is in his early teens when he falls head-over-heels in love with Abra, the daughter of an acquaintance whose family visits his father's farm. The feeling is mutual. Together they create an imaginary world of endless bliss and confine themselves to their naïve story of life. Eventually, Abra grows up and the fairytale no longer fulfills her needs. She confides: "When we were children we lived in a story we made up. But when I grew up the story wasn't enough… Aaron didn't grow up… He wanted the story and he wanted it to come out his way… He couldn't stand to have it come out any other way."[40] Emotionally, Aaron is incapable of moving on and convinces himself that he can make life come out right.

Both boys push themselves to succeed. They are fixated on the need to make their indifferent father proud. Aaron's return from college for a brief visit ushers in a series of tragic consequences. Adam arranges a special Thanksgiving dinner for the return of his "perfect" son. Cal has spent months earning a large sum of money, which he plans to give to his father on Thanksgiving. It is to be his special day, not his brother's. In all innocence, however, Aaron arrives home and steals their father's attention. Cal's revenge is sinister and spiteful.

Late at night, Cal tricks his vulnerable brother into visiting a house of ill repute. He knows their mother is the proprietor there. The plan is to shock Aaron with a radical dose of reality. When Aaron learns that their mother is a prostitute, the lie he has accepted his entire life comes to an abrupt and brutal end. The pretence is over and he collapses inside. His whole world comes crumbling down and there is no one to help him pick up the pieces.

Aaron's reaction is altogether predictable. Swimming in a sea of disillusionment, he yells obscenities at his mother. Then he knocks his brother down as he turns and blindly rushes out, running away from himself. Desperate to escape from life, he enlists in the army. The heart has gone out of him and his spirit is dead. If his only recourse is to act out being alive, he may as well do it fighting some tangible enemy.

Aaron is a fictional example of a gut person. Like him, gut people romanticize about life and fastidiously wrap their identity in angelic innocence. Their world is an unreal and superhuman world. They can make others feel inadequate and inferior, never quite good enough. Their world has no room for failure or weakness or sin. In the real world, assumptions about absolute goodness and innocence are destined to crumble. Instead of facing failure and growing from it, perfectionists come up with one pretext after another. Their inner battles rage on until they finally grow to understand that "evil must constantly respawn, while good, while virtue, is immortal."[41]

Redeemed gut people discover a sense of freedom in their focus. They learn to see the bigger picture, the bigger truth. When they soften the harshness of their principled stance, they develop the virtue of patience. While they "dream the impossible dream," they are able to bring others on side by affirming rather than criticizing.

The second style of being is to get one's energy from the head. Head people are powerful, strong, independent, and highly intelligent. Because they relate to the world on the academic level, they come across as distant and aloof. It is more important for them to know the right answer than the right people. Focusing their energy on knowledge, as opposed to people, they have difficulty in relationships.

Head people pride themselves on their powers of observation, their ability to take in and digest information, their patient search for insight and clarity, and their good natural instincts. They know how to assess a cause objectively, finding its merits and stepping around its pitfalls. Enterprising and bold, they are the world's thinkers, analyzers, visionaries, and achievers. Because they habitually get things done, we refer to them as movers and shakers.

The path of head people is the path of power. They know how to play the crowd to advance their mission. Nothing fuels their energy like grand achievements. Because they believe they can make a difference, they approach their cause with tenacity and passion. When winning becomes an end in itself, there is no room for the opinions and feelings of others. Uncompromising and tenacious, head people can easily make themselves indispensable. Sometimes, they entrench themselves as leaders of the group. Taking charge in time of need is admirable. Clinging to power corrupts, because it makes the leader intimidating, threatening, controlling, and domineering.

People who are extremely self-reliant seek their own counsel. They tend to see only one way to achieve a specific goal—their way. They need no one. Those who reach the pinnacle of power lose perspective. Human values are sacrificed for the sake of the cause. The slightest suggestion is viewed as criticism and must be eliminated at all cost. Head people condemn themselves to loneliness and isolation because they spend little time building personal relationships. They have a hard time trusting others.

We are into the third week of the semester when Janet springs into my class like a whirlwind. Bright and self-confident, she uses a tone of superiority in introducing herself. She tells the group that she is strong in math and science, an accomplished pianist, a seasoned traveller, and a powerful debater. With time, she will learn that trumpeting her achievements is not the most effective way to make new friends.

Within a month, contradictory forces come into play. While Janet wants to fit in, she lives life in her mind. That is her reality. In group situations, she selectively alters her position depending on the opinions of people she needs to have on her side. In social settings, she plays the crowd in search of the most powerful prospects. It is important to align herself with the "right people." It's her trump card, should the need arise.

Exam time instils new life in gifted students. Knowledgeable and confident, they have no need to fuss and stew. Janet breezes through exams like a pro. She knows when she's done exceptionally well and she makes sure everyone else knows it too. Her need to compare results is an obsession. She collects and displays her consistently high marks like trophies.

Driven to be on top, Janet has little time for the interests of others. Small talk bores her, so she becomes a silent observer. A few girls try to befriend her but are quickly turned off by her aloofness. Because she is stingy in sharing thoughts and ideas, defensive and controlling when challenged, other students describe her as pretentious and arrogant. Blinded by pride, she fails to forge meaningful relationships.

Any semblance of a reasonably balanced emotional life comes tumbling down in a single weekend. Following the Saturday matinee, a group of classmates heads off to Sheila's house and orders pizza. Innocent enough. Except that no one remembers to invite Janet. To add insult to injury, the girls talk about it on Monday. Janet shrivels up inside. She needs to have a few girls on her side before student council elections. Disappointment lurches just beneath the surface. She copes by losing herself in a series of energy-draining activities. All the while, she is scheming her revenge.

Later in the week, a torn piece of paper mysteriously shows up on the washroom vanity. The heading is cruel in its bluntness: "If you hate Janet, sign here." In the course of the day, most of the girls sign it. Janet hangs around for a long time after school before going to check the washroom. The list has deliberately been left on the vanity. She snatches it up as though it were a hundred dollar bill. She combs through the signatures and carefully adds the missing ones. Driven to the edge, she brings it to my office.

There is something that smells strangely suspicious about the whole affair. Janet's penmanship is a dead giveaway. In a dejected voice, she tells me categorically that she hasn't seen the note before. I know it will hurt, but Janet needs to face the truth. I pull out a recent essay and compare the handwriting. A perfect match! Feeling a deep sense of defeat, Janet slumps into a chair and breaks into tears. After a long time, she queries: "Why can't I have friends like the other girls do? I'm smart and good-looking. I get high marks. What more do they want from me?" The Mona Lisa smile is gone, perhaps forever.

Janet is an example of a head person still in the making. Redeemed head people develop the virtue of acceptance. While they remain faithful to the task, they make room for others and their opinions. As they become more outgoing and learn to connect with others on a variety of levels, they become more joyful and carefree.

The third style of being is that of heart people. Relationships are paramount to people of the heart. They spend little time in inner reflection and a whole lot of time reaching out to others. Their energy comes from interacting with others.

Heart people relate to the world through feeling. Their energy is expressed in: astuteness, perceptiveness, warmth, generosity, and incessant activity. Their path is the path of relationships. Kind and compassionate, they are the world's caregivers, artists, musicians, and poets. A healthy sensitivity alerts them to the pain of others. In their strong sense of caring, they add beauty and warmth to a world that is often harsh. Positive in their observations, they speak the language of the heart. They know all the consoling words and comforting phrases. They serve well as ministers and health care professionals.

An innate anxiety about relationships drives heart people to excessive worry over their image. They base their sense of worth on others' reactions to them. They need to be needed. Because they take little time to recognize and understand their own feelings, they fail to ask the right questions and find their own centre. Hence, the incessant longing to serve is never far away. While they are known for their generosity, their love can have strings attached. Without realizing it, they tend to make others feel indebted to them.

Highly subjective people find it difficult to assess a situation on its own merit. They see a cause and jump in with both feet. They see a wrong and need to right it. People who overextend themselves move from task to task, from person to person. They become victims of circumstance. When they feel trapped, they are prone to self-pity. The end result is a martyr complex. Like the scriptural Martha, heart people are busy about many things but critical of those who are content just to be.

"By blood, I am Albanian. By citizenship, an Indian. By faith, I am a Catholic nun. As to my calling, I belong to the world. As to my heart, I belong entirely to the Heart of Jesus."[42] Born into a poor family, Gonxha Agnes experienced both love and a sense of discipline in her early life. With her strong faith as a guide, she felt the call to be a missionary at age twelve. By the time she was eighteen, her path was set. She left her homeland to join the Sisters of Loretto in Ireland because they were a missionary community. From 1931–1948 she taught at St. Mary's School in Calcutta. There she was known as Mother Theresa.

She may well have remained a teacher but for the excessive poverty she witnessed in Calcutta. The servant of God felt driven to proclaim the kingdom by loving and caring for those whom nobody was prepared to look after. This mission became the driving force of her life. Going into the slums of Calcutta, she visited families, washed the sores of children, cared for the sick and dying. She never looked back. A humanitarian and an advocate for the poor and helpless, she believed that time was of the essence.

In order to respond better to both the physical and spiritual needs of the poor, Mother Theresa founded the Missionaries of Charity. The rapid growth of her congregation soon drew the attention of the world. Her greatest tributes came from an unlikely source, the English soldier, spy, and journalist Malcolm Muggeridge. He popularized her work as "Something beautiful for God." Mother Theresa garnered numerous awards, including the Nobel Peace Prize in 1979. It was the world's reply to her efforts on behalf of the sick and suffering, including drug addicts, prostitutes, and battered women. The whole of her "life and labour bore witness to the joy of loving, the greatness and dignity of every human person, the value of little things done faithfully and with love, and the unsurpassing worth of friendship with God."[43]

A heart person by nature, Mother Theresa was blessed with the ability to win others to her cause. An effective and forceful leader, she moved directly from idea into action. God made a suggestion and she followed through. Nothing was too much for her. She played to win the hearts and souls of people who would further her work. A humble woman, she shared her spirit of prayer, simplicity, sacrifice, and dedication with her young followers.

Mother Theresa's legacy as a mystic began only after her death. The interior doubts and uncertainties that plagued her soul were hidden from all eyes during her life. Her personal journal revealed deep spiritual suffering. It described a feeling of painful separation from God throughout most of her life. She referred to it as "the darkness." She believed that suffering and pain gave her a mystical share in the interior desolation of the poor. She trusted God explicitly. In everything, she complied with the divine invitation to serve the needy of the world.

To many, Mother Theresa was known as "the little woman of faith." But she was not without her critics. Some took exception to her view of suffering. They could not grasp its redemptive value. Others found her style of leadership domineering and controlling. The little missionary of the poor would be the first to confess her inner reality. Like the rest of us, she was touched by original sin.

Redeemed heart people learn to turn inward and discover God in all things. As they uncover their real beauty, they accept their limitations and live in the present moment. Single-minded, they care for others simply because it is the right thing to do. As they unearth their own inner simplicity, their need to write scripts for their relationships diminishes. Their tranquil spirit serves as a balm to a tired and disturbed world.

Gut people, head people, and heart people have powerful inner strengths. All are gifted in their own ways. They also face unique weaknesses that variously express themselves. To be human is to be fallible, to be broken. Divergence can be found in everyone's life. We all digress. We step off the path that leads to life. We choose chaos over right living. Our motives are mixed. We do things for the wrong reasons. We are imperfect creatures. But God accepts us in our goodness and our sin and raises us up to become the person we are destined to be. All God asks of us is that we speak tenderly, act kindly, and radiate love and compassion wherever we go. In the end, all that really matters is that we love.

Original sin and original blessing are the flip sides of the same coin—the human soul. In some mysterious way, our most remarkable strength is intimately connected to our greatest weakness. Both accompany us through the journey of life. The most natural tendency is to wipe the slate clean, to burn out our original sin. No one succeeds. It remains part of us until we come full circle in death. Recognizing our errant inclinations makes us humbler, more genuine, and ever open to the promptings of our original blessing. Grace beckons us to draw on our personal resources, go beyond our shadow, and harmonize the apparent opposites of our inner reality.

Wisdom invites us to surrender to grace. We do not become holy by the sheer power of our own will. It is the work of something Greater than the self. Like the grain of wheat that falls into the ground and dies in order to bear abundant fruit, so the human spirit must turn to God for strength and inspiration. When we surrender to the Spirit, we find the capacity to be compassionate with ourselves.

> *Deep in the soul the acres lie*
> *of virgin lands, of sacred wood*
> *where waits the Spirit. Each soul*
> *bears*
> *this trackless solitude.*
> *…*
> *The soul that wanders, Spirit led,*
> *becomes, in His transforming*
> *shade,*
> *the secret that she was, in God,*
> *before the world was made.*[44]

Chapter 11: Forgiveness

1971. As I walk into the classroom, I notice that the energy level is abnormally high. Four or five conversations are going on simultaneously. The exchange centres around *Love Story*, a movie based on Eric Segal's novel. Having read the novel, I wonder what all the excitement is about. I did not find it particularly inspiring. Yet the movie captured the interest of my students. Seventeen-year-olds are already quite astute in giving their stamp of approval to books and movies. Why does *Love Story* speak so poignantly to them?

At the students' request, I go to see the movie. It develops the heart-rending story of love between two college students who are complete opposites. Oliver Barrett IV is born into wealth and privilege. Jennifer Cavilleri is born into a middle-class American family of Italian descent. Oli, a popular football star, is strong, handsome, likeable, and magnetic especially to the girls. Jenny, a music major, loves Mozart, Bach, and the Beatles. In addition, she is brilliant, beautiful, confident, and self-assured. He has a difficult and strained relationship with his father. Her father adores her and dotes on her every wish.

The story moves along quickly. Amiable and exceedingly sociable, Oli can't resist the simple charm of the lovely Jenny. A single, casual meeting changes both their lives. He pursues her with all the energy and charm he can muster. While she likes Oli, she wonders about the inner cloud that seems to cast a shadow on his carefree and jovial manner. Sensing an unresolved issue in his soul, she stands on guard. She worries about his ongoing bouts of melancholy. Secure in a warm and loving relationship with her father, she cannot understand the deep-seated and bitter resentment Oli bears toward his father. She resolves to help him mend the familial bond that appears to be so badly broken.

Within six months, love leads to marriage. Jenny's father is elated and prepares an elaborate dinner to celebrate the occasion. Knowing his father would never approve of his intimate friendship with a woman of humble stature, Oli doesn't bother inviting him to the wedding. The wheels of gossip grind on whether Oli likes it or not. Soon Oliver Barrett III learns the "awful" truth.

There is only one thing the distraught father can do and he swings into action immediately. He threatens to cut off all financial support until Oli puts an end to the insanity. Passionate love for Jenny wins the day and months of wedded bliss ensue. Cash strapped and with no source of new income, the young couple begins hunting down bargains. Their priority is to keep a roof over their heads. Oli naturally misses the material plenty he has been accustomed to from childhood. Jenny flows with it.

Every marriage ushers in its own challenges whether the couple is rich or poor, beautiful or plain, brilliant or merely average. Youthful marriages end in failure more often than not. Oli and Jenny, however, manage together.

Then, out of the blue, tragedy strikes. Jenny is diagnosed with a rare form of leukemia and the prognosis is not good. Initially, they are able to shore up each other's spirits. But Jenny's prolonged and intense suffering takes its toll. Sometimes they argue over the best treatment. Following a particularly hurtful fight, Jenny storms out into the night. Oli believes she needs time to think, to regroup her resources. He expects she will return within the hour.

Jenny needs to be alone to clear her head. Sitting in the dark, she mulls over her predicament. She worries about the effect the disease will have on their marriage. Meanwhile, Oli sits alone, waiting. Several hours drag by and still there is no sign of Jenny. He panics. Worried about her safety, he sets out to look for her.

The night is dark. The rain pelts down unrelentingly. Oli finally spots Jenny sitting alone on the cold steps of the Arts building. She is shivering inside and out. Seeing the pain and misery on her beautiful face, he has no words to make things better. He longs to take her in his arms and assure her that everything will be all right. But he has his own doubts and says nothing.

Jenny looks suddenly sadder. Tears fall steadily down her pale cheeks. Finally, she cries out: "Love means never having to say you are sorry." He is stunned into a deeper silence. His mind races as he tries to figure out who was at fault. He can't even remember who started the fight and it doesn't much matter now. Gently, lovingly, he takes her into his strong arms and kisses her sorrows away. Arm in arm they walk home together.

As the leukemia becomes more invasive, Jenny clings to a semblance of hope. Her courageous spirit refuses to give up. While her physical life is draining away, her love remains indomitable. Love is her refuge—a strong, paternal love and a tender, supportive, spousal love. Sick with worry, Oli continues to keep his father in the dark. He is too proud to ask for help. It takes Jenny's untimely and heart-rending death to bring father and son together. When the harsh reality sinks in and Oli realizes that the light of his life has gone out, he breaks down and turns to his father. The reconciliation brings emotional and spiritual healing for both of them.

My students are absorbed in the romance and tragedy of the movie. Many have a hard time wrapping their minds around Jenny's comment: "Love means never having to say you are sorry." Some are in complete agreement; others vehemently against. It raises classroom discussion to a whole new level. Does love mean never having to say, "Thank you?" Does it mean never having to say, "I love you?" What does it mean to really love someone?

We all participate in human brokenness. We have the scars to show it. Guilt, a by-product of sin, is never wanting. However, it also pushes us to cry out for healing. Our emotional and spiritual lives follow an unrelenting cycle: budding enthusiasm, false starts, miniscule steps forward, giant steps back, good choices, and wrong directions. Guilt intensifies while hope diminishes. Sometimes, it is hard to see beyond our spiritual ineptness. Most of us are more wounded that we like to admit. But there is a Power beyond us, directing and guiding us, walking with us through the light and the darkness.

Our raw drives stem from both our blessing and our sin. Life calls us to risk growth, to bear the tension between sin and grace. While we cannot heal ourselves, we are indeed healable. Conversion is the work of the Spirit but it does not take place without us. The Spirit invites, inspires, calls, and pursues, but the grunt work comes from us. Inner healing begins with absolute honesty—a humble and sincere acknowledgement of our sin. It is the essential first step to change and spiritual rebirth.

We seek inspiration from those who have gone before us. The Bible provides countless incidents of people who turned their lives around: the great King David, Nicodemus, Zacchaeus, and St. Paul, among others. The fundamental biblical role model is God's chosen People. One would expect them to be forever faithful to the God who led them out of slavery in Egypt and into the land of promise. Not so. Time and again, their history is etched in infidelity to the Covenant, destruction, chaos, and grave injustices within the community. They continually sought easy answers. When life became too demanding, their reflexive reaction was to turn to false gods. It didn't solve anything. In fact, it demoralized them even further.

God might have looked the other way and left them to themselves. But our ever-faithful God took pity on them and repeatedly raised up a prophet in their midst. The prophet served as a mirror for the people—pointing out their infidelities and calling them to repentance. Some prophets spoke a harsh language; others pleaded, beseeched, cajoled, and implored. All called the people to mend their ways and reminded them of God's healing love.

God chose the prophet Hosea because his personal life epitomized selfless love and forgiveness in the face of gross infidelity. Married to the prostitute Gomer, Hosea knew the frustration and hurt of betrayal and the renewed hope of forgiveness. Personal experience prepared him to speak passionately about God's devotion to the Covenant. He presented God as one who extends a forgiving hand to an incorrigible and obstinate people. He described God's compassionate attitude in powerful, poetic terms. "I will now lure her, and bring her into the wilderness, and speak tenderly to her. From there I will give back her vineyards... she shall respond as in the days of her youth... And I will (reach out) in righteousness and in justice, in steadfast love, and in mercy."[45]

Jesus exemplifies God's forgiving, healing love. Early in the morning, he sat at the temple gate. Before long a crowd of people gathered around him. They hung on his every word. Unannounced, the protectors of the law dragged a young woman before him. In vindictive and condescending tones, they announced that the woman was caught in the very act of committing adultery; no mention of her partner in crime. First, there was a clear, icy statement about the Law of Moses and its direct command to stone such a woman. Then came the trick question: "Now what do you say?"

What was Jesus to do: obey the law and condemn the woman? It flew in the face of his values of acceptance and forgiveness. The woman lay helpless in the dirt. Frightened for her life, she kept her gaze fixed firmly on the earth. When the silence dragged on, she slowly raised her eyes and looked into the face of Jesus. Hope crept into her heart as she detected the compassion there. Slowly, Jesus bent down and placed himself on a level with the woman. Then he began to write on the ground. Standing up at last, he looked directly at her accusers. In an authoritative voice, he said: "Let anyone here who is without sin be the first to throw a stone at her."

Jesus bent down again and continued writing on the ground. The woman was lying languid, half-dead with fear. She closed her eyes and steeled her body to receive the first stone. It never came. One by one, her accusers covered their faces and silently stole away. Aware that he was alone with the woman, Jesus stood up. He took her gently by the hand and raised her up. Then he asked: "Woman, where are they? Has no one condemned you?" Relieved beyond imagining, she replied, "No one, sir." Jesus' eyes filled with kindness as he said, "Neither do I condemn you. Go your way and do not sin again."[46]

Things are not always what they appear to be. In Brazil, teen gestations were an ongoing saga in every village. I met many women who were prostitutes by force of circumstance. Most bore children as a result of a debasing, shameful rape. Still, people in the village shunned them. They believed the woman was somehow at fault: out alone too late at night, on the beach too early in the morning, or wearing skimpy, provocative clothing. Condemning eyes followed these women wherever they went. In the face of reproachful looks and accusing fingers, most carried their pregnancy to full term. Left alone to rear their children, they turned to prostitution as a means of survival.

Jeda is a striking woman with a gorgeous mulatto complexion and ebony black eyes. She and her two-year-old son, Mingo, live in the red light district. When I meet her, she is going on nineteen. Her life stretches out before her but most opportunities are completely out of reach. Her best attempts to better her life are short-circuited. It is unfair. Unjustifiable. She deserves better.

On Mondays, I deliver bread and milk to the women who live in the shanty huts on either side of the open sewer. While I don't pry into their private lives, I am aware of the holy gossip that is always there. Jeda, a strong, young woman, is quite indispensable to the others. Several times a week she picks more shellfish than she needs. The extras find their way to the most needy women. They see kindness in her youthful eyes and trust her completely. She fascinates me in a curious way. I like her charm, her openness, her courage, and her fierce intelligence.

As I enter the "district" one morning, I notice Jeda's door ajar. A comforting arm around a distraught, pregnant teenager, she looks up as I pass. She blows a kiss in my direction. In a whisper she asks me to come back later. On my return, the beam in her eyes is still there. She is relaxed and talks freely. Mostly, it's about her roots. Raped by an uncle, she struggled through a long, hard pregnancy. Her family was extremely poor and an older sister spoke disparagingly about "yet another mouth to feed." Jeda couldn't wait to move out on her own. Her hut came from an anonymous donor, most likely the uncle. She accepted it gratefully and asked no questions. Details were immaterial. She had a home for Mingo and that was all that mattered. "Edite," she said, "life is too short to

bear grudges. I look at my darling Mingo and forgive his father
from my heart."

Life challenges us to accept its vicissitudes without bearing
resentment and hatred. The kind of person we become is the result
of an inner decision. Life merely shapes our circumstances. With
the help of the Spirit, we shape our soul. The Paschal Mystery offers
a distinctly discernible pattern: light, darkness, light; life, death,
new life. Life forces us to face the naked reality of who we are. Self-
deceptions are washed away. We discover reality—we create our
own road to inner freedom. It involves honest discernment: which
part of our shadow leads to integration and vitality and which part
merely burrows a hole inside us? Until we win the victory over our
own heart, we cannot extend a healing hand to others. The spirit of
forgiveness begins in small things.

It is 1973. The gifted, handsome Sasha is playing the lead
role in *H.M.S. Pinafore*. Several grade twelve students and
I volunteer to do the costuming for a cast of two hundred.
We spend many Saturdays in the sewing lab designing and
making costumes. Louise, diligent and precise, works on
the captain's suit. Sasha's face brightens considerably as he
models it for the rest of the cast. His strong baritone voice
and his exceptional charm make him a spectacular captain. It
is his first major role and he can't wait for his parents to see
him perform.

Excitement runs high on opening night. A hundred sailors
put on their costumes in the home economics lab. Ten short
minutes to curtain call and the boys are ready. As we walk
past the four-foot wall between the cafeteria and the main
hallway, I hold my breath. Surely, no one will think of jumping
the wall tonight. I quickly dismiss the thought. Then, I see
Sasha running back toward me, his face lined with embarrass-
ment. Clutching at his pants, he blurts out the awful truth: "It
was just one jump. I slipped. Now what?"

There is only one thing to do. Back to the lab, a quick
mending job, and all will be well. Irritated inside, I bite my
tongue. I can't spoil opening night for Sasha. As I throw the
restored pants over the dressing room door, I sing: "He is the

captain of the Pinafore and a right good mate is he." Sasha emerges as attractive as ever. His spirits lifted, he puts an arm around my shoulder and whispers: "Sister E, I'm so happy you are okay with this." Sasha renders an awesome performance. A standing ovation erases the heartache that went before.

God takes the ambiguities and paradoxes in life and fleshes them out in order to take us to genuine love. God beckons us to let go of the images we have of ourselves and the images others have of us. With grace, we grow to realize that the negative is not destructive. It is merely a part of us. People who accept and forgive themselves radiate an inner beauty, a deep peace and tranquility. Refusing to dwell on the fact that they are broken and incomplete, they see their shadow as a threshold of grace and transformation. It takes time and a lot of thought to learn to appreciate that reality. In this life, we remain a promise never quite fulfilled.

Children are generally much better at correcting their hearts with compassion than we are. They may be stuck in the blame game for a brief time. But it hardly ever lasts. Friends turn back to each other in short order. It all works out in the end.

The morning bell summoned teachers and students to their classes half an hour ago. I let my thoughts drift for a while, and then I turn to the mail on my desk. A timid knock at the door interrupts my concentration. It is Will. Again. I see the confusion and hurt that lie beneath the surface. It is Will's fifth trip to the office in as many days. "Something of a record," I tell myself. His face is lined with bitterness, as he admits, "Mr. C. sent me. He claims I was disturbing the class." A gesture of helplessness says it all.

How do I salvage this troubled young lad? He already feels teachers think of him as a troublemaker. After a long silence, I ask him to get his jacket and meet me in the front foyer. The anger moves up a notch or two. I know what he is thinking. I assure him that I do not plan to suspend him. We are simply going for a walk. That does not spell relief and Will replies, "But I don't want to talk to anyone, not even you. I have nothing to say."

Keeping my voice deliberately calm, I respond, "We don't have to talk. I feel comfortable walking in silence. Is that okay?" When he answers in the affirmative, I feel the relief inside.

We are hardly half a block from school when the verbal floodgates open. Will pours out his frustration. It runs deep. As the story goes, he did not initiate the incident. Chuck shot a rubber band at him. No one noticed, so Will used it as a slingshot. Mr. C. turned just in time to see an eraser flying from Will's desk to Chuck's. No questions asked. Will must be the instigator. Without further ado, Mr. C. dismisses him from the classroom.

I believe Will and I tell him. It is important to let him know I trust him. I play down the misdemeanour. Relief registers on his boyish face. Still, we need to come up with an acceptable solution. Knowing an apology from Will could go a long way toward smoothing the troubled waters, I suggest he find it in his heart to say he's sorry. Perhaps Mr. C. will come round and express his regret for misjudging Will. I secretly hope so. You can't force people, children or adults, to say things just because you want them to. You can only hope. When I see Will's spirit instantly lifting, I am reassured. It is a good sign.

On arriving at school early Friday morning, I am surprised to find a torn piece of paper in my mailbox. In a child's scrawl, it reads: "Dear St. Edith, I forgive you. Signed Will." A thoughtful gesture from a troubled student. The hurt of yesterday seems to have receded. On further thought, I begin to question the intent of Will's message. I should be forgiving him. Not the other way around. A light slowly goes on in my head. Understandably, I am part of the unjust system that made him feel the culprit over and over again. He was not at fault and still I suggested that he apologize.

I am not quite sure how to interpret the note. However, it is an expression of forgiveness and that should count for something. I feel it imperative that I acknowledge its author. He deserves at least that much. At recess, I seek Will out on the playground. I thank him for his note. On behalf of the school, I ask him to give us another chance at being fair.

The gospels are charged with the Christian call to forgiveness. In biblical terms, forgiveness means: to wipe away, to be gracious to an offender, to show compassion. The need to forgive was a never-ending theme in the life and teaching of Jesus. His entire mission was to demonstrate, not only God's eagerness, but also God's need to forgive. Forgiveness is the very nature of God. Before every miraculous physical healing, Jesus boldly proclaimed the forgiveness of sin. It pointed to the powerful connection between physical and spiritual healing.

Jesus holds up three moving parables on the theme of forgiveness. In each case, the focus is on the joy and delight of the one who finds what was lost. The good shepherd leaves the ninety-nine sheep and goes in search of the one gone astray. And when he finds it, he stoops down and lifts it up, placing it on his shoulders and carrying it home. The woman who lost her precious coin crawls on her knees searching until she finds it. Then she calls her friends and neighbours to come, rejoice, and celebrate for her treasure has been found.[47]

The prodigal sons serve as two quite different examples of human sinfulness. Their parents were farmers who worked hard coaxing growth out of a few acres of rich, black soil. Over time, they bought more land and built a splendid mansion on the hill. But what gratified them most was the sight of their two sons growing into manhood. Jared was the devoted, faithful elder son; Gabe, the affable, fun-loving younger one. Both worked the land day after tedious day.

While still a youth, Gabe took his parents by surprise with a startling request: "Father, let me have the share of the estate that will come to me." Incredible. Destined to inherit half the huge estate, the boy had everything handed to him on a silver platter. What more could he want? The father, more than a little disappointed, promised to think about it.

Gabe was unrelenting. He needed an answer quickly. After tossing and turning throughout the night, the father reluctantly signed over Gabe's share of the property. The ink was hardly dry on the page when Gabe sold it all off to strangers. The following day he took his money, along with everything he had, and set out for a distant country.

His adoptive land was rugged and unyielding. Rains came sporadically. But to Gabe it spoke of freedom and he abandoned himself to wanton self-indulgence. His time was his own. He was, in every sense of the term, master of his soul. Giving no thought to the future, he opted for a carefree and reckless life. Still, life failed to satisfy him. Alienated and lonely, he turned to alcohol and loose friends who helped him squander his entire fortune. When the money was gone, so were the friends. Without the faintest spark of light in his dark night, Gabe slumped into a state of deep depression.

At the same time, the entire country experienced a severe famine. For Gabe, the timing was poor. The pinch of hard times lay heavily on him. He knew something about farming, but little else. So, he sought employment with a local pig farmer. On his father's farm, feeding and caring for the pigs was a demeaning task, the lot of servants. But he had little choice here. Eventually, he saw the irony of his situation. Even the pigs on his father's farm ate better than he did.

Gabe lay awake at night. Flashes of home lingered in his mind. He remembered the love and security he felt there. Suddenly, there was no place like home. Exaggerated memories of bygone years led him to the most important decision of his young life: "I will leave this desolate place and go back home. I will tell my father how sorry I am. I will admit that I no longer deserve to be called a son. I will beg him to treat me as one of his hired men." The next day he set out for home.

The trip took its toll on Gabe. His ragged clothes and faltering steps spoke of a long and painful journey. His energy was running low as he came within sight of the family farm. He felt his heart clench. His father saw him in the distance and ran out to meet him. Clasping his younger son in his arms, the father kissed him and welcomed him home. Gabe's selfish mistakes were forgotten. Washed away. Still, Gabe needed to blurt out his well-rehearsed confession: "Father, I have sinned against heaven and against you; I no longer deserve to be called your son." The tight grip of his father's arms remained firmly around him.

Ignoring his son's apology, the father called to his servants and asked them to bring out the finest robe, the family ring, and expensive sandals. Beside herself with joy, Gabe's mother organized a sumptuous feast in honour of the homecoming. The fattened calf was killed and delectable fruit and full-flavoured wines decked the tables. "This son of mine was dead and has come back to life," declared the father. "He was lost to us and now he is found. Come, let us celebrate."

Faithful, reliable Jared was still out in the fields when the festivities began. Overhearing the carousing in the distance, he returned home. He was utterly shocked to learn the reason for the feasting. How could his parents betray him by opening their hearts and their home to his errant brother? Seething with anger, he refused to enter the house.

When the father came out, he put his arms around Jared and assured him of his love. Gently and sensitively, he invited him to come and join in the feasting. Jared's reaction was icy cold: "All these years I have remained faithful to you. I worked for you; I slaved for you and never once disobeyed your requests. Yet, you never offered so much as a young calf for me to celebrate with my friends. But, for your younger son who returns after he has squandered the fortune you gave him and has nowhere else to go, you kill our fattest calf and make a feast for him. I don't get it!"[48]

The father found himself in a terrible dilemma. He was overwhelmed with love and understanding for both sons. He could not understand the terrible jealousy between them and he felt helpless in the face of it. Still, he never gave up trying. His approach was consistent with his paternal nature. He did not force the hand of either son. He exerted no pressure. In the face of the younger son's heartless and cruel denial, he clung to the dream that someday his son would return. Despite the older son's cold and calculating rejection of familial ties, he reaffirmed his eternal love.

The real focus of the parable is on the father's forgiveness. It gave both sons the spiritual freedom to overcome their fears, to let go of imagined hurts, and to put aside past resentments. It opened the door to self-acceptance and self-respect. The forgiving father presents a concrete example of divine compassion. Those who experience the intensity of God's acceptance and forgiveness learn how to love both self and others. God reaches out to embrace the sinner with both hands. The one protects the vulnerable side, while the other reinforces the strength and desire to get on with life.[49]

The God who created us cannot help but receive us with forgiving love. From the beginning, God has consistently stretched out both arms in merciful blessing, letting us know that the love we seek has been, is, and always will be there. Forgiveness gives us the grace to cultivate an intimacy with self. When we turn back to God with all our heart, love bursts forth and touches our lives and the lives of others in intimate, humble, and honest ways.

To forgive from the heart is humanly impossible. It is a gratuitous gift that only God can give. Human willpower alone cannot effect genuine change. The mind is capable of envisioning the thought, but it is a long road from the head to the heart. That journey originates and finds its completion in love. The first step is an awareness of our emptiness. Sin cuts us off from others and our true self. Left to ourselves, we don't know how to deal with the resulting barrenness. Some people seek peace by losing themselves in work or leisure activities, but it never lasts. Some turn in on the self, nurse their grudges, and blame others. There are no effective escape routes. The human heart remains forever restless until it rests in God. "Who is a God like you, pardoning iniquity and passing over the transgression of the remnant of your possession? He does not retain his anger forever, because he delights in showing clemency."[50]

Sincere forgiveness is a miraculous process: painful in a way, beautiful in another. We remember past hurts not to let them fester inside, but that we might let them go. Some things are too ingrained, too deeply rooted to erase from the memory. Recalling painful moments is not akin to probing old wounds. It is to let forgiveness soften our hearts and lead us to acceptance and healing. In response to grace, we eventually feel the pain beginning to dissipate and we look on our hurts with kinder eyes. When we understand our personal role in hurtful situations, we are less inclined to condemn others.

1956. I am in grade eleven and I play the lead role in *The Two Mothers*. The legend explores the themes of vengeance and forgiveness. A wealthy Spanish widow Lucretia has an only son Roberto. He is the centre of her world. She shelters and protects him with her wealth and power.

The play opens with a distressing scene. Messengers bear the painful news that Lucretia's son was found murdered in a family field. Beside herself with grief, Lucretia turns to the virgin mother Mary and pours out her soul. Perhaps a mother whose son was crucified before her eyes can help her deal with such a cruel fate.

Lucretia is still at prayer when servants drag in the murderer. The grieving widow recoils at the smell of blood on his clothing. She recognizes him as the slave Antonio from a neighbouring fazenda. Like a vulture, she circles around her prey. The black slave lies still and helpless before her. His fate is in her hands. When she can no longer stand looking at him, she turns her gaze back to the statue. No prayer escapes her lips. No heavenly power brings comfort to her broken heart.

She turns back to Antonio. Her dark eyes swoop down as she reminds him that the law demands "an eye for an eye and a tooth for a tooth." He cringes visibly as she describes the rack and the wheel in the castle's dungeon. She threatens: "It can stretch your body until the last ounce of life seeps out of you. I have the power and the mind to do it."

A deep darkness descends on the sorrowful mother. She shivers at the evil thoughts in her soul. Can a mother be so brutal? Unsure of herself, she turns back to Mary and cries out in agony, "What am I to do? He killed my only son. He deserves to die."

Mary's response is couched in kindness: "They killed my son too. And he was utterly innocent."

Lucretia retorts, "You don't understand. My son was defenceless. He carried no weapon."

Mary continues, "My son was defenceless too. Still, they whipped him and crowned him with thorns."

Lucretia's final attempt is weak. "I am the mother of an innocent victim. I am expected to bring about vengeance."

Mary's final argument is strong: "They nailed my son to a cross. And he cried out and forgave the soldiers who crucified him." A woman of faith, Lucretia is all too familiar with the proverbial Christian message: "Whenever you stand praying, forgive, if you have anything against anyone; so that your Father in heaven may also forgive you."[51]

The human battle rages on. To forgive or not to forgive, that is the question. We cannot have it both ways. We can get into the area of revenge and reprisals and stagnate there. Or we can exercise our humanity to the extent that we forgive from the heart. When we are deeply hurt, we instinctively want to inflict pain on the aggressor. Vengeance smells sweet, but it is not what it is touted to be. It brings no lasting relief. Sincere forgiveness does. It bears abundant fruit in the one who forgives and in the aggressor. It turns an enemy into a friend. At the very least, it disarms a foe and makes him/her defenceless. To forgive is to lower the barriers and open the door to acceptance.

To forgive is to let go, to respect our adversary's freedom and leave retribution to God. The Christian is called to forgive, not seventy times seven, but eternally because that is the way God forgives us. Like Sudoku, a young Japanese girl who responded to the bombing of her city by making paper cranes, we can reach out in true forgiveness. The white origami birds have become a symbol of peace and forgiveness throughout the world. We would do well to create our own symbol of peace and reconciliation—something to remind us of our inner experience of forgiveness and our call to forgive those who "trespass against us."

> Wilt Thou forgive that sin where I begun,
> Which was my sin, though it were done before?
> Wilt Thou forgive that sin through which I run,
> And do run still, though still I do deplore?
> When Thou hast done, Thou hast not done,
>   For I have more.

Wilt Thou forgive that sin which I have won,
Others to sin and made my sin their door?
Wilt Thou forgive that sin which I did shun
A year, or two, but wallowed in a score?
When Thou hast done, Thou hast not done,
   For I have more.

I have a sin of fear, that when I have spun
My last thread, I shall perish on the shore;
Swear by thyself that at my death Thy Son
Shall shine as He shines now, and heretofore;
And having done that, Thou hast done,
   I fear no more.[52]

Chapter 12: Grace Creeps in through Weakness

When I consider how my light is spent,
Ere half my days, in this dark world and wide,
And that one talent which is death to hide
Lodged with me useless, though my soul more bent
To serve therein my Maker, and present
My true account, lest he returning chide,
"Doth God exact day labor, light denied?"
I fondly ask; by Patience, to prevent
That murmur, soon replies: "God doth not need
Either man's work or his own gifts; who best
Bear his mild yoke, they serve him best. His state
Is kingly: thousands at his bidding speed
And post o'er land and ocean without rest.
They also serve who only stand and wait.[53]

Aware of his blindness, John Milton refused to turn away from life. He used his poetic genius to share his thoughts and insights with the world. Helen Keller contracted meningitis when she was only nineteen months. It left her deaf and blind. After a very lonely childhood, she met Anne Sullivan who taught her sign language and opened the door to a whole new world for her. Apartheid was very much alive, and fiercely defended by the ruling class, when Nelson Mandela was born a black man in South Africa. Mandela spent twenty-seven years in prison before he was elected president of South Africa. His "long walk to freedom" continues to this day.

Nothing is perfect this side of heaven. Indeed, life is often far from it. We make plans and dream dreams. Our expectations are larger than life. In our mind's eye, all will be serene and peaceful. The sun will shine the radiant beauty of its light and warmth on a friend's wedding. Everyone will be ecstatic about our homecoming. Friends will lavish us with compliments on our latest achievement. The family reunion will bring everyone closer together. Our good health will last forever. In a positive and confident spirit, we drive away any fleeting thought of imperfection. But reality catches up with us and we see that life falls short of our imaginings.

The longing for freedom and fulfillment is innate. As children grow into teens, and teens into young adults, they seek independence. We don't have to live long to realize that absolute autonomy is illusive. Every decision we make affects others. Conversely, their choices can have an impact on our lives. We are interconnected, dependent on each other and on mother earth. Things go wrong. We all mess up. Reality has a way of holding our feet close to the earth and to the fire.

Life happens while we are making plans. It keeps intruding, meddling in our carefully arranged programs and projects. Every now and again, human nature lets us down: a friend betrays us; the end product doesn't reflect our effort; our best resolutions fade and disappear; a sudden illness tests our faith; a close family member dies before we've had a chance to say goodbye. It's a stark reminder of original sin. There is no purely perfect moment or perfect time or perfect life. People of faith absorb it all, live with it, and make the best of it. In a life that most would describe as the pits, they spend their time savouring the cherries. In a spirit of confident faith, they refuse to take life and love and friendship for granted.

How do we walk the journey of life with dignity and grace in the face of adversity? It entails living in the present, cherishing the blessing of each moment, trusting our instincts, and listening carefully to the voice within. Real happiness lies in the present: in our thoughts and feelings, projects and activities, relationships with family and friends. Goodness and peace are found in the very act of living. God does not withhold them until we reach the end of our journey. The real focus is on the journey itself.

The old Baltimore Catechism began with the timeless question: "Why did God make us?" And the answer was: "To know him, to love him, to serve him, and to be happy with him in this life and in the next." At age ten, I was expected to commit this to memory. But it left me in a state of confusion. Surely, an all-loving God intended life to be a journey filled with peace and contentment in the here and now. Yet so much preaching and teaching in my young life merely focused on the afterlife. I was looking for happiness in this life: here on earth, in my daily encounters, in the countless joys embedded in my childhood, in the midst of everything that was happening in and around me. I wasn't so much concerned about getting somewhere; I simply wanted to enjoy where I was.

Children naturally trust life, themselves, and people around them. Everything appears to be a marvellous gift. If something appears enticing, it probably is. That is all the invitation they need. So, they go exploring with total abandon. They give little thought to danger or insurmountable obstacles. The tempting fruit is there, waiting to be plucked. They do not ask whether or not it is theirs. They assume it is.

It is midday and the sun is high in the cobalt blue Brazilian sky. I arrive home a bit tired after walking the length of the village. As I approach the gate, I hear the joyous laughter of little boys. The sound comes from my backyard. I wonder what is giving them so much delight? Then I hear the thump, thump, thump of mangoes falling to the ground. Two nine-year-olds are perched on the pinnacle of a giant mango tree. They shake the tree vigorously until another mango falls to the ground. Six little brown-skinned bodies scurry to snatch up the savoury fruit. One has a paring knife. I watch in admiration as he deftly peels a mango and hands it to a friend. They eat with passion, and tiny rivulets of juice flow down thin dark arms.

On seeing me, the two climbers shout down: "We're okay." Then, they slide down the tree trunk like monkeys. But Flavio lands in a broken tree stump. Blood gushes from an enormous gash in his right leg. As I try to stop the blood, I send Antonio to find his friend's mother. Five hours later, the gash has been cauterized and bandaged. Flavio half apologizes: "You weren't picking the mangoes. Someone had to eat them before they spoiled."

He was right. Fruit ought to be eaten when it is perfectly ripe, no sooner and no later. The optimum time has a narrow window. One has to seize the moment while it is there. Between the curtains of birth and death, life offers us countless opportunities and beckons us to create our own Camelot. Of course, there are wounds, but they go with living. As we learn to live each day, we discover that most joys come with some pain. Everything that happens to us has a purpose. Trials, tribulations, handicaps, and disappointments have the potential to enrich and deepen us.

Some things in life are simply incomprehensible. Full of mystery, they have the power to move us deeply, to make us kinder, more generous people. Everything that happens to us is a moment of grace, sometimes glaringly obvious and sometimes subtle and indiscernible. All has the potential to deepen us. Awakening us to the element of surprise, events and circumstances call us to approach the whole of life with abandon and unabashed enthusiasm. Challenging us to relinquish our tight hold on the way we think things ought to be, life moves us to surrender heart, soul, mind, and spirit into the hands of Providence.

1970. My students and I visit a nursing home three blocks from school on a weekly basis. I look upon it as an opportunity to emphasize the spiritual value in reaching out to suffering humanity. Each of us is assigned a special patient. Heather is mine. At twenty-nine, her unadorned beauty goes deeper than the skin. One would say she has it all, until you see that she is in a wheelchair. A severe case of multiple sclerosis keeps her confined to the nursing home.

I take an immediate liking to Heather. We have a lot in common: the same age, a similar rural upbringing, members of the Catholic Church, and patrons of the arts. Before I know it, I am visiting her after school every Wednesday. My admiration grows as I witness her self-acceptance in the face of a horrible, crippling disease. She knows how to focus on the blessings in her life. One afternoon we talk about the rich musical culture in the city. Moved by her comment that she hasn't been to a concert in five years, I promise to make some inquiries.

It is a piece of cake. All I have to do is purchase the tickets, book the handibus, and accompany Heather to the concert. Her naturally sunny disposition beams brighter when I tell her I have tickets for *Swan Lake*. Her brown eyes open wide in anticipation. At the conclusion of the concert, she takes my hand and whispers, "That's the nicest thing anyone has ever done for me. Thank you."

Heather and I attend monthly concerts for a period of three years. She glows every time I pick her up. The theatre is accommodating. They arrange a seat on the side aisle, second row from the front where I can easily wheel Heather close beside me. Her deteriorating physical condition tears at my heart. Within the second year, she asks me to lift her right arm so she can rest her chin on it. It takes the strain off her neck. When her arm involuntarily drops, she doesn't have the strength to raise it up again. I do that for her. Cordial and gracious, she never fails to express her gratitude.

I admire her positive spirit and wonder how I would fare under similar circumstances. Would I be so accepting? Would I have the fortitude to befriend the negative effects of a debilitating illness and see them as a source of inner growth? Heather is a powerful witness to a fundamental and simple truth: I can choose how I will regard the unfortunate circumstances in my life. If I see them as curses, I become dejected. If I see them as blessings, they become a source of personal and spiritual riches.

The Jesuit philosopher Teilhard de Chardin got it right when he observed, "We are not human beings having a spiritual experience. We are spiritual beings having a human experience." As spiritual beings, we are created for love and the fullness of life. Naturally, we long to leave our mark, to do extraordinary things, and to fix everything that is broken in our world. But God calls us to do simple things, to approach the ordinary, daily events of life with intensity, passion, and conviction. God doesn't ask us to do extraordinary things, merely to make the most of the simple things that are part of life. If we do them with heart and soul, we give them enormous spiritual value. Eternal happiness begins with the ability to enjoy the ordinary blessings of each day.

Saints and heroes are not only people of long ago and far away. Most often, they are found close to home. We stumble on them within our own family and in our neighbourhood. They are the people who inspire us with their faith, hope, and love. Magnanimous people. Benevolent people. Selfless people. Resilient people. Fearless people. People who understand life celebrate the blessings of each day and bear the "slings and arrows of outrageous fortune" with equal grace.[54] And the world is richer by far because they have the courage to live life to the full.

As a mere boy, my brother Jerry embraces life with pizzazz. Everything delights him. Wild summer storms are an invitation to walk barefoot in the rain. Trees are there for kids to climb and dugouts for them to explore. Every rock hides some secret: an ant, a beetle, a cricket. It doesn't matter. All needs to be examined with care. Jerry's favourite tool is a small magnifying glass. He is drawn to the natural world like steel to a magnet. Nature is pure gift, a gift to be unwrapped with care.

Jerry's playful spirit discovers joy in the most mundane task. He makes a game out of hoeing the garden, drying the dishes, washing the car, and carrying in firewood. He has an organic connection to his world. He is, indeed, a free spirit. I see a passionate purity in him. Unfamiliar with subtleness, he accepts people at face value. His greatest asset is his ability to put the best spin on things. Despite the negativity of a few neighbours, he refuses to affix blame. There isn't a mean bone in his body. Carefree, good-natured, friendly, and outgoing, he has many friends.

Jerry has an inner light that guides him. From childhood on, he has been blessed with an amazing faith. Dogmatic theory is not important. Faith practice is. His approach to God and to life is best described as observant, faithful love. In an eminently active life, he finds time for God and others. Love is not something to be weighed and measured. It is a precious gift to be shared unstintingly.

The casual observer could never guess that a chronic heart condition has plagued Jerry all his life. A long bout of rheumatic fever at age two left him with an enlarged and severely damaged heart. Still, nothing daunts him. An audacious spirit compensates for any lack of physical energy. Neighbours describe him as "full of spit and vinegar." Self-pity never crosses his mind. An acute will to live took over after his first serious illness and filled him with an inner drive to live in the present moment, wholly absorbed in its riches.

Two months after his thirteenth birthday, Jerry becomes more and more listless. When Mom's nursing skills can no longer stave off the feverish spells, Jerry is hospitalized. I am shaken to the core the first time I walk into that antiseptic room with its anemic lights. My brother's diminutive body is curled up in an oversized bed. There is the familiar mop of blond hair, but the effervescent spirit has escaped. There is tiredness in his eyes and a hint of sadness in his frail voice. Ruefully, I recall the countless blessings in both our lives and keep thinking: "We have shared a lot of history. How will it continue?"

For the next six months, the family ritual revolves around Jerry. My routine quickly takes on a new shape: rush home from school, prepare supper, gulp it down, and drive with Mom and Dad the twenty-two miles to the Wilkie hospital. It is a privilege to help my younger brother with his homework. I prepare him to write the grade eight departmental exams at the end of June. The bond between us grows stronger.

Jerry's troubled face brightens and breaks into a smile when he sees us at the door. He is suddenly tired when it is time for us to leave. Joy and sadness entwine to weave an intricate design of his young life.

I am engulfed in a strange foreboding the night Dr. Cherry asks to speak to Mom and Dad in private. The doctor's tone is urgent. Quietly, unobtrusively, I linger at the door and listen carefully. The information pierces something inside me. Jerry is not expected to live beyond the next ten to fifteen years. "Dubious analysis," I call it. How can such an eminently active life take such a sudden turn for the worse? I turn to the only person I know who can change my brother's fate and I pray for a miracle.

At long last, early in July, Jerry is strong enough to come home. He's confined to bed rest, but home is where he belongs. He longs for the outdoors with its wonders and delights. By the end of the first week, he comes up with a strategy. It involves bending the rules a bit. My siblings and I are up for it. While Dad works on the farm and Mom minds the store, we stealthily lift Jerry from his bed, out through the window, and carry him to the ball diamond. The August summer sun and the fresh, clean air are a balm to body and spirit. The friendship of Jerry's peers proves to be an added bonus. Before long, he is "all boy" again. These clandestine escapades become the norm and life is almost perfect.

By age twenty-three, Jerry is assistant manager for a large paper company. There he meets the love of his life, Valerie. Their friendship flowers into a deep and lasting respect that carries them through many trials and tribulations. Children arrive in rapid succession—three boys and, finally, a darling baby girl. While Jerry's health problems are far from over, the young couple resolves to have their children grow up in a normal, relaxed, and secure home.

Despite countless heroic efforts and numerous medical advances, the spectrum of illness continues to spread a dark shadow over my brother's life. Two open-heart surgeries, two major heart attacks, a pacemaker, a defibrillator, several strokes, deteriorating lungs and kidneys, and ten surgeries over the last eight years, and the "energizer bunny" keeps on going. Jerry's tenacious will to live defies death and holds fear at bay. With Val faithfully at his side, he accepts his tentative hold on life with faith. He is living proof that while "cowards die many times before their deaths; the valiant never taste of death but once."[55]

Recently, I've had the opportunity to sit with my brother in ICU. As he sleeps, I look intently on that gentle face lined with suffering. A quiet energy of spirit seems to surface every time he needs it. There is nothing self-absorbed about him. I reflect on the ways the goodness and love of God impact on our lives. I am amazed at the way life continues to open my younger brother to the surprise of God.

The memory of miracle following miracle, tells me that while power kills, weakness creates. When Jerry awakens, there is a thoughtful expression on his tired face. Then he says, "Despite the troubles that surround us, the sun still shines. When I look around this ICU, I can always find people who are worse off than I am. They need our prayers."

I share my reflections. Jerry needs no epiphany to validate his faith. It is always there. In fact, he believes his poor health and indomitable faith go hand in hand. One serves as a catalyst to the other. It isn't cheap "God talk." It's about courage and strength, faith and love, and the affirming presence of Mystery in life. Jerry has attained a high degree of wisdom, a dynamic kind of knowing.

We burst into life full of grace and light. This is our original blessing. But blessing does not translate into instantaneous perfection. A gift from God, it is more than the energy that moves us. It is the ability to live well. "Becoming a human being involves more than conception and birth. It is a mandate and a mission, a command and a decision. We each have an open-ended relationship with ourselves."[56] We do not appear on the stage of life ready-made, complete, crowned in glory. Our mission is to "make" ourselves by responding to grace and letting God transform us. In some way, we are all fragile and weak. But it is through weakness that grace creeps into our lives.

The Christian journey takes us into many amazing places that fill the soul with wonder and delight. At times, it also leads us into personal darkness and anguish. All of it is necessary as we journey toward self-realization and the fulfillment of God's dream for us. While we prefer to walk in the light, life teaches us that darkness is a great teacher. If we hope to realize our destiny, it is necessary to risk all and walk fearlessly into unknown territory. When we are open to the Spirit of God, we come full circle. The things we so desperately want to avoid in the beginning take on a whole new meaning at the end.

God continually comes to us through the quiet stillness and peace we feel in our own centre. God sustains us through the darkness of sin and suffering, teaching us the way to compassion and inner freedom. We bring meaning into our lives when we discover the meaning in suffering. New energy springs from our wounds. Suffering trains us to approach others with gentleness. Grace creeps into our lives through the cracks, through the dark night of the soul.

> *Out of the night that covers me,*
> *Black as the Pit from pole to pole,*
> *I thank whatever gods may be*
> *For my unconquerable soul.*
>
> *In the fell clutch of circumstance*
> *I have not winced nor cried aloud,*
> *Under the bludgeonings of chance*
> *My head is bloody, but unbowed.*
>
> *Beyond this place of wrath and tears*
> *Looms but the Horror of the shade,*
> *And yet the menace of the years*
> *Finds, and shall find me, unafraid.*
>
> *It matters not how strait the gate,*
> *How charged with punishments the scroll,*
> *I am the master of my fate;*
> *I am the captain of my soul.*[57]

Part 4

Spirituality: Opening to Transformation

God of little buds just now wearing green sleeves,
God of lilac limbs all full with signs of flowering,
God of fields plowed and black with turned-over earth,
God of screeching baby bird mouths widely awaiting food,

God of openness, of life and of resurrection,
Come into this Easter season and bless me.
Look around the tight, dead spaces of my heart
That still refuse to give you entrance.

Bring your gentle but firm love.
Begin to lift the layers of resistance
That hang on tightly deep inside of me.

Open, one by one, those places in my life
Where I refuse to be overcome with surprise.
Open, one by one, those parts of my heart
Where I fight the entrance of real growth.
Open, one by one, those aspects of my spirit
Where my security struggles with the truth.

Keep me open to the different and the strange,
Help me to accept the unusual and also the ordinary;
Never allow me to tread on others' dreams
By shutting them out, closing them up,
By turning them off or pushing them away.

God of the Resurrection, God of the living,
Untomb and uncover all that needs to live in me.
Take me to people, events, and situations
And stretch me into much greater openness.

Open me. Open me. Open me.
For it is only then that I will grow and change.
For it is only then that I will be transformed.
For it is only then that I will know how it is
To be in the moment of rising from the dead.
                                        —*Joyce Rupp*

Chapter 13: Letting Go

Once upon a time a young woman was walking along the edge of the Grand Canyon. In order to peer down into the depths of the canyon, she stepped closer and closer to the edge. The dark abyss had no end. Suddenly, she slipped and total panic invaded her soul. Down, down, she went. Certain disaster awaited her. But Providence was on her side. On her way down, her shirt caught on a twig sticking out of the canyon's rugged interior. A momentary reprieve. It gave her time to think.

Gathering her wits about her, she quickly grabbed hold of the twig and hung on for dear life. It could be her salvation. After a long time, she looked down into the darkness below. Nothing but a black hole! What was she to do? Her situation seemed absolutely hopeless. If she was to get out of there, she needed help. And the help had to come from above. So, she called out in a very loud but unmistakably feminine voice: "Is there anyone up there?" When a deep, kind voice assured her that someone was, indeed, up there, she quickly asked, "Who are you?"

The "Voice" replied immediately, "It is I. I am God." Now the woman knew her faith wasn't strong. Why would God even bother with her? She had done nothing to deserve God's attention. In fact, she never took time to whisper so much as a prayer of gratitude on her birthday. She couldn't remember the last time she'd talked to God or asked forgiveness for her wayward ways. She hadn't darkened the church steps in years. Then, a few faint childhood memories surfaced. She recalled how she prayed with her mother before closing her eyes at night. Maybe that counted for something.

When the terrified woman wondered if the Voice could actually help her, someone echoed back: "Of course, I can help you. Remember? I am God and I can do anything."

Feeling somewhat embarrassed, she asked, "But will you help me? Do you even want to help me?"

God's voice reverberated loud and clear: "I created you out of love, didn't I? I loved you from the beginning. I will love you forever. Of course I want to help you."

Now that was the kind of reassurance she needed. It brought comfort to her soul. She responded in her most sincere voice: "I will do anything you say. Just tell me what to do."

Having heard both her request and her promise, God threw her a lifeline: "Let go of the twig." And God waited patiently for her reply. It was a long time coming.

Finally, she called out, "Is there anyone else up there?"[58]

Like forgiveness, trust is an essential virtue for living. It is a necessary attitude for all of us, regardless of age or religious affiliation. But unshakable trust does not come easily. When we are born, we rely completely on others. Somewhere, between birth and moral consciousness, our trust in others and in life begins to fade. Reasons are copious and complicated. The problem grows in the mind. The more often others let us down, the weaker our ability to trust becomes. We learn early on that people are imperfect and inconsistent. Parents and teachers make promises they cannot keep. With time, siblings and friends join the foray. Plans change. Promises are broken. Grown-ups tell us one thing and mean another. We hang our heart on something and it never materializes. Friends come and go. Nothing seems certain. The circumstances of life program us to distrust our environment. The end result is an abiding sense of insecurity.

When we are young, we seek rules and formulas, guidance and role models—anything that might give us some assurance. We believe in a better world and chase after it. Eventually, we learn that better has a lot to do with wholeness. Enduring love stretches the mind, one trusting moment at a time. It helps us discover the natural cohesiveness in the human soul. While human nature is precarious, it is also rich in goodness. Love abounds; kindness breeds peace; contentment expands the heart. The more we come to that understanding, the sooner we cease polishing our doubts and anxieties as if they were diamonds and begin trusting life. To trust is to live in freedom—to think our own thoughts, arrive at our own decisions, and chart our own course. It is to believe in our heart that, in the end, everything comes out right.

Those who live in faith develop a deepening awareness of their utter dependence on God and they are okay with that. Trust teaches us to protect our inner truth and find God in the depths of our own soul. To trust is to reach toward our ideals and know that we are capable of living them from day to day. Some days, the journey goes "all uphill." When we find ourselves in muddy waters, we instinctively tread harder just to keep afloat. Each tough-minded and independent response makes us stronger. Like Solomon, we learn to believe in the Lord's promise that he will be there for us, in the thick darkness.[59] Spirituality empowers us to rise above the inconstancies of our situation and tap into the resilience that is part of our original blessing. Behind every life and its challenges lies a call to greatness.

> At fifteen she is vibrant and impressionable, academically bright but socially insecure. Other students' attempts to initiate a personal conversation with Patti are met with a hesitant silence. Often, she stares at the floor or the wall, anywhere but directly into a pair of human eyes. Patti frequently stays after school, sewing a little and talking a lot, when other students are not around. The talk is mostly about Opa Tommy. They are close.
>
> "My Mom had me when she was seventeen. I've never met my Dad. He doesn't even know I exist. I don't get it." Patti lives with her Mom and her maternal grandparents, Oma and Opa.

"I remember how Opa taught me to ride a two-wheeler. I fell a lot... He was the one who picked me up. He bought me my first pair of skates... I love hiking with Opa. He knows about plants, mostly about trees. I love hiking in the woods with him. He is my best friend."

It is early Monday morning. I walk back to the home economics lab to set things up for the day. "Thought I left the lights on. Guess I didn't." I reach in and flick the switch. Laboured, painful sobs emanate from the other side of the room. Then, I see her crouched on the floor. Her eyes are tired, as though she's seen too much of life. Hurrying to her side, I carefully sit down beside her. Patti falls into my lap and the floodgates open wide.

Amid intermittent sobs, she pours out the story. "I was hurrying to catch an early bus. The garage door was open and the light shone out onto the walkway. I reached around the frame to switch it off. The rope went around his neck and up to the rafters. He was just hanging there lifeless. My Opa was dead. I tried to scream, but nothing came out. I had to get out of there. So I ran and caught the bus. I feel safe here."

Opa Tommy's funeral is on Friday. My heart bleeds for the three of them—sad, lonely women. Each is engrossed in her own pain. For a long time, Mom cradles her daughter's head in her lap. When Patti stands up, there is intense pain in her eyes. She stares off into the distance. All seems surreal to her. The graveside ceremony drones on far too long. As the casket is lowered into the earth, the sun slips completely behind a cloud. It too is in mourning.

Patti is back at school on Monday. Exposed and vulnerable, she slides back into the habit of staying after school. Sewing a lot and talking little, she finds comfort just being there. I know she's in a terrible space. I don't go there. I just hang around quietly. She needs a loving presence, not a preacher. Four weeks later she starts talking again. Initially, it's all about her sewing projects. Then, one day, she remembers the hikes with her beloved Opa. Her courage shatters me.

Patti wants to visit Opa's grave. Rain pelts down mercilessly the Saturday I pick her up. I watch her closely as I drive to the graveyard. Quiet tears tumble down in spasms. When we get out of the car, she takes hold of my hand. The rain stops. She lays a bouquet of golden roses near Opa's headstone. We hover for a long time. The tears stop suddenly when

Patti looks up at the rainbow spreading its soft hues across the sky. "Opa is smiling at us," she says.

There is an intuitive authority in the human soul. We know how things ought to be. Faith helps us accept the things we cannot change and come to the realization that we cannot right every wrong. Patti had a strong, almost childlike faith. It was her bulwark in time of need. While misfortune tested her, she did not succumb. She had an innate strength that carried her through her time of unbearable sorrow. Faith enables us to live life to the full, often on the edge.

Life doesn't bow to our wants and desires or our fears and insecurities. Most often, it seems oblivious to them. Joys and sorrows intermingle, seemingly at will. Now and again, disappointment and failure scratch the surface and dull our enjoyment of life. Some suffering runs deep and we don't always understand why, but, somehow, we muster the courage to hang on. Much later, we learn to value the discrepancies and the pain as opportunities for growth. The seed must die to produce new life. No amount of wishing it were otherwise can change that. In some mysterious way, each obstacle takes us a step closer to holiness. Life has change and growth and transformation written all over it. Like the Buddhists, we eventually learn that "perfection is not achieved in reaching the end of the road, but in walking the journey."

I am a very young teacher when I am hired as principal for a small Catholic school in rural Saskatchewan. I am a full-time teacher and manage the administrative work after school. My class is a high-spirited and energetic group of students in grades seven and eight. Good, wholesome farm kids. I love them. It doesn't take much to challenge them and to keep them content. I know that thirteen- and fourteen year-olds seek adventure. I try to make sure the escapades are healthy. Boredom sets in when routines are too fixed and blasé. The energy and vitality of my students keeps my mind alert and my creativity in constant motion.

We don't have a school gym, so we need to improvise. A group of grade eights and I work at night to build an outdoor rink in the schoolyard. Albeit small, it serves our purpose. All winter, physical education classes and noon hours are spent on that small rink. Girls as well as boys love to play hockey. Early in February Mr. Dobbs, principal of the public elementary school, challenges us to an interschool hockey game. Not one to decline a challenge, I explore the possibility. When I mention it to my students, their enthusiasm goes through the roof. They are fired. We are the smaller school and will be at a decided disadvantage. That is no deterrent. What we lack in size and numbers we make up for in passion for the game.

It's time for the challenge. The entire school comes to cheer us on. It takes no time at all for my students to lace up. All have hockey sticks. Few, if any, have hockey gloves. Only our goalie, Derek, wears shin pads. Danger is not even a remote thought. The moment of excitement arrives with the first whistle and the drop of the puck. The score see-saws back and forth through the first two periods. It comes down to the final fifteen minutes of the game. Cheers go up from both sides. I am just as thrilled with the score as my students are. We are ahead 4 to 3.

Then, a sudden crash changes everything. Peggy hits the ice hard. No, no, this cannot be happening. One split second— that's all it took. Ted, an overbearing and big grade eight student from the public school gave Peggy a hard shoulder check. A bit clumsy but a good-natured kid, Ted skates back to view the damage. I overhear his faint apology as I run onto the ice. To my horror and Peggy's shock, he had skated over her right hand. Blood was gushing through her gloves, forming a dark red puddle on the ice.

I look at Mr. Dobbs and he comes to my assistance. We put a tourniquet on Peggy's arm to stop the bleeding and carefully bandage the open wound. It looks ghastly. A tendon may have been severed. Now what? I don't have a car and the nearest hospital is thirty-five kilometres away. I look around for help. The only spectator with a car is none other than nineteen-year-old Jack. He has a reputation as a speed demon. Not the best option. As though he senses my dilemma, he casually strides over and offers to drive Peggy to the hospital. Sometimes, second best is better than no option at all.

Putting the grade six teacher in charge, I get into the back seat with Peggy. Jack drives well beyond the speed limit but I offer no objection. I just want to get Peggy to the hospital.

When Doctor Bennett examines the wound, he shakes his head. I wait anxiously for the verdict. My heart is in my throat. Ted's skates were sharp and severed not one tendon but three. They can be mended but recuperation will take several months. Peggy is a bright student. She assures me that she can manage without the use of her right hand.

Embarrassed, but deeply relieved, I call her parents. I fully expect them to call me down, telling me how reckless and negligent I have been. To my surprise, they are kind and understanding. In fact, they say they knew the risks when they signed Peggy's permission slip. I'm not sure which is more painful: Peggy's severed tendons or my hurt pride.

We cannot rearrange life. It takes us where it wills. We never know what to expect. We encounter it all: the new and the old, the motivating and the disturbing, the magnificent and the unsightly, the sound of quiet rest and the loud cry of distress. There are issues we cannot resolve, trials that seem beyond us, and embarrassing, personal blunders. Our natural response is to step up our effort. In due course, we learn that effort alone cannot change us.

Transformation is a gift from God. Providence offers us numerous occasions that foster growth. Over and over again, God beckons us to trust our best impulses. In faith, we know that all the energy and wisdom we need to become fully human is always at hand. When we live in trust, we know that every situation has the potential to deepen us. It all depends on our reaction. Holiness is not about doing all the right things and believing everything that others tell us. It is about letting go and running into God's open arms.

Life is a magnificent symphony. Harmony is created when every instrument is responsive to its own special score. One deeply resonant and beautiful instrument enriches the entire symphony. It carries the softer, weaker ones. We are called to "march to the tune of our own inner drum," though not in isolation. Companions on the journey, we need to be in tune with our fellow travellers, neither racing ahead nor dragging behind. Some people, in their striking simplicity, walk into one's life and shed a direct light on the meaning of freedom and love.

Dilma lives along the mountainside behind the church in Saubara, Brazil. Born and raised in poverty, her opportunities have been exceedingly limited. Poverty has crushed her. Little wonder she wants to remain invisible. When I first meet her, her dispassionate expression says it all. A single mother of three, she ekes out a meager existence harvesting wild fruits and weaving lace. Her hut is one undersized room. The roof consists of palm branches thrown one upon the other. The hut is bare, stripped of furniture except for one small chest of drawers. At night, Dilma and her children unroll their mats and spread them on the earth floor. Three of her children died of malnutrition before reaching the tender age of two.

I stop at Dilma's on Thursdays when I make my rounds distributing fresh bread and powdered milk to the poor along her side of the mountain. The local mothers' club raises enough money to pay the annual tuition fee so Dilma's children can attend school. She is home alone every afternoon, usually sitting in the shade working on a lace project. She designs her own patterns and works assiduously to make metre upon metre of lace. At market time, she sells her creations to tourists along the beach.

It is a sweltering day. The sun beats down mercilessly. By the time I arrive at Dilma's door, the perspiration is running into my eyes. As always, she is waiting for me. A loving, tender soul. Today her welcome carries an irrepressible hint of delight. She has a surprise. She takes my hand as she leads me into the backyard. An old blackened pot sits steaming on the open fire. The unmistakable scent of coffee floats through the air. No longer able to contain her enthusiasm, she explains how she saved enough money to buy a little coffee. Then she stops abruptly. Something is amiss. To her dismay, she has everything but the cups to serve the coffee.

I can't allow her generous act of hospitality to diminish into nothing, all for lack of cups. Seeing the look of sheer disappointment in her eyes, I suggest that we walk a little ways down the mountain. "Surely, something will turn up," I offer. Not more than four to five hundred metres down, Dilma spots two rusty old tin cans. They don't look all that appetizing but she thinks they will do. Relief spreads across her face as she scrambles to pick them up. In her eyes, it's a miraculous find. Once again, I am confronted with my need for cleanliness.

Drinking coffee from rusty old cans seems a bit much. But, for friendship's sake, for Dilma's sake, I push revulsion aside. I pick up the rusty can and start to drink. Coffee never tasted so good. Tim Horton's best brand pales in comparison.

God knows where and when we need to be stretched. The letting go that opens us to the transforming power of God holds nothing back. It embodies the smallest act of kindness and the most heroic effort. To let go and let God be God of one's life demands a high degree of faith—a strong, unyielding passion for living right. People of deep faith inspire and move us to greater love. An inner light guides them and fills them with the freedom to live well. Resolute and secure, they take charge of their lives and become all they can be. They lend support to others and use their inner resources to build a better world.

In the early seventies, a military government rules Brazil. Like many dictators and military regimes, the governing party works hard to have the world see their country as a true democracy. An important election is scheduled to take place during the rainy season. Many courageous people put their names forward and run as opposition candidates. This points the way to possible, and even radical, change in the political leadership. Naturally, the military candidates are running scared. They use every means at their disposal to win the favour of the populace. Desperate times call for desperate measures.

The local candidate, Pedrinho Nasimento, is well known for his strong allegiance to the army. The populace is tired of military rule. The reality is that Pedrinho is losing ground. If he hopes to survive politically, he needs to come up with a scheme to win over the people. The combined population in our five fishing villages is well over forty thousand. Pedrinho knows he has to win here. When he comes knocking at my door, I am decidedly uneasy. People have already warned me about his intentions. He wants to use my presence at some significant event to help him score points with the masses. A flame of suspicion ignites and quickly turns into a conflagration.

Pedrinho starts off on safe ground. Extravagant with his praise, he compliments: "Edite, your leadership in the villages is good for our people. Everyone admires and respects you." Coupling the graciousness of the Brazilian and the lustre of the politician, he continues: "I was wondering if I might use the church to celebrate a Mass of thanksgiving for my deceased mother?" An artful opening. I listen carefully but say nothing. My instincts are right. Oblivious to my lack of enthusiasm, he goes on: "I already contacted a priest friend, Antonio, who will preside at the Mass. I thought it would make it easier for you." It's a premonition of what is to come. Questions race through my mind: "Who is this phantom priest? Where does his allegiance lie? Why have I never heard of him?"

After a prolonged moment, I am ready to take my stand. My response is a clear and definitive "no." Pedrinho is not accustomed to rejection. His sullen and defiant look exposes his utter annoyance. When flattery doesn't charm me into a change of heart, he stoops to cajoling. I remain unfazed. It would send mixed messages to the people. He can neither understand nor accept that. "Dull circular thinking," I muse to myself.

He takes a new approach. The dialogue becomes personal when he questions my right to speak on behalf of the people. "How can a foreigner have such power in the church?" he asks. This line of questioning is all wrong. Detecting that, he reverts to beguiling maneuvers and overt threats. To no avail. As he gets up to leave, he stops unexpectedly. Casting a bitter look in my direction, he makes one final request: "Edite, can you meet me at the church in Acupé on Friday night?" An uneasy feeling takes hold of me but I agree. He adds one final proviso: "Come alone."

Acupé is only fifteen kilometres away. The road is narrow and winding. The bamboo trees along either side obstruct the view, making it hard to see wild animals leaping out of the bush in the dead of night. I experience a vague feeling of foreboding as I leave home. I have one notorious bridge to cross. There's no turning back now. It isn't quite as dangerous for a foreigner to cross Pedrinho. A Brazilian could easily disappear in the night. I find it unsettling to be in such a tight spot. I pray for courage and prudence and a lot of wisdom.

As I drive up to the church, I wonder why there are so many cars around. No one in the village owns a car. There is something radically wrong here. As I enter the church, my head is spinning. Twenty-nine military men sitting in a circle with Pedrinho serve to fan my unease. The atmosphere is strained and downright hostile. I have to face this alone, at least that is what I am thinking. Then, close to the door, I spot her, the young catechist Zezé, a cultured woman with a strong personality. Relief at seeing a familiar face quickly turns to a new kind of concern. A young, Brazilian woman should not be here. What is she thinking? She is only thirty-two, a teacher at the local school. This is dangerous territory for her. I quietly walk up to her and whisper, "Go home. Please go home."

She stands her ground and murmurs, "I can't let you face this crowd alone." Then, picking up her chair, she moves it beside the lone empty chair in the circle. She meets Pedrinho's intense gaze steadily. Fear reigns within me as we sit down.

It proves to be the longest and most painful two hours of my entire life. Pedrinho states and restates his case. His tone alternates between bitterness and white rage. A few of his cronies add a tidbit here and there. I stand firm. There will be no pretence of a Mass and no political rally in the church. Finally, Zezé senses the futility of continuing along this vein. A prophetic look in her eyes, she stands up and courageously announces, "We will close this meeting with a prayer song." Mouths fall open. In a strong, clear voice, she intones, "The Word of God does not divide; the Word of God brings unity and love." Succinct and to the point! At the end, Pedrinho and his retinue file out in silence. Zezé and I stand alone.

The problems of the night are far from over. When I ask Zezé where she found the fortitude to chant that provocative song, she gives me a quiet look. Then she says: "Edite, I believe we need to replace comfortable religion with uncomfortable spirituality. I simply threw caution to the wind and followed the Spirit." I hug her tightly. Then our minds revert to the practical side of things.

We need to find a neutral hiding place for the night. It is not unusual for brave Brazilians to disappear under cover of darkness. Zezé knows that. While she is solicitous for my safety, I am deeply concerned about hers. She insists that I cannot drive that lone road after all that has transpired. We lock the front door of the church, switch off the lights, and sit waiting for some way out of our dilemma. Zezé thinks of her father's bakery. No one would imagine anyone sleeping there.

Several hours later, we slip out the back door and make our way along the shadows. Sprawled on sacks of flour and grain, we finally seek rest. I tell myself tomorrow will be a better day, but sleep is elusive. It is no match for my fear.

On Sunday morning, as people are walking to church, Pedrinho and fifteen of his supporters set up mikes in the square in front of the church. To the tune of the national anthem in the background, they invite everyone to join in a political rally. The faithful merrily walk past the camp and enter the church. As the celebration of the Word begins, Pedrinho and company quietly dismantle their mikes and silently steal away. He knows he's lost the election.

We receive a legacy at birth. In our youth and early adulthood, we spend a lot of time and energy watching, observing, questioning, and exploring. Over time, reality takes hold of us and we run into the road-blocks of life. Our reactions to situations sometimes come up short. Lacking effort, taking the wrong direction, missing the point, and veering off course keep us away from the high road. Discouragement percolates underground. We cannot locate the recipe for life because there is none. Some questions remain unanswered. Eventually, we learn to live with that. Love draws us with an irresistible force. Our plans are no longer paramount. Even our regrets lose their hold. We still want to be the seed that yields a hundredfold, but we know we cannot do it on our own. When we risk all in faith, we face every decision in hope and we are prepared to shoulder the consequences in love.

Aging carries its own inner wisdom. It sifts out what is really important and lets the chaff blow away in the wind. While we are no longer at the centre of things, we know there is still a good reason for living. Though our once-vibrant, resonant energy is gone forever, the story of life keeps rolling onward. Life becomes more tentative and death takes on new meaning. What we once saw as a marked distinction between life and death gradually fades into a single reality. We find ourselves in a different world, a world beyond easy answers. We know where we come from and feel a previously unfathomable connection with our past, our families and friends, and most of all with our God. We appreciate the fact that love stretches beyond time and space. It is the reason for our being. We open ourselves to a new moment in time, an unhurried moment.

I cherish the slower pace of retirement. Some days, I take note of the best and the worst in me. I think back to the innocence of childhood. I miss that. Often, I remember how my experience in Brazil defined me in ways that can never be erased. I think of my family and the ways they've inspired me. I am moved to gratitude for my own good health. I reminisce about all the times God was close and I consider the times I sat alone in darkness. All is good. All is blessing.

Throughout 2007 I feel an enormous change in my body. Initially, there is nothing specific, nothing I can put my finger on. I carry on as usual. I exercise, go for long walks, read, garden, and enjoy being alive.

Every now and again, I find myself retiring into silence. My energy is all but spent. The weight of sickness begins to drag me down and restlessness invades my soul. I tell myself that we all have our own bag of pain and this too will pass. Then, one morning, I look in the mirror and see that my eyes are flat. "Where has the sparkle gone?" I wonder. When I see the look of concern in Karen's eyes, I know it is time to confront reality and see my doctor. A variety of exploratory medications do nothing to stop the intense bouts of nausea and diarrhea. Finally, in mid-October, I am admitted to the hospital. Test after test proves inconclusive. Still, I keep inhaling the scent of serious illness.

The mystery of my illness deepens as the tug-of-war inside presses on. At my lowest ebb, I am placed in the intensive care unit. I am barely aware of Karen and two of my sisters, Jean and Phyllis, standing at my side. Their certitude begins to falter. I can see that. Pinning her eyes on me, Karen smiles gallantly and urges me to fight on. But her voice seems like a distant murmur. My thoughts won't coagulate. I want to put a positive spin on things, but my body is too weak for my mind to focus. I listen to the rhythmic drip, drip, drip as three units of blood are pumped into my veins.

Later, I close my eyes and try to sleep. When sleep doesn't come, I look around and the light seems to be fading. Then, suddenly a luminous shaft of resplendent light breaks into the room. It is comforting and reassuring. I feel a spiritual presence. My Dad and my maternal grandmother are bathed in serenity. They gaze lovingly in my direction. I want to reach out to them but they are already vanishing into the distance. I find myself filling with memories of childhood, adolescence, young adulthood, and my declining years. The regrets are washed away by a prevailing sense of gratitude.

Slowly, imperceptibly the light intensifies. Jesus moves into the light—a pale image that gradually comes into sharper focus. Regal, but welcoming and gentle! Goodness and kindness spread out in every direction. I want to say something. Before a word escapes my lips, I hear the invitation: "Let go. Just let go."

I recall the story of the twig. In the course of my adult life, my letting go and trusting in God has run the gamut: reasonable success today and dismal failure tomorrow. But this is different. This is a divine command. This is about letting go of my firm hold on life itself. Grace descends and I know what I have to do. When I finally let go, the light grows faint. Jesus becomes opaque. Enfolded in peace, I drift off to sleep.

Several hours later, I awake feeling considerably rested and renewed in spirit. I hear the distant echo of my favourite hymn: "I will raise you up on eagle's wings; bear you on the breath of dawn. Make you to rise like the sun and hold you in the palm of my hand."[60] It is life affirming. I have been granted a reprieve. That one shining moment of divine Presence is all the comfort and inspiration I need. I know I have turned a corner. Death has receded. As I look around, I see Karen, my faithful friend, still sitting nearby.

I want to go on with my life. But the painful question remains: "What is wrong with my body?" A week later the diagnosis comes: extreme ulcerative colitis. In a conciliatory tone, my doctor reminds me that the prognosis is not good. It is a disturbing discovery. It doesn't matter. I have a hard time separating the reality of my illness from my near-death experience. When I take a wider view, the two are connected. Together, they illumine my future.

There is a depth and complexity about human life that I am still learning to appreciate. Each dying bears the fragrance of new growth. "Where do I go from here?" I wonder. Months of prayer and discernment lay the foundation for this book. I feel called to share my life experiences and my reflections with a wider audience. It gives me a decisive direction.

Once again, Providence has shown me that letting go is liberating. I am not at the end of my journey. I am being called to go further, deeper. The discerning process is ongoing. To let go is to open my hands and let God take control of my life. To let go is to take each moment as it comes, cherishing its inherent blessings. It is this moment in time that carries the potential for growth, the splendour of faith in action, and the miracle of God's presence.

No life is woven in a single colour. The most exquisite tapestry is made up of many threads. A variety of tints and shades, weights and textures, give it a multifarious effect. Body, mind, and spirit are woven into a single unit. When you let go, you and God sing in harmony. You weave the pattern of your life together. It is only when you let go that you find your rightful place in the universe. You learn to step out of your own way and discover the light within. Letting go helps you realize that your spiritual footprint is but one small aspect of the grandeur of God.

> *To see a World in a Grain of Sand*
> *And a Heaven in a Wild Flower,*
> *Hold Infinity in the palm of your hand*
> *And Eternity in an hour...*
>
> *Man was made for Joy and Woe;*
> *And when this we rightly know*
> *Thro' the World we safely go.*
> *Joy and Woe are woven fine,*
> *A Clothing for the Soul divine;*
> *Under every grief and pine*
> *Runs a joy with silken twine...* [61]

Chapter 14: A Persistent God

After all had been fed, Jesus dismissed the crowds. Then, he sent the disciples off in a boat to the other side of the lake and went up into the mountain alone to pray. The lake was unusually calm. Within the hour, the sea grew restless. The wind picked up and stirred the waves. A fierce storm rolled in and the boat was tossed from side to side. As darkness thickened, the boat was near sinking and panic gripped the disciples.

In their time of need, Jesus came to rescue them. All they saw was a vague image far off in the distance. Some said it was a ghost. They cried out in fear. Jesus called to them, "Take heart, it is I; do not be afraid."

Still, the water was roiled by the wind. Peter, ever the impulsive one, responded, "Lord, if it is you, command me to come to you on the water."

Jesus said, "Come."

Should he? Shouldn't he? Suddenly, the daring adventure didn't seem to make a whole lot of sense. A knot tightened in Peter's stomach. He hesitated for a moment. Then he jumped in with both feet. He walked on the water until doubt settled in his mind again. Taking hold of the little faith he had, he cried out, "Lord, save me." Jesus immediately reached out to him and led him to safety.

As Jesus got into the boat, the wind ceased and the boat was back on tranquil waters. The disciples proclaimed, "Indeed, you are the Son of God."[62]

We've all been there. Done that. We've stood at the crossroads. At the invitation to step out into the vast unknown, we are inclined to hesitate. Though we know that all great adventures involve some risk, we don't like to feel vulnerable. So, we waffle. We second-guess our reliance on God. If we could, we'd play both sides forever. To jump or not to jump, that is the question. Do I jump into the menacing waters or do I remain in the safety of the boat? How bold is my faith? The experience of life repeatedly demonstrates that God is in my boat, consistently in my life. God invites, beckons, pushes, and encourages until I risk all in love.

The Hound of Heaven, by Francis Thompson, is a timeless literary classic. A beautiful and detailed autobiography, it is the story of one man's struggle to be faithful to his destiny. Like every sincere pilgrim, Francis was in search of God. It took him down a long and winding road, a road filled with one false start after the other. As a youth, he lacked the necessary fortitude to stand up to his father who was a renowned medical doctor. The expectation was there from the beginning: Francis needed a laudable and financially rewarding profession. College was inevitable. So, the shy and unassuming young student entered medical school only to discover that he had neither the stomach nor the stamina for it. Dropping out of school within the year, he flitted from job to job. And all the while his real passion lay in the writing of poetry. Unable to face himself, he kept on running. The pattern became all too familiar—Francis fled and God pursued:

Across the margins of the world I fled,
And troubled the gold gateways of the stars,
Smiting for shelter on their clanged bars...
Still with unhurrying chase,
And unperturbed pace,
Deliberate speed, majestic instancy,
Came on the following Feet,
And a voice above their beat—
"Naught shelters thee, who wilt not shelter Me."[63]

A series of unfortunate circumstances led Francis to wander the streets of London. There his budding obsession with opium was easily fed and quickly became a full-blown addiction. Unfortunately, it took a powerful hold of his body and presented a lifelong challenge. A deeply wounded soul, alone and destitute, Francis had no one and nowhere to turn. His exceptional talent lay dormant for many years. For all intents and purposes, he gave up on life. There was nothing to live for and nothing worth dying for either.

The long dark days were followed by even darker nights. But Francis was not completely alone. Providence followed him lovingly, persistently. Waiting in the wings, God found the opportune time to give the young poet a gentle nudge. In one of his darkest moments, Francis felt new life slowly surging back into his weary body. He no longer saw himself playing a part on a stage. Life was real—messy, but precious. When one awakens to life, there is only one way to go. Forward. As Francis came alive, his poetic flair discovered its own renaissance.

A poor and humble man, Francis sought out the Victorian editor Wilfred Meynell. Most editors would waste little time on a ragged, pathetic vagrant who chanced to knock on their door. Meynell was different. When he saw the rueful Francis, he was filled with compassion and immediately took him into his personal care and protection. Redeemed at last, Francis took up the pen in earnest and wrote some of his most inspiring poetry. However, a nascent fervour did not protect him from the vicissitudes of life. His ongoing struggle with opium returned to haunt him. It dissipated his energy and paralyzed his magnificent talent.

In an effort to save Francis, Meynell sent him to rest in a monastery in Sussex. A secluded place of peace and tranquility served to wash away years of anguish. Miraculously, it held Francis' addiction at bay. Francis spent hours in the fields where he was deeply moved by a life-size statue of Christ on the cross. A powerful, mystical experience took him to a turning point. It led him to the realization that he alone was responsible for the person he became. This spiritual revival inspired him to write his greatest poem, *The Hound of Heaven*.

The poem moves from tragedy to tragedy, from pain and utter loneliness to salvation and wholeness. A decidedly Christian poem, it serves as a canticle of hope, a hymn of inspiration even to our day:

> *I fled Him, down the nights and down the days;*
> *I fled Him, down the arches of the years;*
> *I fled Him, down the labyrinthine ways*
> *Of my own mind; and in the midst of tears*
> *I hid from Him, and under running laughter.*
> *Up vistaed hopes I sped;*
> *And shot, precipitated,*
> *Adown Titanic glooms of chasmed fears,*
> *From those strong Feet that followed, followed after.*[64]

The poem takes the universal experience of darkness and light, sin and grace, and elucidates it in Francis' personal life. It is an epic account of his faith journey from the dark and menacing streets of London to the safety of his private room in Meynell's home. A template of the spiritual journey of the soul, the poem describes a common human experience. The deepest longing of the human spirit is for God. Francis spent the better part of his life retreating from God. And don't we all!

In splendid imagery, Francis paints a graphic picture of an indefatigable God. Pithy, terse phrases describe the Hound of Heaven as a God who never stops caring, never gives up on love. The discovery of his own inner beauty and goodness enabled Francis to take hold of life and allow it to bear abundant fruit. The God of Francis' earlier days was the eternal judge who condemned his every move. The God of his resurrection was one who walked with him in love and compassion.

Like Francis, we discover that there is nowhere to hide, nowhere to run in order to escape from God. God is not deterred by our stubborn, selfish ways or by our cold detachment. Looking deeper into the human heart, God heals our insecurities and vulnerabilities and reaches out in acceptance, forgiveness, and healing.

> *And human love needs human meriting:*
> *How hast thou merited —*
> *Of all man's clotted clay the dingiest clot?*
> *Alack, thou knowest not*
> *How little worthy of any love thou art!*
> *Whom wilt thou find to love ignoble thee,*
> *Save Me, save only Me?*
> *All which I took from thee I did but take,*
> *Not for thy harms,*
> *But just that thou might'st seek it in My arms.*
> *All which thy child's mistake*
> *Fancies as lost, I have stored for thee at home:*
> *Rise, clasp My hand, and come!*[65]

Good poetry touches on the transcendental directly or indirectly and leads the reader to thoughtful reflection and prayer. Shedding light on our superficial and false self, it invites us to contemplate the infinite possibilities buried deep within. In poignant language, it personifies the divine in the human. Beckoning us to conversion and transformation, grace empowers us to appreciate both our original blessing and original sin. The result is overflowing gratitude and a full, rich life.

Spirituality, our passion for life and our longing for God, is pure gift. We do not find God; God finds us. God longs for us, yearns for us, and seeks us our whole life long. God simply cannot stop pursuing us and calling us to be all we can be. We may be open and receptive but the deeper effort always comes from the God who loved us into life. Happiness, goodness, and wholeness are unsolicited grace. God places the seed into the human soul at conception. As it germinates and grows, we discover a joy and delight in living. Many psychologists believe that powerful periods of spiritual rebirth begin at a very early age.

I am two and a half years old when my mother gives birth to her fifth living child. She is a tiny baby girl, and I name her after my favourite doll, Anne. Initially, I have no idea of Anne's impact on my young life. I do not understand the shift in family dynamics. In an instant, I become the middle child. Not old enough to be helpful, yet big enough to do a few things for myself.

Grandma arrives at our house within the week. She knows without asking that Mom is fatigued. I beam up at her as they talk quietly. She looks every inch a queen. Concern registers in her soft blue eyes as she watches Mom looking after five needy pre-school children. Her thoughts blossom into a plan. She will take me with her and care for me for the next two or three months. After repeated protests, Mom finally agrees to give it a try. I don't know if Grandma wore Mom down or if Mom was too tired to resist.

Many thoughts flit through my mind as we ride in the sleigh to Grandma's house. As our farmhouse recedes into the distance, I experience a vague feeling of trepidation. I already feel the separation from my brothers and sisters. I cope by telling myself to think of other things. I watch the breath of the horses freeze in the cold air. I feel the bumps as the sleigh slides over gently rolling hills. Grandma's warm embrace is a citadel of secure love. The wool blanket around my feet is pleasant, really very comforting. Before I know it, I drift off into a quiet and restful sleep.

I awake just as the horses pull into Grandma's yard. Time passes imperceptibly until suppertime. My teenage aunts dress me in their best clothes. Safety pins secure a lovely pleated skirt under my arms. Aunt Helen's red necklace and dangling earrings transform me into a princess. Aunt Mary's high-heeled shoes add the final touch. I go clippety-clopping up and down the living room to the whistles and shouts of encouraging uncles. But it doesn't take long before the joyful atmosphere gives way to a nagging sense of nostalgia.

That night, and every succeeding night, Grandma kneels beside my bed with me. Her German night prayer sounds strangely familiar. It is the same prayer that Mom and Dad pray with us at home. Tonight, it is an exceptional balm to my soul. As Grandma tucks me in under the warm duvet, she leans over and kisses my cheek. I almost lose myself in her kind eyes. It takes me to a far away place, to the home of God.

When Grandma walks out, lamp in hand, I feel a deep purity and innocence inside. Darkness sets in and, still, I am not afraid. I close my eyes and an inexpressible peace settles over me. I sense the presence of a greater Power. God is with me. I know it. I don't really understand all that God is, but I like what I feel. Bathed in God's warmth and light, smothered in God's loving embrace, I am free of all anxiety. Nothing, absolutely nothing, can invade the deep joy in my heart.

In the ensuing months, my emotions are in roller coaster mode. One minute up, the next down. Grandma keeps a close eye on me every waking moment. A parody of wisdom, she has an uncanny sense of how I am feeling. She always seems to know. When homesickness takes hold of me, she stretches to reach the top of the kitchen cupboard. Down comes the cookie jar. I clap my hands in anticipation. Grandma holds it out to me and I draw out a tasty Jam-Jam. She makes the best cookies in the whole world and her jar never runs out. Go figure.

I feel completely happy. Life can't get much better than this. I am almost as attached to Grandma as I am to my Mom. Like Mom, Grandma knows how to spin a good tale. I love her spirit—open and accommodating, exceedingly kind and gentle. I like her soft hands rubbing flour from my nose and her strong arms hugging me to my breast. There is an extraordinary power of presence in Grandma. In my eyes, she is as close to God as anyone can get.

Like Mom, I responded to the resonance of Grandma's deep faith. A spiritual giant, she passed on her devotion in intangible and unspoken ways. Her legacy lives on years after her earthly pilgrimage ended. When I was two and a half years old, I felt incredibly close to God, thanks to Grandma and my parents. While I could not describe God, or say anything meaningful about God, I knew that God has a lot to do with love.

My spiritual landscape shifts slightly when I am four. My oldest brother Phil and sister Jean invite me on an exhilarating adventure. We plan to walk the four miles to Grandpa Elder's farm. It seems like a cool idea. I have absolutely no concept of the distance. I remember walking to our neighbour's farm a half mile away. And that was okay. Surely, Grandpa lives close by.

Initially, all goes according to plan. I am able to keep up with my siblings. We cover ground relatively quickly to make sure Mom doesn't see us trudging down the road. After the first mile, we feel thirsty. We carry no water bottle and there isn't a single farm in sight. I am beginning to feel that my short legs are a decided disadvantage. The pace is too fast. I am a burden to my trekking siblings. I see no other option but to sit in the middle of the road and cry. And that is what I do.

Jean stops briefly to listen to my woes. I show her the blisters on my tiny feet. Phil is not about to stop just to look at a little girl's sore feet. Convinced that if they continue I will soon follow, he works on Jean. She hesitates, but then they both blaze ahead. I turn to the only person I believe can help me. In guileless trust, I ask God to stop my siblings in their tracks and bring them back to me. My prayer goes ostensibly unanswered. The image of Phil and Jean receding into the distance pokes holes in my youthful faith.

I decide that God has no time for a little girl's woes. His lack of response is a complete letdown. "Whatever happened to the caring God who comforted me when I was at Grandma's house a short time ago? Did God take off or is God merely hiding in some corner of my soul?"

Every tiny, faltering step toward wisdom provides a different perspective. God is like a highly polished diamond. Today we see one angle of love, tomorrow another. Time teaches us that God is consistently there for us. Not always the way we think God ought to be, but lovingly and faithfully nonetheless. A divine Presence carries us through every circumstance even when we are wholly unaware. God shares our intense joy, our tragedy, and our pain.

The great book of Job is an eloquent presentation of one man's journey through brokenness and trauma and chaos. One long dialogue, it expounds the meaning of suffering and the mystery of God. It is a poetic tale that dismisses our common responses to distress and suggests that suffering has many levels of meaning. But, on the deeper level, the book is about the powerful relationship between God and Job. Job is held up as an ideal servant of the Lord, not because he was a patient man in the face of suffering, but because he knew how to ask all the right questions. Job begged, pleaded, lamented, argued, prayed, and challenged God. Despite God's seeming silence, Job poured forth his soul: "Why do you hide your face, and count me as your enemy? Who is to blame for my predicament? Where are you, God? Why do you hunt me down like a wild animal? Why? Why?"[66]

Personal experience reaffirmed Job's understanding of human misery and his trust in God. Job inspires us to move beyond seeking answers to reaching out to the eternal presence of the Spirit. Because God's favour rested on him throughout the course of his life, Job was able to maintain an inner dignity, a nobleness of spirit.

Despite our physical pain, mental anguish, doubt, and uncertainty, we, too, learn to ask the right questions and come to realize that some will remain unanswered this side of heaven. Like the majestic eagle that soars along the sky in search of food, so life takes us on a never-ending search for holiness. But, the eagle teaches another powerful lesson. When the young are old enough to learn to fly, the parents push them out of the nest. Then, they immediately swoop down to catch each little eaglet before it hits the ground. Parents call it "tough love." Somehow, somewhere, God is in every experience of life.

1968. I apply for a teaching position in the public collegiate. The interview rolls along smoothly until the end. Casting an eye on my small gold cross, the superintendent, Mr. Collet, expresses his concern: "We're talking about a public high school. We can't have you pushing your religion on students." When I assure him that I will not initiate any "God talk" in the classroom, I get the job.

What Mr. Collet didn't count on was the large number of Mennonite students bused in from a community south of the city. I take to them like glue to a stick. Their warm eyes suggest a rare kind of purity. In the relaxed atmosphere of the home economics lab, their questions frequently centre on spirituality. Coming from homes where integrity, simplicity, honesty, and personal responsibility are taught, the girls are interested in the big questions. They already know that there are things we owe God and things we owe ourselves.

Graduation comes and goes. Some students set off for trade school, others to secretarial school, and others to college. The Mennonite girls are exceptionally studious. The general expectation is that they will do well wherever they go. Gina, the valedictorian, is blessed with a natural beauty and a keen mind. No one is surprised to hear that she set her sights on medical school. Her kind and gentle personality will be a definite asset in a humanitarian profession.

Following a Bachelor of Science degree, Gina is accepted into medical school. She spends her summer on the farm with her family. I am enjoying the warmth of the July sun when I look up and see her approaching. Her long blonde hair flows like strands of silk and her iris eyes are full of promise. Her bearing speaks of a woman who respects and trusts herself. The conversation flows freely from friends to university life to memories of high school.

On Gina's third weekend home, her long-time friend Tracy picks her up and they go to a movie. They laugh together as they recall personal successes and a few shared blunders. Suddenly, a car comes careening toward them. Tracy veers left. It is too late. The car crashes against the passenger side of the vehicle. When Tracy regains consciousness, the smell of blood is everywhere. Tasting the acid of fear, she hoists herself from the wreckage and frantically searches for her friend.

Gina is pinned in her seat. Her head is smashed, both legs are broken, and her arms are bleeding profusely.

Doctors do their best to save Gina and to keep the damage to her brain to a minimum. She remains in an induced coma for four months. Surgery follows surgery. The first time I visit her, her eyes are glassy and her once-tawny complexion is ashen. Somehow, she has argued her way out of death, but a strange twist of fate has radically changed her life.

The next three years test Gina's spiritual stamina. Physiotherapy goes on forever. Then, it's on to job hunting. The dream of medical school will remain just that—a lovely fantasy. Gina finds fulfillment working in a daycare. She doesn't complain. She only wonders why her friends keep expecting her to be the Gina she used to be. Incalculable suffering taught her to breathe in the power of God. A mysterious encounter with the darkness of adversity defined her in a new way. I stand in awe at her fortitude and resilience.

Every soul is destined to grow deep like a river. Life's events help us reach out to transformation. When we put aside our preconceived ideas, break out of our fantasies, and stop polishing our doubts, God comes to fill our emptiness with unbounded love. The human task is to open the soul to the divine, to all God asks. It's a complex journey. Like a drowning person, we need to let go of our "treasures" in order to take hold of the rope, the lifeline of salvation. We need to lay aside our notions of grandeur and strength in order to rely on God. It is a question of believing that God is always there for us, that God never lets go.

The more we allow God to be the God of our lives, the more we realize that we are incapable of attaining perfection on our own. In the spiritual life, practice alone does not make perfect. We need God for that. Our role is to surrender to grace, to all that God is doing in us. Redemption is about openness, acceptance, humility and abandonment into God's loving arms. It is about discovering our true riches, not in silver and gold, but in the wisdom and love of God. Then God becomes our father, our mother, our source of life and blessing, and the wisdom that guides us. Letting go of original sin, we turn around to behold the reality of life and discover the richness and complexity of our own original blessing.

God never lets go of the divine dream for us. Like the Hound of Heaven, God pursues us, follows us, and invites us to be all we can be. God calls us to let go of superficial and passing values in order to lead us to the fullness of life. In my youth, I frequently bargained with God. I promised God that I would hand over this or that aspect of my life in exchange for the tiny miracle I needed at a particular point in time. I was willing to offer some of my gifts and my time to do things for others. But I held back the real me, my interior self. It took me a long time to realize that what God wants more than anything else is my heart. God takes all.

At seventeen, I am on the verge of walking into the next chapter of my life. This is serious stuff. Like most teenagers, I am convinced that there is more than one path into the future. I am quite certain that I want to be a teacher. What kind and under what circumstances is still up in the air. I love children and I am good with them. As the town babysitter, I have lots of experience. My dream is to get married and have a house full of kids. It is doable in the life of a teacher.

I have gone through life thus far with a single-minded aim—to remain close to God. Tenacious by nature, I generally stick to my commitments. My life is sailing along smoothly. Then, one day, God proposes another way. I am to be a different kind of teacher, a member of a religious community. My initial reaction to God's latest proposal is anything but enthusiastic. I have a flair for life. I love it all: boyfriends, dances, parties, sports, and doing my own thing. I want to be a free agent even though I'm not exactly sure what that is. Convent life would stifle my raw desires. Still, the dialogue with God flows on. Do I leave my cares and ambitions behind and follow wherever God leads me? Or do I keep pushing the truth into the background?

God writes the story. I live it. I know that. Or do I? I have fairly well mapped out my future and it looks awesome. Why can't it play out that way? I spend the next year bargaining with God. "Just this once, can we do it my way?" I pray. I am past thinking of God as a scorekeeper. Still, I want us to be on the same page. I am looking for some wiggle room. But, no matter how I rub my thoughts together, God draws me into the divine orbit. In the end, I take a chance on God.

Time and grace usher in a different way of looking at life. As Thomas Merton maintains: "It is not a question of either-or but of all-in-one... of wholeness, wholeheartedness and unity... which finds the same ground of love in everything." God wins the day and God wins my life. After graduation, I join the Ursulines, a teaching community on the prairies. Convent life is an altogether new experience. It takes self-discipline to a whole new level. There is monastic frugality and feverish work. I have no time to myself. Every minute of every day is programmed. I rise at 5:30 am, work hard, pray even harder all day long, and observe the grand silence at 9:00 pm. Lights are out by 10:00.

But community life also has its rewards. I live and work with some incredibly holy people. As an Ursuline, I volunteer to serve as a missionary in Brazil. Missionary life teaches me what it means to let go, to let God be God, and to serve God with unquestioning loyalty. It alters my way of understanding reality, my way of living life. It helps me fathom the depths of my own heart.

I love Brazil and hope to stay here for a long, long time. But, after five years, I am elected to a leadership position with the Ursulines and recalled to Canada. Four years later, the plot of my story turns the page to a new chapter. A new invitation is set before me: "Go now and work in Canada's north country." Under the guidance of the Spirit and at the urging of the local bishop, Karen and I commit the rest of our lives to the Catholic Diocese of Whitehorse. I know little about the Yukon's geography, its people, and its challenges. Still, when my Ursuline friends caution against this latest move, I remain resolute. None of it really matters in the face of God's single-minded intent. Together, Karen and I co-found a new community, the Companions of Angela and Francis (Koinonia Association). God consistently seems to cast a wide net.

In the changing fortunes of time, we discover that the sun still guards the days, the stars continue to shine through the night, and all is right with the world. Naturally, there is a kind of dying to every rebirth. God beckons, invites, and urges. Then remains silent for a time. In the spiritual life, silence seems to amplify the message. One way or another, we get it. The call is to offer up one's heart and let God take care of the rest. When we are open to God, when we let go of the familiar and launch out into the deep, there is a progressive unfolding that leads to integration and self-realization, to wholeness and, hopefully, to holiness. To walk in tune with God, is to walk in eternal hope.

> *Two roads diverged in a yellow wood,*
> *And sorry I could not travel both*
> *And be one traveler, long I stood*
> *And looked down one as far as I could*
> *To where it bent in the undergrowth;*
>
> *Then took the other, as just as fair,*
> *And having perhaps the better claim,*
> *Because it was grassy and wanted wear;*
> *Though as for that the passing there*
> *Had worn them really about the same,*
>
> *And both that morning equally lay*
> *In leaves no step had trodden black.*
> *Oh, I kept the first for another day!*
> *Yet knowing how way leads on to way,*
> *I doubted if I should ever come back.*
>
> *I shall be telling this with a sigh*
> *Somewhere ages and ages hence:*
> *Two roads diverged in a wood, and I —*
> *I took the one less traveled by,*
> *And that has made all the difference.*[67]

Chapter 15: Living the Beatitudes

Blessed are the poor in spirit, for theirs is the kingdom of God.

Blessed are those who mourn, for they will be comforted.

Blessed are the meek, for they will inherit the earth. Blessed are those who hunger and thirst for righteousness, for they will be filled.

Blessed are the merciful, for they shall receive mercy.

Blessed are the pure in heart, for they will see God.

Blessed are the peacemakers, for they will be called children of God.

Blessed are you when people revile you and persecute you and utter all kinds of evil against you falsely on my account.

Rejoice and be glad, for your reward is great in heaven.[68]

Three powerful scenes followed one upon the other: an all-night vigil, the calling of the twelve, and the proclamation of the kingdom. The backdrop was a mountainside, the place of many great biblical theophanies. The atmosphere alluded to the magnitude of this moment in Jesus' ministry. Surrounded by his disciples and a huge crowd listening to his every word, he proclaimed a series of blessings. The beatitudes were addressed to the disciples for the world. They serve as a mandate for all who wish to follow Jesus down through the ages.

Jesus' key message declared "blessed" some surprising people. The poor, the merciful, the humble, the honest, and the agents of peace are close to the heart of God. Going beyond the Ten Commandments and basic ascetical virtues, the beatitudes are not so much about personal perfection but a loving union. Those who want to share in the sanctifying power of Jesus must conform their lives to the beatitudes. To follow Jesus is to walk in truth and humility, reaching out to the needy in our midst.

The beatitudes are paradoxes, anomalies that fly in the face of everything the world deems important. The world summons us to pursue happiness; God calls us to create it. The world speaks of power and glory; God speaks of humble service. The world finds personal security in material riches; God invites us to poverty of spirit. In the final analysis, we face a radical choice: to humbly accept our innate poverty or become slaves to our fears and anxieties. The beatitudes are a way of life that calls us to go beyond the law and the prophets, to plumb the depths of our reliance on God. When we are poor in spirit, we discover the spiritual freedom that is our destiny.

The beatitudes present a road map for the Christian life. They form a single unit with poverty of spirit as the first and defining beatitude. The other seven delineate the deeper meaning. Blessed are those who know the Spirit of God is alive and active within. They realize that God's grace is bountiful and flows out to others. Conscious of their dependence on the Creator, they walk humbly with their God. It is their acceptance of their innate poverty that enables them to soar to the heights of spiritual freedom. Blessed are those who move beyond anger, envy, worldly ambition, and personal pride, to a life of gentle peace, personal contentment, and humble service.

Life is about spiritual transformation. As human beings, we are incomplete and life beckons us to strive for wholeness and holiness. It is our nature to question, to seek answers, and to look for meaning and purpose. Poverty of spirit empowers us to live with the open questions and the uncertainty that time and changing circumstances bring into our lives. It teaches us to embrace every aspect of life, root as well as blossom. As we move to new stages of growth and maturity, we become increasingly more aware of our weakness and vulnerability. But we also learn to obey the truth of our being. "You shall lovingly embrace the humanity entrusted to you. You shall be obedient to your destiny. You shall not continually try to escape it. You shall be true to yourself. You shall embrace yourself!"[69]

By all external appearances, the life of Jesus was insignificant and inconsequential. Though he was rich, yet for our sake he became poor, so that by his poverty we might become rich.[70] Born in human likeness, Jesus embraced his humanity and became one of us. He renounced his power as God in order to feel our pain, experience our struggles, and know in his flesh what it means to be human. He discovered God in every facet of his humanity: his thoughts, feelings, questions, doubts, and life itself. Growing in wisdom, stature, and favour with God, he learned to see the goodness and love of God in his roots, his time of growth, and the free blossoming of love.

Jesus developed his unique potential and personal outlook in the fertile ground of his Jewish heritage. He spent time in the synagogue, read the Word of God, and reflected on it in the stillness of his own heart. It was by listening to the Spirit within that he learned to understand life and its call to holiness. He encountered beauty and goodness intermingled with the harsh reality of life. Each blessing and every challenge helped him grow into a deeper awareness of who he was. It enabled him to understand the full extent of his mission and the destiny that led to the cross.

Jesus prepared himself for his public ministry by spending forty days alone fasting and praying. The desert experience was his exodus, his time of purification. It was there that God allowed him to be tempted by the power of evil. One colossal temptation, three distinct pretences. Jesus was tempted to reject his humanity, to reclaim his divinity, and to turn his back on the stark reality of human existence. What Satan feared most of all was God himself embracing the poverty of the human spirit. We think of the Creator as full of power and glory. But God's real strength is expressed in weakness, in poverty, and in the wisdom of the pure in heart.

Jesus' unequivocal rejection of earthly power and glory and possessions filled him with inner light and freedom. Placing his trust and his very life in God's hands, he accepted his innate poverty, his human destiny with all the confusion and pain inherent in it. Freely, lovingly, he chose the way of poverty and weakness. He assumed the naked power of the grain of wheat that dies in order to bear abundant fruit. In absolute fidelity and unquestioning love, Jesus seized the poverty of the cross.

For many, Jesus' entire life is shrouded in mystery. The cross is an inconceivable contradiction. But it brought Jesus face to face with the ultimate test of his personal identity and mission. Stretched between heaven and earth, he hung alone and helpless before the powers of this world. In the face of deep darkness and chilling doubt, he commended his spirit into the Father's hands. His Passover was complete. He knew with absolute certainty that he and the Father are one. A few privileged people get the essential message: the cross leads to fullness of life.

The world judges things according to status and rank, wealth and possessions, influence and power. In the eyes of the world, a book is as good as its cover. A person is as good as the image she/he projects. It is all in the impression, the façade. People who are powerful, rich, and beautiful are esteemed and venerated. They become gods unto themselves. But the world demands perfection, absolutely and unequivocally. It refuses to tolerate anything less. In its cold, calculating, and heartless ways, it rejects the weak and the vulnerable. One misstep instantly erases a multitude of past successes. One sin blots out thousands of good deeds.

Human life is never perfect. We age and get sick, stumble and fall. Sooner or later, we lose our lustre and the world deems us dispensable. God is not like that. God loves us categorically, accepting and embracing us as we are. All God asks of us is that we open our hearts, our lives, and our souls to the Love that created us. With God, there are no half measures. Like Jesus, we are to accept our destiny, embrace our humanity, and stand before God in openness and humility. And God fills up what is lacking so that we might seed the world with love.

Becoming a human being involves much more than conception and birth. It summons us to discover our hidden self, to realize that we are, indeed, fearfully, wonderfully made. It is to discern our mission and to trust that God will help us bring it to fruition.

The Gospel presents two very different responses to the mandate of God. The rich young man came to Jesus seeking some guarantee, an assurance of the end prize. When he asked what more he must do to gain eternal life, the emphasis was on his deeds, his good works. He placed himself front and centre in the scheme of things. The invitation to take up his cross and follow Jesus proved too much for him. It spoke of loss and dependence. He had amassed great wealth by the sweat of his brow. The suggestion that he share it with the poor was a new and threatening concept. Detachment, in any form, was completely unacceptable.

Full of illusions instead of truth, the young man chose to place his trust in material riches rather than in God. Because he had no idea of the freedom poverty of spirit brings to the soul, he walked away from the greatest opportunity of his life. He did not grasp the tremendous spiritual power in weakness, in poverty, in vulnerability. All he wanted was to lay claim to paradise. Because he believed he could "earn" heaven, he could not accept the idea of letting go of the tight grip he had on life. He was not prepared to open his hands and let God fill them. He did the only thing he was prepared to do at that time in his life—he went away sad.

The second biblical response is that of the child. When the disciples asked Jesus who is the greatest in the kingdom, Jesus set a little child before them and said: "Truly I tell you, unless you change and become like children, you will never enter the kingdom of heaven. Whoever becomes humble like this child is the greatest in the kingdom. Whoever welcomes one such child in my name welcomes me."[71]

In their candour and simplicity, children demonstrate poverty of spirit. They are not afraid to say, "I need you." They accept everything as a gift. Taking joy and delight in the simple things of life, they mingle with the splendours they see. They don't just see beauty; they become united with it. Receiving it as a precious gift, they immerse themselves in it. They see life as full of possibilities. Their guileless trust becomes the blossoming of surrender to God. Those who are humble in spirit, free in spirit, trust God with their very lives.

Poverty of spirit is a fundamental Christian attitude toward life. It is to put aside all sense of entitlement. The poor in spirit take nothing for granted. Everything is gift. Hence, they have no problem sharing their gifts. In their humility and generosity, they become the pillars of the community.

> Brazil's poor practically live in each others' yards. Because they know everything about their neighbours, they are there for each other. They work together and pray together. They counsel, chide, and discipline each others' children. They share almost everything, including their hopes and dreams.
>
> The sight of all the avocado and lemon trees growing in pockets around the village sets my mind "a-thinking." I purchase a blender and begin experimenting. It is really quite easy. I put avocado, lemon, powered milk, a bit of sugar, and water into the blender. A few seconds of blending produces a mild-flavoured health drink. The children love it and call it "vitamina."

When I tell my next-door neighbour about it, she borrows the blender, passes it on to a woman down the street who passes it on to a cousin across the street. Before long, the blender has been up and down both sides of the street dozens of times. A mother who wishes to prepare vitamina simply stands in front of her hut and claps her hands to a samba beat. Women living further down the street join in the clapping until the blender mysteriously appears. It belongs to no one and to everyone. Like a well-read book, it becomes community property.

People who have little seem to know much more about sharing than the rest of us. When your life is governed by the dictates of material poverty, you learn to rely on those around you. You are not inclined to place yourself above others. Reality teaches you that survival depends on people's ability to be there for each other. The poor remind me of the bamboo that grows everywhere along Brazil's coast. The trunks are hard and sturdy, but the foliage is soft and airy. The inner freedom of the poor reflects nature's beauty and strength.

While some people are born into poverty, others choose it as a way of life. St. Francis of Assisi was born into a wealthy family. Privileged and honoured among men, young Francis was given extraordinary responsibility in the army. Everything seemed to fall into his lap: wealth, status, power. However, it could not shield him from the reversals of illness and disease. When he contracted a serious malady, fortune no longer smiled on the youthful soldier. His high rank disappeared in an instant.

A near fatal illness brought Francis to a turning point. Old ways no longer served to advance his career. Something had to go. Francis embarked on a new journey. Examining his desirable position, his superficial values, and the direction of his life, he discovered how hollow and empty they really were. An inner vision inspired him to commit himself to a life of absolute poverty. He renounced his father's wealth and joined the masses who lived on the streets of Assisi.

Francis' life of poverty was not an easy one. Lonely moments and frightening nights unsettled him. When the clouds covered the sun and the sky poured down incessant rain, he longed to be back in his father's house where he would be sheltered from the wind and the cold. The memory of the cooking meats and the taste of good wine filled him with a yearning for bygone days. His bare feet and ragged tunic were no consolation. But, in time, the rains washed his fears away and Francis felt free again. The dream, once again, shone brightly in his soul.[72]

The poor in spirit accept their humanity with its doubts and uncertainties, anxieties and ambiguities, risks and demands. Because they believe in the power of God's love, they journey into the unknown with a sense of confidence. They know how to "get out of their own way" and let God be God. Day by day, they celebrate the infinite mystery of God, alive and active in their weakness.

Born the third child of young immigrant farmers, my Mom comes face to face with material poverty in her childhood. It clings to her like an old winter coat. Her family has few material possessions. The farm boasts a mere hundred and sixty acres, a few workhorses, and old farm implements, but many willing hands along with many mouths to feed. The family cannot afford the luxury of electricity or indoor plumbing or even a radio. Mom walks to school, often barefooted, with her brothers and sisters. Family meals are simple, and daily portions are carefully measured to make sure everyone is fed.

Poverty invades every aspect of Mom's life and puts huge demands on her: hard physical work, selfless dedication to family, and a very modest lifestyle. She does what she has to do to assist her parents. She works in the fields; helps with the farm chores; cooks and cleans; and plants, cultivates, and harvests the garden. Nothing is beneath her—no task too menial, no person too lowly.

By all appearances, Mom has no great talent, no exceptional passion, and no outstanding contribution to make. Still, she has her youthful dreams. She likes school and is good at it. But the one-room, country school does not go beyond grade eight. Her dream is to become a teacher, however circumstances close that door. "If I would have had a chance, I think teaching would have been a good career for me. I would have liked to do that. I would have liked to teach little children."[73]

Marriage at age twenty brings no relief from the poverty of Mom's early life. It merely takes a different form. She and Dad face the never-ending challenges of a long, hard prairie drought. The Second World War follows fast on the heels of the Great Depression. Still, a strong work ethic, coupled with a sense of kindness and generosity, enables them to share both their produce and their home with those in need. When a close neighbour dies and doesn't have anything suitable for his burial, they clothe him in Dad's wedding suit. When a homeless couple wanders into the yard and begs to stay for the winter, they take them in. No questions asked.

In some mysterious way, poverty is part of Mom's original blessing. It gives her a profound sense of what it means to be human. She does not place herself above others. She tells her story with unmistakable clarity. Nothing is glossed over and nothing is overstated. She accepts her past, trusts the grace of the moment, and finds fulfillment in her future. Unaffected and unpretentious, she is not afraid to be herself. She is on the outside what she is on the inside.

Mom is not afraid to take risks in order to follow her destiny. A mother of nine, she is given a lofty and noble mission. In a sense, she does not belong to herself. She belongs to her family. She learns early on that children are entrusted to her for a brief time. Her first sons, premature twins, die shortly after birth. Years later, she confides: "There was no hope—they were much too small. My tears were beyond comfort, as they lay lifeless in my arms. But, I had to go on living. Life is a precious gift and I had lots to live for."

Keeper of the flame, Mom raises us on Gerein-Elder lore. She is a pillar of faith, and faith is at the centre of our family life. We give thanks to the Creator for new life, bumper crops, personal achievements, and times spent together. We face every obstacle and every challenge with prayer. Serious illness, painful accidents, crop failures, and personal blunders are occasions for prayer. When the going gets tough, we kneel around the kitchen and pray together.

Mom lives her declining years before the backdrop of deep personal loss. She is barely sixty when she begins to lose both her hearing and her vision. It often pains me to see her straining to hear and follow a conversation. The loss of her vision demands a different kind of detachment. An artist at heart, she loves to paint, sew, knit, and crochet gifts for her grandchildren and great-grandchildren. I note the resignation in her voice the day she admits she can no longer do any of those things. It is a new kind of poverty.

On the eve of their sixty-eighth wedding anniversary, Dad has a massive heart attack and dies within minutes. With a steely calm, Mom mourns her deep loss. The love of her life is gone. Alone, handicapped, and uncertain of the future, she negotiates her way through the darkness of loss and uncertainty and discovers a deeper spiritual energy. She knows she is the sole keeper of the flame and devotes herself to keeping her family united.

Within a year of Dad's death, Mom is called to further detachment. She decides to sell the home she has known for over forty years and gives away her cherished possessions—her pictures, family heirlooms, souvenirs, furniture, and the beautiful rose garden she so carefully cultivated over many decades. She moves into a seniors' lodge. Now home is a single room and a private bathroom. By all appearances, she is returning to the material poverty of her youth.

I help Mom move into the lodge. When I am ready to leave, she walks me to the front door. Before getting into the car, I turn to wave a last goodbye. The image of my strong and resolute mother is gone. In its place, I see a small, frail woman, standing alone before the vast unknown. The memory remains forever etched in my mind. As I drive off, I recall Mom's tremendous faith. Love has placed an absolute claim on her heart. All her life, she let God approach her and lead her.

Two months after Mom's ninety-sixth birthday, the inevitable call comes. Mom has fallen and severely damaged her right femur. She is taken to surgery but never totally regains consciousness. As I walk into her hospital room, I take in the smell of death. I am supposed to believe that death always yields to more life, but all I can do is fight back the tears. God is weaving the final threads into the beautiful tapestry of my mother's life.

In her hour of need, Mom feels the presence of her nine children around her. As I sit alone with her one night, I realize that all fear is gone. The mysterious continuity of history is unfolding before my eyes. I remember the way she used to talk about Grandma's incredible faith. Mom loved listening to Grandma read Bible stories. She described Grandma as a good mother—fair, loving, honest, and kind.

I begin to pray the rosary. "Holy Mary, Mother of God, pray for us sinners now and at the hour of our death." Mom gives my hand a weak squeeze. A tear rolls down each pale cheek. She knows the end is near. And I recall a moving verse from St. John of the Cross:

> *"That sweet night: a secret.*
> *Nobody saw me;*
> *I did not see a thing.*
> *No other light, no other guide*
> *Than the one burning in my heart."*

I know that the story of her life is playing itself out in Mom's mind. It puts her in touch with her deepest self: the self that chose one path over another, the self that learned to surrender all to God. Now Mom is moving on to a new horizon where love is still the dominant force and poverty of spirit calls her to surrender herself in death so that she might be immersed in transcendence. She has carried the imprint of God in the earthenware jar that was her body. Now she is going home. The fullness of life bursts forth out of her inner poverty.

To be poor in spirit is to be with God, to find one's hidden self in God. Why, then, are we so afraid to live in poverty of spirit? For most of us, the risk often looms much larger than the spiritual riches it brings. While our original blessing plunges us into the ever-moving stream of life, original sin invites us to a life of comfort and security. It presents us with the image of a nesting place where the forces of life cannot touch us. Poverty of spirit, immersing us in life's wild and wonderful side, alongside its hardships and challenges, leads us to accept the reality of life—our personal world is in constant motion. To be poor in spirit is to recognize that we are not in control of our lives. God is. Blessed be God!

Poverty of spirit is much more than a single beatitude among many. It is the hidden but essential element, the very foundation, of every other beatitude. "All the great experiences of life—freedom, encounter, love, death—are worked out in the silent turbulence of an impoverished spirit."[74] The poor in spirit know they are wounded, limited, incomplete. They understand their need for God and for others. Full of possibilities, they reach for the stars. And in their honesty, they are healed and redeemed. They emerge as the meek and the merciful, the pure and gentle of heart, the peacemakers and peacekeepers.

> *Let your mind be quiet, realizing the beauty of the world,*
> *and the immense. the boundless treasures that it*
> *holds in store.*
> *All that you have within you, all that your heart desires,*
> *all that your nature so specifically fits you for—that*
> *or the counterpart of it waits embedded in the great*
> *Whole, for you. It will surely come to you.*
> *Yet, equally surely not one moment before its appointed*
> *time will it come. All your crying and fever and*
> *reaching out of hands will make no difference.*
> *Therefore, do not begin that game at all.*
> *Do not recklessly spill the waters of your mind in this*
> *direction and in that, lest you become like a spring*
> *lost and dissipated in the desert.*
> *But draw them together into a little compass, and hold*
> *them still, so still;*
> *And let them become clear, so clear—so limpid, so*
> *mirror-like;*
> *At last the mountains and the sky shall glass themselves in*
> *peaceful beauty,*
> *And the antelope shall descend to drink, and to gaze at his*
> *reflected image, and the lion to quench his thirst,*
> *And Love himself shall come and bend over, and catch his*
> *own likeness in you.*[75]

Chapter 16: Prayer

Remember the Sabbath day, and keep it holy. Six days you shall labour and do all your work. But the seventh day is a Sabbath to the Lord your God; you shall not do any work... For in six days the Lord made heaven and earth, the sea, and all that is in them, but rested the seventh day; therefore, the Lord blessed the Sabbath day and consecrated it.[76]

"To keep holy the Sabbath" is a gift rather than a command. God has no need of a sabbatical. We do. Periodically, we need to change our pace, to simply be and let be. The human spirit needs time to pause, to linger in quiet stillness. Taking time out gives us a different perspective, a new lease on life. When we put the pressures of life aside, we free our spirits to wander where they will. In that peaceful rest, we arrive at an inner freedom that empowers us to define and refine ourselves.

To keep the Sabbath holy is to follow the rhythm we find in nature. The earth rotates on its axis right on schedule. The sun rises to announce the beginning of a new day. As night descends, the moon peeks over the horizon, slowly ascends the heights of heaven, and reaches its fullness when all is filled with darkness. The fireweed instinctively plants its seed on the forest floor after a ravaging fire. The human body also sets its own pattern for living. The mind evolves and learns to comprehend. We can safely assume that the soul too has its inner guide. It needs to develop its own measured pace.

God longs for more than an unfocused glimpse. Sabbath is a time to linger, to be still, to be attentive to the peace within, and to listen deeply to life. It is not restricted to a specific hour or even a day. It can be a week, a month, a year, or a moment in time that leads us to resurrection.

Many of us think of prayer as saying prayers. We remember the prayers of our childhood and revert back to them when we are in need. And that is good. But prayer is much more than uttering a few familiar words. In fact, it needs no words, no thoughts, no pleading to make it authentic. In its simplest form, it is being present to God, being attentive to everything in us and around us. It is to immerse ourselves in life, breathing in all that we find there.

It is a strange and wonderful afternoon. The sky has an unusual beauty: deep azure to the north, a gentle turquoise to the south. As Karen and I set out on our daily walk, we wonder what great marvel of creation will be our gift for the day. We turn our steps south toward Schwatka Lake. It doesn't take long for our "blessing" to reveal itself. There, behind the two-metre chain-linked fence of the fish ladder, lies a soft furry bundle. Tinges of red streak down its magnificent golden back. We stop dead in our tracks and drink in the loveliness directly in front of us.

The elegant fox raises his sleepy head and stretches his legs. Turning slowly to face us, he becomes as fixed as the rungs of the ladder. He stares intently at us. As though she reads his mind, Karen says: "We would never hurt a gorgeous creature like you." Seeming to understand, the fox turns and goes back to his fetal position. Once again, becoming a luxurious mound of thick flaxen fur, it serves as a reminder that the entire universe speaks of the grandeur of God.

We come into the world innocent and pure, with an eye for God. In the beginning, our longing for the inner Mystery is undefined and indeterminate. But it gives us an inherent trust in our surroundings and in life itself. It defines our creative and life-sustaining path to God. Our search for God is as natural as breathing. In early childhood, we are already aware of a greater Power at work in our lives. We instinctively turn to this Power and pray for protection and blessings on all those we love.

It is early May, the month dedicated to the Mother of God. At age seven, I have already developed a devotion to Mary. I devoutly clasp her tiny pewter statue in my hand. It's a gift from my maternal grandmother and needs a place of honour in my room. Creative and artistic energy fan the flame of my wild imagination. I take an empty cardboard box and set it on my dresser. Methodically, I walk back into the store and carefully look around. The soft tissue wrapped around oranges will serve my purpose. Delighted with the vision of something beautiful, I pick out several of the tissues and begin turning them into colourful paper flowers. In no time at all, these lovely posies decorate the interior of my "box shrine." I place my petite statue in the centre, stand back, and give it an admiring look. Something is missing. Off I go searching through kitchen drawers. There it is, the little candle I need. Now everything is complete.

About to kneel in prayer, I remember something else. The church is often filled with the glowing light of candles. I like the smell of the wax. I think it helps me pray. I find matches in the kitchen and light my candle. The setting is perfect.

Alas, almost immediately, one of the tissue flowers bursts into flame. Instinctively, I pick up my lovely shrine and quickly carry it into the backyard where I drop it to the ground. In a panic, I frantically stomp on it until all the flames are extinguished. I am filled with utter dismay; I feel I let Mary down. I pick the charred statue out of the ruins. Cradling the tiny figure in my hands, I walk around the yard sobbing profusely. Then a mysterious relief sweeps over me. It could have been a much greater catastrophe. Looking up to heaven, I thank God who spared my cherished statue and me. God always seems to come through for me.

Prayer takes time to unfold. "In the beginning, there is struggle and a lot of work for those who come near to God. But after that, there is indescribable joy. It is just like building a fire: at first it's smoky and your eyes water, but later you get the desired result. Thus we ought to light the divine fire in ourselves with tears and effort."[77] Learning to pray is akin to conversion. The beginning is never easy. It involves letting go and letting God be in us. A long, slow process, it demands a certain degree of ambiguity.

Prayer is a purifying process that often involves some kind of struggle. Like fire tests the purity of gold, events and circumstances bring out our inner strength. When we begin to pray, the smoke gets in our eyes. There are times when we sit alone with our desire to pray and nothing seems to happen. God appears to be watching us from a distance. Sometimes, despite our repeated efforts at prayer, we remember nothing more than the absence of God. We hear God's voice and then we hear nothing but a vacant silence. God is not the one who has moved. We have. Then, just when we are inclined to give up, God's invitation becomes stronger: "Put out into the deep and let down your net" one more time. God knows what lies beneath the surface.

Everyone's prayer sometimes feels unproductive, even sterile. No one is on a "high" all the time. Sometimes God leaves us to our own devices. Then God seems remote and inaccessible, and we feel adrift in the sea of life. We reach out but the anchor seems to have disappeared. No one appears to "be up there." It is then that we are most inclined to give up. We lose interest. Wisdom tells us that it is during the "dry" periods of prayer that fidelity is most important. Somehow, we must believe that God is still with us, still loving us.

I've only had the opportunity to visit the desert once and that left an indelible impression on me. The vast emptiness was frightening. I wondered how anyone could survive in that pounding heat amid mile upon mile of nothing but blowing sand. It was only when the rains came that I began to understand the mystery of that barren region. My observations of the desert, with its alternating barrenness and vibrancy, remind me of prayer. There are intense moments of grace and light in everyone's life. They come to different people in different ways and at different times. Pure gift, they leave us with a deep joy and a profound appreciation of self, of life, and of God. But these intense moments of grace are rare. They are intended to carry us through the times of emptiness and distractions. During the "dark night" of prayer, we need to call to mind the memories of our closeness to God. To persevere in prayer, we must believe that God is simultaneously drawing us within our selves and into the divine presence.

As we do with most things, we make prayer about self. We think of it as our longing for God. To be human is to be filled with a deep desire for God, but that is not the essence of prayer. Prayer has much more to do with God's longing for us. It is God's nature to yearn for us. Who God is and what God does in us is the essence of prayer. God wants to hold a special place in our hearts. For most of us, we come to that realization after a very long period of time. But God is never in a hurry. God is prepared to wait—quietly, lovingly, patiently. Prayer is our response to that waiting. All things come to those who wait.

> 1975. I am to meet one of the ranch hands at the entrance to the fazenda. I know the road is a narrow, winding one. So I set out early in the morning. Two hours later, I come to a dead end. This is the place. I am supposed to wait here. Finally, after three long hours, I see the horse and rider at the crest of a hill. As he approaches, Manuel smiles broadly: "I assume you are Edite." When I acquiesce, he invites me to get on the horse trailing behind him. We ride on together for the better part of an hour. I admire the trees heavily laden with oranges, lemons, limes, and tangerines. The tantalizing smell is an invitation to stop and eat. As though he's reading my thoughts, Manuel announces, "We'll stop here and give the horses a break." The

juice of a luscious orange runs down my arms as I savour it to the last morsel.

Following a refreshing drink of water from a nearby spring, we mount our horses and continue the journey. An hour and a half later, we arrive in the heart of the fazenda. Everything is abuzz with life. This is "baptism" day and that means fiesta time. Amid the cries of young children, the smell of beans cooking on an open fire, the drumbeat of the samba, and the chatter of parents and godparents, I baptize eleven newborns. The celebration extends into the wee hours of the night.

As I prepare to set off the next morning, the landlord, Jaimé, invites me to visit the fazenda on the first Tuesday of the month. Naturally, I agree. It will present many opportunities to form bonds with the people and discern their needs for spiritual support.

I know the routine and I prepare myself for the long waits. I am not particularly good at waiting. Over the months and years, I crochet an entire tablecloth as I sit waiting for Manuel. In hindsight, I realize my mistake. I lost many a golden opportunity. I might have spent my time drinking in the wonderful sights and sounds and smells around me. I might have enriched my hours of waiting simply breathing in God.

Prayer is life. It takes many forms and is not necessarily confined to a specific place. The divine mystery reveals itself in: people, nature, music, art, poetry, life, and the passion within the human soul. Remembering special moments, contemplating God, meditating on the meaning of life, practising centring prayer or affective prayer, pondering icons and symbols, all touch the heart of God. But God also comes to us in the ordinary events and circumstances of life: when we are doing the dishes, hanging out the laundry, cleaning and dusting, picking weeds, raking leaves, and just plain living. All have the potential to enrich the soul and animate the spirit.

God is as close to us as we can risk being close to our real selves. Every intimate encounter with the divine liberates something within us—a source of strength and power, a hope, a dream, a capacity for life, and the ability to bounce back after every loss. Prayer stimulates our capacity to grow and change, to accept explicitly who we are and who we might become. When we are vigilant and attentive, we discover the richness and beauty of God in all times and places. God pervades the universe, nurturing, strengthening, and bringing all things to completion.

It is early June. It is, indeed, a perfect day—warm and sunny and clear. Part of my teaching assignment is to help a group of teenagers prepare for the celebration of confirmation. We decide to spend a day in the wilderness near Marsh Lake. Reflection periods are followed by sharing and, then, enjoying free time. Most of the youth walk quietly along the edge of the lake or in the surrounding forest. Like them, I drink in nature in all her glory.

In preparation for the closing prayer, I invite the students to find a symbol of nature that best describes their faith. Their responses are deeply moving. Peter brings a small branch with several budding leaves. Alice carries back a large solid rock. Mike displays a piece of soft moss he found on the forest floor. Tricia returns with a tiny crocus. Gabe holds an eagle's feather that he found resting on a branch. Robyn carries a fine blend of sand and dirt in her hand. I display a pebble I found along the shore. It has been washed smooth as silk.

Everyone's journey to prayer follows its own unique path. The way we pray has everything to do with the way we understand God and self. Jesus illustrated this in his graphic parable of the Pharisee and the publican. Both men believed in God. Both understood their duty toward God. Both went to the temple to pray. The difference was in their attitude toward self and others. The Pharisee, believing himself righteous, praised his healthy spiritual state. His stance was not about deception. It was about an overblown self-image. His prayer had little to do with God and everything to do with self. "God, I thank you that I am not like other people: thieves, rogues, adulterers, or even like this tax collector. I fast twice a week; I give a tenth of my income."

Conscious of his sinfulness, the tax collector stood afar off, not daring to look up to heaven. He was cognizant of his helplessness and his need for God. He knew that he could not earn love, least of all divine love. His approach was that of a child, open and receptive, genuinely sincere. His prayer reflected a deep awareness of the goodness of God and his own unworthiness. He staked his life on God and relied completely on the compassion and mercy of God. "God, be merciful to me, a sinner."[78] It was a simple, uncomplicated prayer—an honest and humble admission of his ignoble state and a sincere acknowledgment of God's unconditional acceptance and love.

Many things colour our prayer: hopes and dreams, desires and aspirations, feelings and fantasies, and the inner law that is our personal measuring stick. It helps to set a quiet, restful, and peaceful atmosphere. Most often, God's voice is not heard in the midst of a whirlwind, but in the gentle breeze. To pray, it is necessary to wrap a mantle of stillness around one's self and simply listen.

Symbols are an unspoken language, the language of the heart. They move the senses, stimulate the memory, increase our longing, and set the imagination in motion. Any place can be turned into a sacred space, a place of prayer. Light a candle, open the Bible, or place a sacred object nearby. The right atmosphere fosters a sense of peace and inner quiet. A quiet mind is receptive to the outpouring of the Spirit.

1992. I volunteer to teach a grade three religion program for a colleague. The school is crowded to the rafters. The only available space is the front foyer. A school's atrium is always bustling with activity. It's hardly conducive to prayer.

While I believe that holy ground is everywhere, it helps to create the right ambience for prayer, especially for children. I want a space where my students can drink in the presence of God. We need a focal point—something to gather our thoughts and aspirations. I share my feelings with the students and leave it as an open-ended question.

The next day Alex arrives with a rather unusual bundle under his arm. There is a long roll of Tyvec, several carefully peeled willow sticks, and a bunch of twine. I can see that his enthusiasm is bubbling over as he announces: "I got this idea. We'll build a huge tent. We can put a Bible in the middle and add some special stuff. It'll make it easier to pray." The idea mushrooms. The tent is completed within the day.

The following day I bring my Bible and a favourite candle and place them in the centre of the tent. Students catch the spirit. Before the week is out, the tent contains a most unusual blend of precious objects: a flask of Lourdes water, a medal of St. Christopher, a young artist's version of love, a rosary, a hand-written poem, a key chain, a pair of work gloves, a pitcher of water, and a flaming red geranium.

An atmosphere for prayer cuts deeper than externals. The essential element is the aura of the heart. It has everything to do with the harmony of body, mind, and spirit. Spiritual gurus speak of the need to leave behind one's fears, frustrations, guilt, regret, anxieties, and daydreams. Only an empty heart is able to absorb a portion of the immensity of God. The problem for most of us is in the emptying. We manage it on rare occasions and then for relatively short periods of time. Distractions come to all of us but they need not interrupt our prayer. Gently placing them in God's hands sanctifies them while it frees us to breathe in God and life.

Thomas Merton says the simplest way to come into contact with the living God is to go into one's centre and, from there, pass into God. God's power runs from the depths to the surface. The object of all prayer is silent awareness. The prayer of surrender takes us beyond images, thoughts, words, and feelings into the heart and life of God. In prayerful silence and stillness, we find the living God bringing us forth in creative love. At our centre, we come to know both our own being and the being that is God. In a simple "being there," we experience a presence that is complete adoration and absolute love.

> The beginning is a gift of light—
> a tiny shaft, almost imperceptible.
> As we grow older the flame becomes more complex:
> we see dimly, as through a glass darkly;
> then, illumination springs over the horizon.

Love is approaching—
demanding little; demanding much;
calling us to go further, deeper,
until we come to perfect communion.

The journey inward is our natural birthright. Prayer is that journey. It takes us back to our origin and the God who created us. Our natural response is an outpouring of love and adoration. In prayer, we travel back to the moment when we were created and forward to the time when we will enter our eternal home. The more we get lost in prayer, the more we are moved beyond the things we can see and hear and touch. Prayer takes us directly into the arms of God. There, we encounter Love and infinite Mystery. Open to love, we inhale its beauty so we can breathe it out on the world. That is the reason for prayer. That is the gift of prayer.

In the silence and stillness of prayer, we contemplate God without giving God a shape or confining God to our narrow images. God cannot be contained in this or that place. God is nowhere. God is everywhere. God is the air we breathe, the thoughts we think, the life coursing through our veins, and the passion we feel in our soul. God is in our mindfulness and in our heedlessness, in our wholeness and in our brokenness.

Prayer is more than giving our time to God. To pray is to become familiar with God. All we need to do is open ourselves to the present moment and let prayer flow naturally. In prayer, we acknowledge our dependence on God. We remember who we are and what we need. We trust that God will lead us. To pray is to stand before God with open hands and open hearts, letting God enter and fill our emptiness. When we respond to God's invitation, we begin the journey into profound and eternal union.

Prayer is presence. Uninterrupted. Unabridged. Consummate. When we pray we do not stand before God, we stand with God. We do not kneel before God; we kneel with God. Prayer brings divine and human presence together. To pray is to be attentive, to be aware of the divine at the centre of everything—to see people, things, and events from the perspective of eternity.

Prayer takes us deeper and deeper into the realm of relationship. When we listen attentively to God, the message becomes clear. God is continually asking us: "Will you have me? Will you let me be yours? Will you be mine?" To love is to accept the other with our whole mind, heart, and soul. To love is to abandon one's self to the other. Genuine love carries us to the heights of ecstasy. To pray is to know our emptiness and to appreciate the divine mystery that fills it. With every "I love you," God promises intimate presence. That presence has the power to renew and deepen us at every level. To pray is to run into God's embrace, to become aflame with the passion for life that is our original blessing. It is to discover the goodness within.

Prayer ultimately leads to union with God. When we are faithful to prayer, we become more and more like God. When we pray, we let God be in us—in the thoughts we think, in the feelings that move us, in the look of kindness in our eyes, and in the love that pours from our hearts. Life is about seeking and discovering who we are in God. Prayer is about life with God and in God.

The holy one stood watching the young child going back and forth from the ocean to the same small hole in the sand. Time after time, she filled her little pail with water from the sea and poured it into the hole. When the holy one asked what she was doing, she replied, "Don't you understand? I'm emptying that ocean into my tiny hole." The holy one remembered his younger days and how he thought he could contain the great mystery of God in his finite mind. Today he understood—prayer takes us into the heart of God. We become immersed in that immense love. Together we become: "The sun and its light, the ocean and its waves, the singer and her song. Not one. Not two."[79]

Prayer is intimate union with God. It is to find God in all of life—in one's body, mind, heart, and spirit. It is to appreciate the divine in everything around us. To pray is to believe that God is in all things drawing us to our own inner truth and light.

Prayer is enlightenment. It brings each of our spiritual histories to life. To pray is to listen to the sacred story of your life and to commit yourself to shaping it into the story God wants to tell. It is to accept both your original blessing and original sin so that your real self can emerge. It is to move beyond following the rules and playing it safe. To pray is to surrender to the circumstances of life and to find what is liberating, clarifying, and invigorating. It is to take the path that conforms to your deepest longings, the path that leads to eternal love. To pray is to breathe in the beauty and goodness of God in order to breathe them out on the world.

All prayer begins with God, spills over into the heart, and leads outward to the world. The nature of prayer is to let Love increase and grow until it becomes a light to others. Like love, prayer has a ripple effect and sends messages of hope and peace to the world. "To keep holy the Sabbath day" is to allow love to spill over and touch the lives of our families, friends, neighbours, and the universe.

> It isn't you who shape God;
> it is God who shapes you.
> If then you are the work of God,
> Await the hand of the Artist
> who does all things in due season.
> Offer the potter your heart, soft and tractable,
> and keep the form in which
> the Artist has fashioned you.
> Let your clay be moist,
> lest you grow hard
> and lose the imprint of the Potter's fingers.[80]

Conclusion: The Light Within

There is a candle in your heart,
ready to be kindled.
There is a void in your soul,
ready to be filled.
You feel it, don't you?
You feel the separation
from the Beloved.
Invite Him to fill you up,
embrace the fire.
Remind those who tell you otherwise that
Love
comes to you of its own accord,
and the yearning for it cannot be learned in any school.[81]

Spirituality is about the unseen connection between our Creator, our sisters and brothers, and ourselves. It is our innate longing for God and God's desire to form an eternal relationship with us. Our yearning, our passion, comes from the light and love God breathes into us at conception. Every one of us has an inner light. God dispenses blessings freely and equitably. We all receive more than we need to live a full and happy life.

Light does not choose one path over another. Even the faintest light casts its glow in every direction. Divine light shines into the deepest recesses of our soul. In the clarity of that light, the beauty and goodness that are deep within become transparent and we recognize our essential blessing. Because it brings everything into clearer focus, our inner light enables us to see the infinite possibilities open to us. When we are in touch with our inner self, we allow our natural goodness to burst into flame and we become all fire, all love.

Despite the divine light within, we often walk in the shadow. We get mired in selfish ways. We waver between our blessing and our sin. Though the blessing far outweighs the sin, we focus on the sin. We reinforce our narrow views, agendas, and biases. Original sin lures us into a false sense of self. It blurs our vision and we lose perspective. As a result, we ask: "Why me, Lord? Why am I not as good or beautiful or kind as my sister or my best friend? Why do I have this particular cross to bear? Why is there so much obscurity in my life?"

God's light turns our questions around and raises them to a new level. When we listen to the heartbeat of God, we ask: "Why me, Lord? Why do you fill me with so much goodness and light and love? How can I serve you?" Spirituality calls us to deal with the negative in light of our original blessing. As the sage cautions, "never start counting your troubles until you've counted at least one hundred of your blessings." When we start with the blessing, we appreciate how amazing life truly is. We are fundamentally good and the world is essentially good. Each positive thought fills us with a profusion of light, of love, of energy, of passion.

Life is an odyssey from the womb of God, through an earthly pilgrimage, and back to God in death. To help us remember that journey, we make pilgrimages: to sacred shrines, to places where miracles occurred, to memorial sites, to places that hold special memories. To undertake such an adventure is to turn on the pause button and listen deeply to life.

Brazil 1976. The idea of going on a pilgrimage is born out of local folklore. Tradition has it that a poor young man was searching for food and water for his family and for his donkey.

José trekked over twelve kilometres into the mountains over-looking Saubara. Suddenly, he came upon a spring of fresh, clear water. He called the place Milagré.

Tonya, Lika, and Catita plan to make a pilgrimage to the Milagré on Saturday. They invite me to join them. We set off just as dawn is breaking. Walking in silence, we are engrossed in our own thoughts. I listen deeply to the wonder of nature's sounds around me. Step-by-step, I feel earth's triumphs and struggles beneath my feet. As we near the Milagré, the geography of the place moves my heart to praise. The trees are a luscious, vibrant green. Birds sing their joyous melodies. The underbrush becomes less dense. Here and there, I see a profusion of wild flowers. Then, there is the gentle sound of flowing water.

Tonya places a hand on my arm as she advises, "Edite, from here on we travel on our knees." I get down and follow the lead of my friends. We light our candles and journey on together. It isn't easy to "walk" on your knees, but I find it a cleansing experience. Close to the earth, I feel the beating of my heart resonating with the pulse of the earth. Life is good.

As we reach the place of the Milagré, the women prostrate themselves on the ground. Once again, I follow their example. The sound of the flowing water is somehow clearer at this level. It reminds me of the prophet Ezekiel who described the renewal of the earth as coming from a life-giving river spring-ing from the throne of God. "I will sprinkle clean water upon you, and you shall be clean... A new heart I will give you, and a new spirit I will put within you; and I will remove from your body the heart of stone and give you a heart of flesh."[82]

The four of us step deeper and deeper into the water until we are immersed in it. We pray in silence; we pray together. Some time later, we walk out of the pool in quiet peace. The return trip is rich in the candid sharing of insights. I tell the women about the pilgrimage I made on the prairies when I was six years old. So many memories flood into my soul. A lot of water has gone under the bridge since then. But God's love has remained my anchor of strength and love.

The whole of life is a pilgrimage. Whether we are conscious of it or not, God walks with us every step along the way. Spirituality beckons us on the greatest adventure possible, the journey back to God. En route, we search for love, for communion, for relationship. As the wheel of life turns forward, we discover the Spirit breaking through our defences and challenging us to greater love. Whenever we dare to leave the familiar path, we open ourselves to the unpredictable, to the surprise of God. Every step we take in faith draws us back to life's centre where we experience an inner harmony, a unity with the deity. Life from the centre takes us into the very heart of God.

Spirituality is God's personal gift. We don't need some great epiphany to teach us that we are created for relationship. Life does it day in and day out. All it asks of us is that we pay attention. Wounded and broken, we stand in need of guidance. But we know that we have an inner light to point the way. In our open-ended search, darkness and light flow seamlessly into one another. In the midst of death, we find life. In the midst of failure, we find growth. In the midst of despair, we find reason to hope. The journey is an adventure into the unknown that becomes sanctifying and renewing.

The self is not a finished product at birth. We create our own self by going all the way on our path to fullness of life. On that path, everything has the power to replenish us, enrich us, and make us whole. The stages of life, the ecstasies, and the dark nights serve as lessons for the soul. Heart learning takes place as we walk in faith and hope and love. It helps us look at life and everything in it with reverence. As Marshall McLuhan says, "we become what we behold."

The Spirit calls us to finish what the Creator left undone in our soul and in our universe. Sooner or later, we all meet something greater than our own needs. The way we respond marks us and continues to move us throughout life. No one can walk another's journey. No one can fulfill another's purpose. No one can take another's place. Spirituality is about finding our place in the world and discovering our special mission. When we become who God intended us to be, we have the power to set the world on fire.

Life takes us on a wonderful spiritual quest, an ongoing search for God, and a commitment to each other. Thinking, feeling people, we discover our awesome gift all along the way. The flame, the fire in our soul draws us beyond ourselves into the heart of life. The interminable call of spirituality is to keep reaching down to our inner roots and pulling out the things that are uplifting and enriching. The end result is charity, alive and active in us and in our world.

Spirituality is a gift that takes us inward. It entrusts us with life and empowers us to see the essential unity between the secular and the sacred, the body and the soul, the obvious and the mysterious. It is the soul power that sustains us and summons us to fulfill our dreams. The divine mandate is clear: find your blessing and go with it!

> *Let God enter*
> *the deepest recesses*
> *of your soul.*
> *There*
> *to shine the divine light*
> *on the astonishing mystery that you are.*
>
> *Let God whisper*
> *words of eternal love*
> *to your soul.*
> *So*
> *to remind you*
> *of your inner truth, goodness, and beauty.*
>
> *Let God touch*
> *the innate longings*
> *of your spirit.*
> *Thus,*
> *to arouse you*
> *to stretch and grow, to be all you can be.*

Notes

(Endnotes)

Poems/Prayers/Reflections used as epigraphs at the end of chapters that do not have an endnote are my own compositions.

Introduction

J. Philip Newell, *The Book of Creation: An Introduction to Celtic Spirituality* (Mahwah: Paulist Press, Inc., 1999), p 94-95. Reprinted by permission of Paulist Press, Inc. www.paulistpress.com

Part 1

Edite, *The Road Home*. (Whitehorse, E.V. Elder, 2011).

Chapter 1

Psalm 139:13. (NRSV)

2   Indian Artifacts, Arrowheads, Ice Age Indian Art; accessed May 4, 2008, http://www.iceageartifacts.com/ #6 Reflecting Man.
    Speigel Online International. <www.Spiegelonlineinternational.com>

3   James Conlon. *At the Edge of Our Longing: Unspoken Hunger for Sacredness and Depth* (Ottawa: Novalis Press, 2004). Conlon presents ten spiritual practices for growing our soul.

4   Abraham Isaac Kook, *Abraham Isaac Kook: The Lights of Penitence, Lights of Holiness, the Moral Principles, Essays and Letters, and Poems,* translated and introduced by Ben Zion Bokser. (Mahwah: Paulist Press, Inc., 1978), p 207. Reprinted by permission of Paulist Press, Inc. www.paulistpress.com

Chapter 2

5   Adapted from Luke 10:10. (NRSV) For clarity sake, I wish to point out that, while Jesus chose twelve apostles, he had an additional seventy-two disciples who supported his mission.

6   Thomas Kelly, *The Eternal Promise,* excerpt from: *Quaker Spirituality: Selected Writings* edited and introduced by Douglas V. Steere (Mahwah: Paulist Press, Inc. 1984), p 306. Reprinted by permission of Paulist Press, Inc. www.paulistpress.com

Chapter 3

7   Adapted from Ephesians 1:4. (NRSV)

8   Adapted from Micah 6:8. (NRSV)

9   Isaiah 43:1–2. (NRSV)

10   1 Corinthians 13:1–7. (NRSV)

Chapter 4

11   Adapted from Luke 6:6–12. (NRSV)

[12] Movie: *Pay It Forward*, based on the novel by the same name by Catherine Ryan Hyde.

[13] Victor Frankl, *Man's Search for Meaning* (Boston: Beacon Press,1959, 1962, 1984, 1992), p. 23.

[14] Genesis 28:14–15. (NRSV)

[15] Genesis 32:31. (NRSV)

[16] I recommend Brooke Newman's book: *The Little Tern: A Story of Insight* (Mahwah: Paulist Press, Inc., 1999) www.paulistpress.com

[17] Alfred Lord Tennyson, *Ulysses*. Taken from: *The Top 500 Poems: A Columbia Anthology* edited by William Harmon. (New York: Columbia University Press, 1992), p 645-646

Part 2

George Washington Doane. *Life Sculpture*. Taken from: Life Sculpture—George Washington Doane. accessed September 30, 2010, http://www.reastro.tripd.com/life.htm

Chapter 5

[18] Adapted from Genesis 1 and Isaiah 49:15-16. (NRSV)

[19] Peter Van Breemen, *The God Who Won't Let Go* (San Francisco: Ave Maria Press, Inc.), p 24. Used with permission by Ave Maria Press.

[20] Adapted from Luke 7:37-38. (NRSV)

[21] Luke 7:39. (NRSV)

[22] Rumi, *Hush: Don't Say Anything to God. Passionate Poems of Rumi* by Shahram Shiva. p 29. Used with permission by Shahram Shiva. For more information visit www.Rumi.net.

Chapter 6

[23] I highly recommend two books on personality types: Howard Addison, *The Enneagram and Kabbalah: Reading Your Soul* (Woodstock: Jewish Lights Publishing, 1998)

Richard Rohr, *Enneagram II: Advancing Spiritual Discernment.* (New York: Crossroads Publishing Company, 1993)

[24] Richard Rohr, *Enneagram II.*

Chapter 7

[25] Philippians 2:6–8. (NRSV)

[26] Adapted from Matthew 4:18–22. (NRSV)

Chapter 8

[27] Jean Vanier, *Man and Woman God Made Them.* English translation by Darton, Longman and Todd. London. p 49 Used with permission of Darton, Longman and Todd.

[28] Story of Moses adapted from Exodus 2, 3, and 4 (NRSV)

[29] Story of Ruth adapted from the Book of Ruth 1:16. (NRSV)

[30] Book of Wisdom 7:22–30. (NRSV)

Part 3

Shamus-ud-din Muhammed Hafiz, *I Heard God Laughing: Renderings of Hafiz,* Compiled by Daniel Ladsinsky. (Toronto: Penguin Publications) Used with permission by Daniel Ladsinsky.

Chapter 9

[31] Romans 7:15 and 20 (NRSV)

[32] John Steinbeck, *East of Eden* (New York: Penguin Group, 2002), p 264

[33] Adapted from Genesis 4:1-16. (NRSV)

[34] Romans 8:28 (NRSV)

[35] George Herbert, *Love Bade Me Welcome.* Taken from: *The Top 500 Poems: A Columbia Anthology* edited by William Harmon. (New York: Columbia University Press, 1992), p 645-646

Chapter 10

[36] John Monbourquette, Adapted from *How to Befriend Your Shadow: Welcoming Your Unloved Side*. (Ottawa: Novalis, 2001), p 10. Used with permission of Novalis Publishing.

[37] Adapted from Matthew 13:24-30. (NRSV)

[38] Adapted from Ephesians 4:23-4. (NRSV)

[39] Alcoholics Anonymous.

[40] John Steinbeck, *East of Eden* (New York: Penguin Group, 2002), p 575

[41] John Steinbeck, *East of Eden* (New York: Penguin Group, 2002), p 413

[42] Beatification of Mother Theresa of Calcutta, 19 October 2003, accessed April 14, 2011,
<http://www.vatican.va/news...ns_lit_doc20031019_index_madre-teresa_en.html>

[43] Beatification of Mother Theresa of Calcutta. Homily of John Paul II, 19 October 2003. Vatican News, accessed April 15, 2011, <http://www.vatican.va/news/_services/liturgy/saints/>

[44] Jessica Powers, *This Trackless Solitude*. Taken from: *Songs out of Silence: 99 Sayings by Jessica Powers*. (New York: New City Press, 2010), p 1. The complete poem is originally found in *The Selected Poetry of Jessica Powers*, (Washington, ICS Publications, 1988). Used with permission of the Carmelite Monastery, Pewaukee, WI.

Chapter 11

[45] Based on Hosea 2:14-16, 19-20. (NRSV)

[46] Adapted from John 8:11. (NRSV)

[47] Adapted from Luke 15:1–10. (NRSV)

[48] Adapted from Luke 15:29. (NRSV)

[49] Background on God as forgiving Father gleaned from: Luke 15 and Henri Nouwen, *The Return of the Prodigal Son*, (New York: An Image Book published by Doubleday, 1992)

[50] Micah 7:18-19. (NRSV)

[51] Mark 11:25. (NRSV)

[52] John Donne, *A Hymn to God the Father.* Taken from: *The Top 500 Poems: A Columbia Anthology* edited by William Harmon. (New York: Columbia University Press, 1992), p 135

Chapter 12

[53] John Milton, *On His Blindness.* Taken from: *The Top 500 Poems: A Columbia Anthology* edited by William Harmon. (New York: Columbia University Press, 1992), p 210.

[54] Excerpt from: *Hamlet* by William Shakespeare. Taken from: *The Complete Works of William Shakespeare*, Volume Two. Published by Nelson Doubleday. N.Y. p. 613.

[55] Excerpt from: *Julius Caesar* by William Shakespeare. Taken from: *The Complete Works of William Shakespeare*, Volume Two. Published by Nelson Doubleday. N.Y. p. 580.

[56] Johannes B. Metz, *Poverty of Spirit* (Mahwah: The Missionary Society of St. Paul the Apostle in the State of New York, 1968, 1988), p 3. Reprinted with permission of Paulist Press, Inc. www.paulistpress.com

[57] William Ernest Henley, *Invictus.* Taken from: *Best-Loved Poems*, edited by John Boyes. (Toronto: Arturus Publishing Limited, 2007). p 532.

Part 4

Joyce Rupp, *Watered Gardens.* Taken from *May I Have This Dance?* (Notre Dame: Ave Maria Press, 1992), p 55-56. Used with permission of Ave Maria Press.

Chapter 13

[58] Author Unknown.

[59] Adapted from 1 Kings 8:12. (NRSV)

[60] Michael Joncas, *On Eagle's Wings,* based on Psalm 91. Take from: *Journeysongs.* (Portland: OCP Publications, 2004), p 704. Used with permission of OCP Publications.

[61] William Blake, *Auguries of Innocence*. Taken from: *The Top 500 Poems: A Columbia Anthology* edited by William Harmon. (New York: Columbia University Press, 1992), p 368-371.

Chapter 14

[62] Adapted from Matthew 14:22-33. (NRSV)

[63] Francis Thompson, *The Hound of Heaven*, excerpts taken from: *The Top 500 Poems: A Columbia Anthology* edited by William Harmon. (New York: Columbia University Press, 1992), p 844.

[64] Francis Thompson, *The Hound of Heaven,* p. 843.

[65] Francis Thompson, *The Hound of Heaven,* p. 848.

[66] Adapted from the Book of Job 13:20–22; 19:25–27.

[67] Robert Frost, *The Road Not Taken*. Taken from: *The Top 500 Poems: A Columbia Anthology* edited by William Harmon. (New York: Columbia University Press, 1992), p. 844.

Chapter 15

[68] Matthew 5:3–11. (NRSV)

[69] Johannes B. Metz, *Poverty of Spirit*, p. 31.

[70] Adapted from 2 Corinthians 8:9 (NRSV)

[71] Adapted from Matthew 18:2–3. (NRSV)

[72] I recommend *Francis: The Journey and the Dream* by Murray Bodo. (Published by St. Anthony Messenger Press, 1972)

[73] Magdalena Frances Gerein-Elder, *My Memories* (Lethbridge: Diane Miedema, 2003), p. 8

[74] Johannes B. Metz, *Poverty of Spirit*, p. 49.

[75] Edward Carpenter, *The Lake of Beauty*. Taken from: *The Creation Spirit: An Anthology*. Complied by Robert Van de Weyer & Pat Saunders. (Huntingdon: Little Gidding Books, 1990), p 167. Used with permission by Darton, Longman and Todd Ltd.

Chapter 16

[76] Exodus 20:8–11. (NRSV)

[77] Amma Syncletica. (2009) Words from the Desert. <http://www.wordfromthedesert.squarespace.com>

[78] Adapted from Luke 18:9–14. (NRSV)

[79] *Some Wisdom from Anthony de Melo*, SJ. The entire Sufi story can be found on: Anthony de Melo's One Moment Wisdom site: Topic of Identity, accessed June 1, 2011, <http://suzelly.opf.slu.cz/~perzina//demello/>

[80] St. Irenaeous. *It Isn't You Who Shape God.* (120-202 AD)

Conclusion

[81] Rumi, *There Is a Candle in Your Heart,* Taken from: *Hush: Don't Say Anything to God. Passionate Poems of Rumi* by Shahram Shiva. p 37. Used by permission of Shahram Shiva. For more information visit www.Rumi.net

[82] Ezekiel 36:25–26. (NRSV)

About the Author

From prairie girl to teacher and principal, from missionary to pastoral assistant and retreat facilitator...

E.V. Elder's humble roots helped keep her feet on the ground and opened her spirit to the living God present in the ordinary and extraordinary events of life. While her life has been rich and varied, her commitment continues to revolve around community service. In 2002, Premier Fentie presented her with the Queen's Golden Jubilee Medal in recognition of her significant contribution to the Yukon. In 2007, the Yukon Women's Directorate featured her as one of four Yukon Women Leaders.

Her post-graduate studies took her from the University of Saskatchewan to Assumption University and, finally, to University of Alaska Southeast. Though she values her formal education, she believes that life has been her greatest teacher. In a spirit of gratitude, she shares her personal experiences in her writing.